THE NONGRADED
ELEMENTARY SCHOOL

TO THE READER

This edition of *The Nongraded Elementary School* has two distinct sections which are paginated separately. In the first section, written in 1986, we seek to provide a current perspective on nongradedness and its enduring importance for the well-being of young children. The second section is an exact photo reproduction of pages 1 through 248 of the 1963 (revised) edition of the book that appeared first in 1959.

That earlier work, especially in the 1963 version, has had a significant influence upon practice and scholarship over several decades, and it continues to be cited in discussions of nongraded organization, individualized instruction, promotion-versus-retention, progress reporting, and related topics. Sales of the foreign-language editions continue to be recorded. However, at a time when there is a strong resurgence of interest in these topics, English-language copies of the book are no longer available, and we have been urged either to reprint the 1963 edition or to prepare a new, 1980s-oriented statement.

We elected to do both. We are grateful to Harcourt Brace Jovanovich, the original publishers, who reassigned the copyright to us, and also to Teachers College Press, who agreed to publish the 1987 version.

In the first section, especially in the "Dialogue," we indicate that although an updating is appropriate, the philosophy we espoused several decades ago and our suggestions for dealing with children remain both important and pertinent. After you as readers have consulted our recent statement, we hope that you, too, will find the ideas in the 1963 material to be salient and perhaps even a welcome spur to action.

JIG
RHA

THE NONGRADED ELEMENTARY SCHOOL

REVISED EDITION
Reissued with a New Introduction

John I. Goodlad
Robert H. Anderson

Teachers College, Columbia University
New York and London

Published by Teachers College Press, 1234 Amsterdam Avenue,
New York, NY 10027

Library of Congress Cataloging-in-Publication Data

Goodlad, John I.
   The nongraded elementary school.

   Bibliography: p.
   Includes index.
   1. Nongraded schools.   2. Education, Elementary—
United States.   I. Anderson, Robert Henry, 1918–
II. Title.
LB1029.N6G66   1987   372.12′54   86-30055
ISBN 0-8077-2845-4 (pbk.)

Manufactured in the United States of America

92 91 90 89   3   4   5   6

CONTENTS

To The Reader   vii

New Introduction to the Revised Edition   ix

1 • The Child and Procrustean Standards   1

2 • To Promote or Not to Promote   30

3 • Today's Nongraded School Emerges   44

4 • The Nongraded School in Operation   61

5 • Modern Theories of Curriculum
    and the Nongraded School
    of Today and Tomorrow   79

6 • Reporting Pupil Progress
    in the Nongraded School   102

7 • Toward Realistic Standards
    and Sound Mental Health   142

8 • The Establishment of the Nongraded School   170

9 • The Nongraded School Today and Tomorrow   203

Comprehensive Bibliography   227

Index   245

NEW INTRODUCTION
TO THE REVISED EDITION

A Little Bit of History

The first edition of *The Nongraded Elementary School* appeared in 1959. We had started serious work on it in 1956 and the book was essentially complete by the end of 1957. One of our problems was to persuade a publisher (we were rebuffed by six) that the topic was both timely and important. When Harcourt, Brace finally took it on, thanks to the venturesome spirit of Paul F. Brandwein, the book was seen as a commercial gamble in the interest of promoting a worthy idea. Happily for both the publisher and us, the gamble paid off and the book enjoyed reasonable sales, especially for a non-textbook, for nearly twenty years. In fact, as the sales in the United States were dropping off, sales of translations in several other countries were picking up.

In the 1959 edition were included not only a comprehensive bibliography, but also an appendix listing communities reporting nongraded programs in existence (43 in number); descriptions of seven somewhat similar programs; and information about programs that were discontinued, nonexistent, or were likely to be converted to nongraded ones. This material had been collected through several questionnaire studies in 1957 and 1958. Within a year or so of publication, however, we became painfully aware of the illegitimacy of some of the presumably nongraded programs we had cited, and we realized that there had been an overemphasis by schools in the programs we surveyed on reading-levels approaches and homogeneous classroom groupings—practices not recommended by us. Also, most programs embraced only the primary years, as contrasted with the entire K–6 (or K–8) spectrum. We therefore pressed the publisher for permission to issue a second edition that would eliminate the Appendix, alter the operational explanations (in Chapter 4) and expand the discussion (in Chapter 9) of the future potential of nongradedness.

The second edition appeared in 1963, and our confidence in its authenticity and usefulness was, and remained, high. Within two or three years, foreign-language editions were made available in Hebrew, Japanese, Spanish, and Italian. Sales of the English edition were also extensive abroad. We have never ceased to be amazed at how many educators throughout the world have read (and, they say, appreciated) the volume. In fact, the durability as well as the universality of faith in nongradedness are among our reasons for issuing this reprinting and updating of the second edition—nearly 30 years after publication of the first.

Probably the most notable shift in our thinking between the 1950s and the early 1960s is reflected in pages 68–78 of the 1963 edition. There we made a strong commitment to the concept and practice of multiage or interage grouping, which assures that the basic participation of each child will be in a heterogeneous group. More restrained was our advocacy of team teaching as a correlative organizational structure, although we gave wholehearted support to it and to related patterns of differentiated staffing. The discerning reader was free to conclude that in the best of all worlds, elementary-age children would be educated within a team-taught, multiage, nongraded framework; however, this concept was not urged upon the reader with the force that we would now exert.

In the twenty-some years that followed, nongradedness and team teaching became buzzwords and both the literature and conference/workshop programs forwarded discussions pro and con. By the early 1970s the flood of writing had begun to taper off, but by then literally hundreds of research reports, doctoral dissertations, books of readings, and other records were available. Current literature searches, such as one we conducted in 1985–1986, show a preponderance of studies in the late 1960s up to 1971, after which the term "nongraded" appears infrequently. The 1970s witnessed the beginning of a return to the traditional ways of thinking about schooling from which we had sought to depart.

Although our own publication dealt almost exclusively with nongrading in elementary schools, we have received a lively and supportive interest in efforts at the secondary level. We perceive that there has been, and continues to be, considerable success in introducing many of the concepts and practices of nongradedness in early secondary programs. The strong movement away from the literal junior high school and in the direction of "middle schools" has been one of the most positive forces in this trend. The literature of the middle school, which emerged in nearly the same period as that of nongradedness, is based upon essentially the same value system, the same assumptions about optimal learning conditions for pupils, and the same approaches to grouping pupils and managing their academic progress that have been associated with nongrading. In a few instances, such as Fazzaro's 1975 article, there was an actual effort to associate the label "nongraded" with efforts at modifying the structure and the atmosphere of schools for young adolescents. Even when the term is not used, however, the rhetoric is very consistent with that of elementary-school reform. For example, a 1985 National Association of Secondary School Principals (NASSP) publication that pulls together views and developments about middle level education is altogether congruent with what we and others have said about elementary-level nongradedness.

One of the unanticipated consequences of the emergence of team teaching, which had begun to flourish at about the same time as our 1963 edition was in production, was the adoption of multiage (or more accurately in those days, multigraded) grouping arrangements. Most schools that were eager to pursue team teaching had too few pupils to populate a three- or four-teacher team at a single grade level, and so practical necessity called for combining two or more grades. Almost automatically, this caused teachers to adjust in more flexible ways to the reality of individual differences, and even in situations where there had been no advance commitment to nongradedness the conventional labels (and associated mindsets) began to disappear. Teachers found themselves more free to arrange for the continuous progress of their pupils without regard for graded expectations, and it became common to refer to each team as the "Comets," or the "Astronauts," or the "Kappa Group," rather than the Grade 5-6 Team. Although not as powerful a concept as nongrading, team teaching proved to be a useful strategic device for breaking down the grade barriers.

Another major force, largely for good, in the late 1950s and 1960s was the architectural revolution that was triggered by team teaching and related organizational plans. Although the monitorial/Lancastrian plan in the previous century had already involved the use of large common spaces, almost all American school buildings prior to about 1960 featured small, equal-sized, self-contained classrooms, each intentionally insulated from the others and fostering a mentality of privacy and independence. It was with great difficulty that teachers under such circumstances managed to respond to the enormous range of individual differences that confronted them daily. These were the circumstances of isolation which those seeking to nongrade encountered necessarily. Once the space was opened up and teachers were brought together in a common space, many more grouping and space-use options became available and the complexity of individualization was reduced. Even more important, teachers gained control over a wider range of factors impinging on their work and became engaged in a dialogue regarding these conditions.

Nongrading never became a movement as such, nor did it ever

succeed in weakening the stranglehold of the publishing industry, whose fortunes were (and are) geared to selling complete sets of textbooks for each grade level. Whatever their many virtues as resource materials for pupils and their teachers, textbooks nurture conformity and tempt teachers to cover material whether or not it is appropriate for the wide range of individual differences among pupils.

Textbooks tend to be geared in content to the lower levels of ability in each grade, are extremely repetitious year by year, and are often puffed up with filler material to accommodate approximately 180 days of assignments. Ellison's (1972) comments about graded textbooks as stumbling blocks to educational progress are relevant in this connection.

One of the things that happens with teaching teams is that teachers require fewer copies of basic texts for each grade level, and there is more awareness of the stifling impact of texts upon the progress of children, especially those of average and above-average potential. On the other hand, teaching teams usually make more of their own instructional materials and they request more expenditures for other kinds of books and artifacts than do teachers in self-contained classrooms. The explanation for this is simple: there is much more sharing of alternative ideas, and appetites are created for a full range of resources.

One of the greatest stimulants to the growth of nongradedness was what became known, in two different but related contexts, as Individually Guided Education (IGE). Both the University of Wisconsin and the Institute for Development of Educational Activities (/I/D/E/A/) have utilized the terms and produced written and media materials related to them.

The /I/D/E/A/ staff in 1978 published a booklet (Paden et al., 1978) describing a decade of experience with the /I/D/E/A/ Change Program for Individually Guided Education and concluded that the program yields positive results in schools where it has been well implemented. In a section reporting the beginnings and growth of IGE, the co-involvement of the Ohio and Wisconsin groups through a 1969 agreement is briefly noted. Among the statistics in the booklet is that 1,700 schools—1,500 of them elementary—became involved with IGE between 1969 and 1977.

Although there are some minor programmatic differences in the Ohio and Wisconsin programs along with contradictory perceptions of ownership and credit, suffice it for us to say that from both sources have come excellent, useful, and theoretically sound materials that have significantly advanced the cause of better education for children.

The passage of time has caused the tide of nongradedness to recede, but schools that have been linked with either source apparently have maintained their momentum to a notable extent, and it seems reasonable to claim that conceptually Individually Guided Education as a practical illustration of nongradedness is still a factor on the national scene. However, both the extent of interest and the authenticity of identified programs would be difficult to determine. Good ideas have a way of remaining pervasive long after the forms conveying them have faded.

In 1971 the Wisconsin Research and Development Center for Cognitive Learning issued a directory of IGE/multiunit elementary schools in the United States. It identified over 500 centers in 18 states. In a 1985 newsletter, the Wisconsin Center for Education Research announced two books summarizing a longterm multiphased evaluation of the impact of Wisconsin's IGE on elementary schools. It was noted that as many as 3,000 elementary schools identified themselves as IGE schools in 1975. Many different patterns and definitions of IGE were found to be in use. Among the findings of one study (Romberg, 1968) was that, although about 60 percent of the schools in a sample of 900 could be called at best "nominal adopters" of IGE, only about 20 percent could be called true implementers. Another conclusion was that the more successful IGE schools were those in which the program had been installed in a well-planned fashion, with prior staff commitment, parent approval, and provisions for sufficient training.

Excerpts from the Romberg-edited report seem almost excessively negative, reflecting disappointment that too few schools using the IGE label understood and agreed with the goal of shifting instructional planning from the group to the child. The impact of IGE was limited because most schools did not see as their goal the meeting of individual student needs and did not recognize IGE procedures as means to that end. Furthermore, grouping and regrouping of students was a poorly implemented aspect of IGE: Rather than frequently, regrouping was done annually; the age-graded self-contained classroom remained the norm; and shared decision making about meeting individual pupil needs was rare. As a result, both program content and instructional approaches remained essentially unchanged.

A related publication (Popkewitz, Tabachnik, & Wehlage, 1982) indicated that some schools (labeled "technical") focused upon the mechanics of IGE, while others ("illusory") seemed effective on the surface, but their use of IGE practice was mostly ritualistic, whereas a third group ("constructive") was concerned more with IGE's spirit than with its mechanics. These schools, it was noted, stressed learning how knowledge is acquired and emphasized self-discovery and multiple ways of knowing. That such an emphasis was lacking in the majority of schools is of course disappointing but is characteristic of most efforts directed at fundamental change.

As of 1986, statistics on nongradedness, either separately or as a component of programs such as IGE, are unobtainable. The language of current educational reforms makes only rare reference to the various synonyms for nongrading, and very few recently reported research and development projects seem to have been focused directly upon alternative organizational structures. However, interest in individualizing or personalizing instruction seems to be on a steep increase, along with questions about evaluation and reporting of pupil progress (both academic and personal/social), about effective grouping arrangements, about promotion/failure policies, about how to maximize pupil learning, and about using teachers more effectively. These questions have deeper meaning than they had in the 1950s and their resolution seems to be at least as challenging as it was thirty years ago. We dare to hope that the crusade we joined long ago will pick up new support and lead to an array of related changes in schools before this century ends.

Toward a Conceptual Model

Definitions and Guidelines

Several doctoral dissertations have focused on nongradedness as an aspect of school productivity and effectiveness. These, as well as studies conducted by school- or university-based researchers, have generally come up with mixed results, although there has been a trend for the researchers to claim some slight advantages or superiority for the nongraded models. The reported advantages have to do with both academic achievement and pupil mental health. However, a serious flaw in most of these studies is that the investigators fail to collect and report sufficient evidence of the authenticity or legitimacy of the so-called nongraded (experimental) unit. That is, they spend little or no time confirming that criteria of nongradedness are met. Similarly, they fail to confirm that the graded (control) unit is in fact an authentic example of a school/classroom as yet uncontaminated or influenced by nongraded philosophy and/or practices. It is therefore not useful when a researcher says that there *were* achievement (or other) differences, or that there *were not* any such differences, if that researcher has not demonstrated that the procedures of the two units were in fact different from each other and corresponded with their labels.

The general absence of precise operational definitions of nongradedness, and especially the failure of both practitioners and researchers to employ them, prompted Barbara Nelson Pavan to develop a comprehensive ideal model in terms of assumptions and behavioral implications. For her dissertation in the Graduate School of Education at Harvard University (Pavan, 1972), she derived 36 statements of principles divided into six categories: (1) goals of schooling; (2) administrative-organizational framework; (3) materials; (4) curriculum; (5) evaluation and reporting; and (6) methods. This list of statements was then distributed to 48 educators who were well known at that time in the nongraded literature. The group also included a number of writers who had described the British informal or open educational schools. Thirty-nine of these persons responded, and their overwhelming agreement with the statements (except for negligible editorial suggestions) suggests that the statements represented an excellent and authentic overview of the assumptions on which nongradedness is or should be based. In 1987, we consider them to be no less useful. The statements, taken from Pavan's dissertation, follow. We are grateful to her for permission to reproduce an adaptation of them here.

I. GOALS OF SCHOOLING

1. The ultimate school goal is to develop self-directing autonomous individuals.
2. The school should help develop individual potentialities to the maximum possible.
3. Each individual is unique and is accorded dignity and respect. Differences in people are valued. Therefore the school should strive to increase the variability of individual differences rather than stress conformity.
4. Development of the child must be considered in all areas: aesthetic, physical, emotional, and social, as well as intellectual.
5. Those involved in the school enterprise are co-learners, especially teachers and students.
6. The school atmosphere should allow children to enjoy learning, to experience work as pleasurable and rewarding, and to be content with themselves.

II. ADMINISTRATIVE-ORGANIZATIONAL FRAMEWORK

A. *Vertical Grouping*

7. Each individual works in varied situations where he or she will have opportunities for maximum progress. There are no procedures for retention or promotion, nor any grade levels.
8. A child's placement may be changed at *any time* if it is felt to be in the best interests of the child's development considering all five phases of development: aesthetic, physical, intellectual, emotional, and social.

B. *Horizontal Grouping*

9. Grouping and subgrouping patterns are extremely flexible. Learners are grouped and regrouped on the basis of one specific task and are disbanded when that objective is reached.

10. Each child should have opportunities to work with groups of many sizes, including one-person groups, formed for different purposes.

11. The specific task, materials required, and student needs determine the number of students that may be profitably engaged in any given educational experience.

12. Children should have frequent contact with children and adults of varying personalities, backgrounds, abilities, interests, and ages.

III. OPERATIONAL ELEMENTS

A. *Teaching Materials—Instructional*

13. A wide variety of textbooks, trade books, supplemental materials, workbooks, and teaching aids must be available and readily accessible in sufficient quantities.

14. Varied materials must be available to cover a wide range of reading abilities.

15. Alternate methods and materials will be available at any time so that the child may use the learning style and materials most suitable to his or her present needs and the task at hand (including skill building, self-teaching, self-testing, and sequenced materials).

16. A child is not really free to learn something she or he has not been exposed to. The teacher is responsible for providing a broad range of experiences and materials that will stimulate many interests in the educational environment.

B. *Curriculum (knowledge)*

17. The unique needs, interests, abilities, and learning rates, styles, and patterns of each child will determine his or her individual curriculum. Conformity and rigidity are not demanded.

18. The curriculum should be organized to develop the understanding of concepts and methods of inquiry more than specific content learning.

19. Process goals will be stressed: the development of the skills of inquiry, evaluation, interpretation, application—"the skills of learning to learn."

20. Sequence of learning must be determined by each individual student and his or her teacher, since:
    (a) no logical or inherent sequence is in the various curriculum areas.
    (b) no predetermined sequence is appropriate to all learners.
    (c) individual differences in level of competence and in interest are constantly in flux.
21. Each child will formulate his or her own learning goals with guidance from his or her teachers.

C. *Teaching Methods*
22. Different people learn in different ways.
23. Learning is the result of the student's interaction with the world she or he inhabits. Individuals learn by direct experience and manipulation of their environment; therefore the child must be allowed to explore, to experiment, to "mess around," to play, and have the freedom to err.
24. The process is more important than the product. *How* the child learns is stressed.
25. All phases of human growth—aesthetic, physical, intellectual, emotional, and social—are considered when planning learning experiences for a child.
26. The teacher is a facilitator of learning. She or he aids in the child's development by helping each one to formulate goals, diagnose problem areas, suggest alternative plans of action; provides resource materials and gives encouragement, support, or prodding as needed.
27. Children should work on the level appropriate to present attainment and should move as quickly as their abilities and desires allow them to.
28. Successful completion of challenging experiences promotes greater confidence and motivation to learn than fear of failure.
29. Learning experiences based on the child's expressed interests will motivate the child to continue and complete a task successfully much more frequently than teacher-contrived techniques.

D. *Evaluation and Reporting*
30. Children are evaluated in terms of their past achievements and their own potential, not by comparison to group norms. Expectations differ for different children.
31. Evaluation by teacher and/or the child is done for diagnostic

purposes and results in the formulation of new education objectives.

32. Evaluation must be continuous and comprehensive to fulfill its diagnostic purpose.

33. A child strives mainly to improve his or her performance and develop potential rather than to compete with others.

34. Teachers accept and respond to the fact that growth patterns will be irregular and will occur in different areas at different times.

35. Individual pupil progress forms are used to record the learning tasks completed, deficiencies that need new assignments to permit mastery, and all other data that will show the child's progress in relation to past achievements and potential or that will help the teacher in suggesting possible future learning experiences for the individual.

36. Evaluating and reporting will consider all five areas of the child's development: aesthetic, physical, intellectual, emotional, and social.

In the balance of her study, Barbara Nelson Pavan deduced a total of 170 behavioral implications from the 36 assumptions, and again the items were authenticated by several authorities in the United States and Great Britain. Pavan and Robert H. Anderson are currently updating the behavior implications, or indicators, as part of a publication project on implementing nongradedness. Among Pavan's important conclusions was that, in terms of their underlying philosophies, there are no differences between nongraded and open education. Anderson (1973), in a publication about open education, argued essentially the same point.

Another set of guidelines for understanding and implementing nongradedness was provided in 1969 by Lewis. Included in his useful volume were chapters defining the nongraded concept, discussing pitfalls to avoid when nongrading, suggesting how to initiate a nongraded program, and proposing evaluation procedures. An important chapter discussed the implications of the nongraded concept for the culturally different child, to whom a nongraded environment can offer "a new chance in school." Very practical were Lewis's suggestions for organizing the classroom, for reporting pupil progress, and for developing individual study units. These units are one of three basic formats recommended for the nongraded curriculum, the other two being a Skill Concept Sequence Plan and a Multiple Phase Plan. Eight appendices provide various illustrative and source materials.

One of the most scholarly discussions of nongradedness as related to school organizations is contained in a yearbook chapter by Heathers

(1966). He notes the general absence of well-formulated theory; of attention to the motivation and training needs of teachers who become involved in school reorganization activities; of university efforts to develop adequate research designs; and especially of appropriate university programs geared to the training of leaders and teachers involved in local improvement projects. Heathers cautions that the worthy goals and the great promise of attempts to replace gradedness and self-contained classrooms are unlikely to be realized unless these fundamental needs are met.

A very important contribution to the cause of organizational reform was made by Purdom, whose 1970 monograph represented a major step toward a more accurate and precise definition of the nongraded concept. After a review of the distortions and accommodations that have prevented true ungradedness from being developed and tested, Purdom spells out a conceptual model and then describes the "engineering" tasks required to implement each of the model's components. The latter are stated in eleven propositions (pp. 15–19):

School function: (1) The school assists each learner in developing his or her potential to the maximum.

Curriculum: (2) The curriculum emphasizes the development of the broad structural concepts and modes of inquiry in the disciplines.

Instruction: (3) Learning opportunities are provided on the basis of individual needs, interests, and abilities; (4) all phases of human growth are considered when making decisions about how to work effectively with a learner; (5) learning opportunities are paced so that each child can progress in relation to his or her own rate of development in each area of the curriculum.

Evaluation: (6) An evaluation of all phases of human growth is made for each individual; (7) evaluation of each learner's progress is carried on almost constantly; (8) the adequacy of each child's progress is an individual matter determined by appraising his or her attainments in relation to estimates of his or her potential.

Organization: (9) The school is organized to facilitate continuous and cumulative learning for each learner throughout his or her schooling; (10) the school is so structured that there are alternate learning environments available to the individual and alternate opportunities within these environments to progress at different rates and work at different levels in each area of the curriculum.

Role of the Learner: (11) Learners use their own interests and needs to establish the objectives they will pursue.

Therefore it cannot reasonably be argued that nongradedness lacks operational guidelines or that practical suggestions for implementation have been lacking. However, it remains doubtful whether the /I/D/E/A/ materials and the publications of the scholars noted above have reached a sufficiently large audience, particularly through university courses in curriculum and administration. Because almost two decades have elapsed since these useful sources were produced, and especially because interest remains high as supportive research is being produced, it would seem that the time is ripe for another generation of advocative and illustrative literature. We hope the updating of our own work will serve as a stimulant to such activity.

Research Findings

Inquiry into the extent and the effectiveness of nongraded schooling, and of those versions of open education that seem synonymous with nongradedness, ran its course primarily through the late 1960s and early 1970s; however, specific aspects such as competitive versus noncompetitive marking, promotion versus retention, and efforts to individualize instruction continue to receive attention. A brief review of the major reports may be useful.

In a fairly thorough treatment of the topic, DiLorenzo and Salter (1965) provided a composite picture, based on the literature, of nongraded primary schools and of the available research reports. They also described a cooperative experimental study then underway in New York State, which sought to compare graded and nongraded schools in operation. Later, somewhat equivocal results were reported by McLoughlin (1967), who in subsequent publications (1969, 1970, 1972) served as a critical although useful commentator on the generally superficial and, in his view, sometimes empty efforts that were represented in the reorganization literature. His 1972 statement regarding "the basics of viable individualized instructional programs" remains a forceful charge to would-be innovators of the 1980s. In brief, the basics include concern for individual differences, not group similarities; school and district-wide commitments; a basic recasting of the teacher's role; systematic development of individualized instructional programs; continuous, carefully developed in-service programs for teachers; and detailed evaluation procedures.

Barbara Nelson Pavan served for a time as principal of the Franklin School in Lexington, Massachusetts, famed as the site of the first major research and development project in team teaching at the elementary school level. That project, as did most of the significant team-teaching efforts, involved multiage pupil teams within which grade-level labels and distinctions were muted if not ignored. Pursuant to the completion of her doctoral study of nongradedness, Pavan published several articles reporting research studies comparing schools with graded classrooms and those with nongraded or open classrooms. The first of these (Feb. 1973) traced the history of the century-long movement to respond more appropriately to the realities of individual differences and the need to maximize each child's unique potential. She observed, as did Anderson (1973), that progressive education, nongradedness, and open education represent successive stages of such efforts, and she urged educators to become both more familiar with, and committed to, the philosophies and psychological concepts upon which these movements rested, lest pedagogical amnesia cause such awareness and commitment to be lost. In subsequent articles (Mar. 1973, Dec. 1973), Pavan provided detailed information about 16 research studies published between 1968 and 1971, a period that in retrospect was the high-water mark for attention to nongradedness. Later (1977), Pavan surveyed all comparative research studies reported between 1968 and 1976, for a cumulative total of 37. She reported five general conclusions:

1. Comparisons of graded and nongraded schools using standardized achievement tests continue to favor nongradedness.
2. Attendance in a nongraded school may improve the students' chances for good mental health and positive attitudes toward school.
3. Longitudinal studies indicate that the longer students are in a nongraded program, the more likely it is that they will have positive school attitudes and better academic achievement. One study found that 5 to 10 percent more children in primary-level nongraded programs reached fourth grade with their entering class than did children in graded primary structures.
4. A nongraded environment is particularly beneficial in terms of academic achievement and mental health for blacks, boys, underachievers, and students of lower socioeconomic status.
5. Further research is needed that includes an assessment of the actual practices in the allegedly graded or nongraded schools in order to determine if the labels as described are accurate. (Pavan, 1977, p. 93)

Several of the studies advocated multigraded classes as a step in the direction of nongradedness. Within 51 comparisons using standardized achievement tests, only two favored the graded school.

Bob Steere (1972), who compared nongraded and graded secondary schools in his doctoral dissertation, used an approach similar to Pavan's and reported on twelve studies which he concluded "clearly indicate(s) that a nongraded school organization has the potential for breaking the shackles which wantonly bind children of the same chronological age and force a lockstep movement of youth through a rigid curriculum" (p. 711).

In a recent newsletter (Harvard, 1986), researchers from the Harvard Graduate School of Education examined the question "Repeating a Grade: Does It Help?" and concluded that "we have no persuasive evidence that retention helps children to learn" (p. 3). Also noted were both social and academic implications, as well as cost factors, associated with retention practices. The beneficial effects of "readiness" classes (a more appropriate way of providing an extra year of preparation), multiage grouping, biannual promotions, and other efforts to meet children's growth needs more flexibly were discussed.

Other recent reports concerning grade retention versus promotion have been presented by Lindelow (1985) and Walker (1984). Holmes and Matthews (1984) reported a meta-analysis of 44 studies on the effects of nonpromotion on elementary and junior high pupils. The dimensions of academic achievement, personal adjustment, self-concept, and attitude toward school were examined, and on all counts the negative effects of retention consistently outweighed positive outcomes. The results led the authors to challenge "proponents of retention plans to show there is compelling logic indicating success of their plans when so many other plans have failed" (p. 232).

As we have already noted, among the most serious problems afflicting all of the research on nongradedness—and indeed all efforts to redefine structural and operational elements in schools—is the absence of relevant and appropriate measurement tools. Especially absent are measures of the aforementioned elements as they either do or do not exist in the experimental and control groups being compared. As often as not, researchers seem to accept the labels that are attached, without bothering to confirm that what is happening within the class or school is in fact consistent with the label. As a result, School A (which recently has been labeled a nongraded school, but which is very little changed from the graded school that it was) may turn out to be doing much less well than School B (which is called a graded school but within which the principal and staff are deviating significantly from literal gradedness). It is therefore highly important for researchers to examine the extent to which the essential features of nongradedness, as a system, are found within each environment being examined.

Otto (1969), after reporting on a study in two schools in Texas and reviewing some 40 other studies, concluded that the research does tell us several things. First, teachers differ widely in how they teach and how children become involved in the instructional program; these differences prevail among teachers in nongraded as well as in graded programs. Second, how teachers teach and how they work with children is more important than any single feature of organization. Third, the classroom practices of teachers are influenced by the scope and variety of resources available to them. Fourth, if the resources are restricted, one should not anticipate major advantages accruing to a nongraded program. Fifth, a nongraded program cannot be mandated; it must have teacher insights and dedication appropriate to the nongraded philosophy. Sixth, if a nongraded program is to fulfill its mission, many related facets of the internal organization of the school must be altered simultaneously (pp. 125–126).

In one segment of a report on British primary schools, Stanton (1973) describes how vertical grouping, also known as family grouping or vertical streaming, is used to promote pupil growth and well-being in infant programs (ages 5–7) and in junior departments (ages 7–11). Flexible and staggered entry arrangements, continuation of groups with the same teacher for more than one year, highly individualized learning programs, heavy use of self-sufficient pupil groupings for skills work, and shared total-class experiences are noted as features. The healthy and mutually supportive relationship between "older and more mature children" and "newcomers and the less able" is said to be both social and academic in context. Tracing the philosophy of vertical grouping to the work of Jean Piaget, Stanton observes that the arrangement reduces anxieties, promotes social and intellectual growth, and facilitates the progress of both slower and brighter children without "the disgrace of staying back and repeating a grade," on the one hand, or on the other, of sacrificing social-peer interactions when going ahead academically more rapidly.

Evidence from ethnology, anthropology, and educational history and research indicates that age segregation, which is in effect what graded classrooms provide, is neither necessary nor natural. In studies of primates and more simple human societies, it becomes clear that age segregation is a relatively recent social invention, and, worse, it appears to have far more negative than positive consequences. Pratt (1983), in summarizing 27 empirical studies in multiage grouping in the United States and Canada from 1948 to 1981, concluded that although there is no consistent relationship between multiage grouping and academic achievement, it has a generally benign effect on social and emotional development. Whereas same-age groups create increased competition and aggression, multiage groups promote increased harmony and nurturance. Companionship patterns outside the multiage classroom are also healthier. Younger members benefit the most, although many observers in other studies have noted that the more mature and experienced members of multiage groups offer opportunities for leadership and mentoring.

In a recent (1986) condensed revision of his paper, Pratt extends his study and concludes that multiage classrooms, though more arduous for teachers to manage, provide socially and psychologically healthy places for children. In a personal letter (June 12, 1986), Pratt also reported that there have been no adequate summaries or syntheses of the research on nongrading: He located more than 50 empirical doctoral theses, but rarely are more than 20 or 30 reviewed.

As a final commentary on mixed-age grouping, it might be noted that it is employed within the highly respected Montessori system for early education.

In the research that will be needed in the future, the extent to which children are comfortable and happy in the school environment should receive more emphasis. In fact, a reasonable hypothesis is that children who are experiencing and developing a capacity for *pleasure* within the school will be more diligent and productive than those who are not. It is of special interest that this conclusion was reached by Bloom and his associates (1985) in their study of the early development of 120 young adults who have reached the top of their fields in music, sports, arts, and sciences. In addition to noting the strong influence of parental commitment and attention, and the hard work and sacrifice involved in succeeding, the researchers identified the very critical role of pleasure (the parents', the child's, and the teachers') in the development of exceptional talents. Although some children had greater natural ability or talent, those who practiced with enthusiasm, persistence, and pleasure surpassed them. In the early years, the influence of teachers who genuinely enjoyed working with children and who made lessons pleasant was strong. The building of early foundations under pleasant conditions prepared children well for the more demanding and rigorous training that followed after a few years. It is easy to translate this research, done with highly competent and successful people, into implications for early elementary schooling more universally defined: The capacity of all children to derive satisfaction from earnest effort and the gradual, incremental improvement of skills underlies most accomplishments. Parents, teachers, and children ought ideally to reinforce and stimulate each other through the enthusiasm that both precedes and follows upon achievements.

In a similar vein, in describing behavioral sets that can be learned, Bloom (1986) uses the term "automaticity" for the state when the individual's array of habits and skills provides a peak response with one stroke of attention. In order for young children to develop desired automaticity in language use, Bloom asserts, there should be a great emphasis upon voluntary reading "for pleasure and for the pupil's own purposes" (p. 77). Similar comment is made about promoting reading habits, writing for personal use, arithmetic as a tool for outside the classroom, safety rules and skills, and the basic idiom and skills of the various arts, learned in an enjoyable way. It seems reasonable to claim that nongraded classrooms are more likely to support such learning.

One of our strongest original convictions, reflected especially in Chapters 6 and 7 of the 1959 and 1963 editions, had to do with the importance of building self-esteem and ego strength, for example, through whatever procedures are used to assess and report on pupils' academic progress. Bloom (1981) comments in several ways about the impact upon children and their self-concept of teachers' evidenced opinion of their academic progress, and he implies that standardized achievement test scores, received less frequently and within a less relevant framework, have less influence upon self-image. Repeated success over a number of years, he concludes, "increases the probability of the student's gaining a positive view of himself and high self-esteem" (p. 19). The reverse is also true. Equally impressive is Bloom's conclusion that repeated success enables children to withstand stress and anxiety (emotional illness) more effectively, whereas repeated failure has the opposite effect.

A pervading theme in the nongraded literature, and also in the broad field of early childhood development, is that the preschool and primary years are of crucial importance. Again, Benjamin Bloom is a preeminent source of information derived from research on this topic. Among his conclusions, which we heartily endorse, is that primary teachers should be the best trained, the most carefully selected, and the best paid teachers in the system (Bloom, 1981, pp. 106–108). He also recommends a lower adult–child ratio, especially in the case of children with learning difficulties, and the use of highly developed diagnostic and evaluation techniques. He then proposes:

> The work of the pupils in these early years must be one of constant success. This will probably mean that great care must be taken in planning learning tasks which children can successfully complete. Failure of children to succeed with learning tasks should be regarded as a failure of curriculum and instruction rather than as a failure of the children. It is likely that some children will need more time and assistance to complete a specific learning task than will others. However, the repeating of a grade or year of work at this level would seem to be an inappropriate procedure. In contrast, the ungraded school[5] has much merit if this plan is accompanied by teaching methods and curriculum programs which encourage each child to move to his highest level of capacity and continually rewards him for his accomplishments. (p. 108)

Bloom's footnote number 5 refers to our 1963 edition. Later, in a section dealing with "The Variables for Mastery Learning Strategies," he notes that such strategies may be derived from the work of John B. Carroll, supported by the ideas of H. C. Morrison, Jerome Bruner, B. F. Skinner, Patrick Suppes, Robert Glaser, and Goodlad and Anderson.

The section discusses five variables: (1) aptitude for various kinds of learning; (2) quality of instruction; (3) ability to understand instruction; (4) perseverance; and (5) time allowed for learning. The nongraded school is acknowledged as one attempt to provide an organizational structure that permits and encourages mastery learning (p. 166).

Overall, therefore, it would seem that there is a large body of research data and informed scholarly opinion, some directly related to organizational variables and some related to basic underlying concepts, which supports the structure and approach we have advocated. If, as seems at least possible, the time has arrived for reinvigoration and reapplication of nongraded arrangements, it is to be hoped that significant additional studies will soon be under way.

Why is Nongradedness Still Alive?

Beyond the theoretical validity of the nongraded school concept, at least a dozen reasons exist for its persistence and its currency. The most important reason is that the graded structure, whatever its usefulness in the nineteenth century as an aid to the development of universal public education, has been an anomaly with which conscientious educators have had to contend for over a century. The simple fact is that a literally graded approach to instruction does not work, and teachers and administrators must constantly subvert it in order to deal with the realities of individual differences. Compromise, invention, adaptation, and thoughtful disregard for grade-level standards are invariably practiced in graded schools, even though many teachers probably do not realize fully how unfaithful to gradedness they find it necessary to be in their daily work with children. That each child's unique needs must be accepted in good spirit is rarely resisted by such teachers, although abandonment of the labels and the administrative practices (for example, competitive marking systems) that contradict such a view does not generally seem feasible to them.

Probably the abandonment—or more accurately the softening—of graded administrative practices has occurred most widely in schools where team teaching or some variant thereof has replaced the literal self-containment of teachers. Especially in situations where two or more grade/age levels are served by the same group of teachers, there is much greater flexibility for dealing with individual differences when teachers share and collaborate. In fact, it is probable that the most valid examples of nongradedness in practice are to be found within multiaged (or multigraded), team-taught situations. This is true even though graded levels and marking practices may still be used to some extent. We perceive that over time those labels and practices tend to become almost invisible.

The most thorough discussion of team teaching that has appeared in the literature is the multiauthor volume edited by Shaplin and Olds (1964). A chapter on "Theory and Practice in Team Teaching" in Anderson (1966) remains a useful operational statement, but a much more recent and work-group-oriented discussion appears as Chapter 6 in Snyder and Anderson (1986).

The methodologies and procedures associated with both non-gradedness and team teaching appear to permeate many schools and classrooms, even though the two labels are not commonly used. Of interest is that the educational literatures in other countries apparently pay considerable attention to the two organizational constructs, and it seems that related American publications (including our own) continue to circulate quite widely. We occasionally communicate, for example, with educators in the British Commonwealth nations, Japan, Israel, and Central European countries. Of the five translations of the 1963 edition, the Italian version is still being purchased in quantity. Muzi (1980) indicates in a journal focusing on Western European education that the "two educational innovations" have become increasingly popular as a means of modernizing traditional educational environments.

The American love affair with British-style open education—which reached its peak in the late 1960s and early 1970s—tended to steal the spotlight from nongradedness for a while, and the word "open" came to be used in much the same way that the less attractive word "non-graded" (a litotes) had been. This is not to say that the terms and the concepts they represent are synonymous; however, there is enough overlap in the philosophies they represent and the practices they commend, so that advocates of nongradedness have regarded open education and its literature as a welcome and compatible phenomenon.

A major force in the weakening of graded practices was Public Law 94-142 (The Education for All Handicapped Children Act, 1975), which we regard as one of the most important and beneficial pieces of federal legislation in American educational and social history. However difficult this law has been to implement, however clumsy (and sometimes reluctant) have been the implementers, and however idealistic it has seemed to be, PL 94-142 established forcefully that each child, being unique, must be given learning opportunities logically related to a carefully assembled definition of his or her needs and possibilities. That the law focused upon exceptional children was a long-overdue correction, but the relevance of both the assumptions and the requirements of this law to *all* children should not be lost upon educators. An additional observation is that the type of training and behavior required of teachers (counselors, administrators, and other involved professionals) in "special" education, spurred by PL 94-142, can and should become the standard in "regular" education as well. Meanwhile, the influence of special education professionals upon their colleagues in the mainstream has already advanced the cause of nongraded education in countless ways.

Since the late 1950s, when we organized the first edition, there has been a staggering amount of research and informed commentary about child growth and development, human learning, "effective" schools and schooling, and about the usefulness of various materials and schemata. Publications from medicine, physiology, psychology, social psychology, anthropology, and other fields have fertilized and enriched the bodies of knowledge now available to educators as they seek to understand their objectives and opportunities. Notable among the works with which educators ought to be familiar are several books by Benjamin Bloom. His advocacy of mastery learning for all children, his optimistic conclusion that under the right conditions nearly all children can in fact master the school's offerings, and his recommendations concerning classroom practice are consistent with and supportive of nongradedness as we have sought to define it.

In fact, looking at the entire array of literature growing out of recent educational research, we find an overwhelming preponderance of evidence and argument to support nongradedness in all of its dimensions. There is simply no research that says graded structure is desirable, or, for that matter, that single-age class groupings and/or self-contained classrooms are to be preferred. The debate about promotion versus nonpromotion, which heats up every so often, rarely comes down on the side of nonpromotion. Similarly, studies of the effectiveness of competitive marking systems fail to sustain or support that aspect of graded schooling. If the advocates of gradedness were to stake their professional reputations on research, or even on responsible commentary in the literature, they would all be unemployed educators within a few hours. Put positively, the advocates of nongradedness have virtually no counterevidence with which to contend.

Teacher education, both preservice and in-service, is another force—despite its being a relatively weaker one—for a sustained interest in nongradedness. The aggressive advocacy of the self-contained classroom that was common several decades ago is much less in evidence today. Exposure to the extensive research literature, to systems of individualized instruction, to computer-related technologies, to realities such as Public Law 94-142, and to other forces causes newly prepared teachers to have greater zeal for nongraded and cooperative learning approaches. Related to this is the growing strength of the teaching profession and the increasingly enlightened behavior of major professional organizations in (1) their advocacy through contracts of better in-service growth opportunities for their members; (2) their sponsorship of instruction-based workshops and clinics; and (3) their support of legislation that promises better schooling conditions.

It seems to us that the sometimes furious national debate in the 1980s about the quality of American education, spurred by numerous commission reports and much-discussed publications such as *A Place Called School* (1984), has resulted in unprecedented awareness of both the failures/weaknesses and the strengths/merits of schooling as it is now practiced in America. To some extent the pressures toward back-to-basics curricula, tougher academic standards, higher test scores, and other manifestations of serious educational effort may have hurt the cause of nongradedness. On the other hand, advocates of nongraded schools have never supported soft standards or low test scores as if they were a reasonable price for helping all sorts of learners to feel better about themselves. Studies that Pavan and others have reported tend to show that nongraded approaches actually *increase* scores and productivity, and that tougher nonpromotion practices result in *less* learning. While parents may need a harder sell before they will believe this, it would seem that one outcome of all the fury must eventually be greater enthusiasm among the citizenry for nongradedness as the way to go.

In our mention of open education, as well as in discussions of team teaching, the impact of more flexible school-building designs upon individually more appropriate instructional arrangements should be noted. Although there has been a noticeable swing back from the totally open designs that were popular in the 1960s, flexibility and functionality remain central to school architecture, and the fact that so many American schools are designed to facilitate open and collaboratively taught arrangments is a positive gain for nongradedness. The significant success and durability of pilot efforts in school reorganization, such as the multiunit schools associated with Individually Guided Education, remains another positive gain for nongradedness.

One point of confusion for us, as we seek to assess the current status of nongradedness, is the condition of pupil progress reporting. The views we presented in Chapter 6 of the first two editions remain both valid and practical, in our minds. We suspect, however, that the increasing use of computers in the process of issuing reports to pupils and parents has led teachers and administrators to depend far more heavily upon numbers and scores, to become much less descriptive in the messages sent home, and to heighten parental awareness of grade norms and grade-level expectations. Whether this tendency is being counterbalanced by more effective one-on-one parent–teacher conferencing, by informative supplementary messages, and by other elaborations of the child's progress is a question we must investigate. The relative dearth since the 1960s of doctoral dissertations, articles, book chapters, or other publications dealing with reporting pupil progress is lamentable. Our hope is that such investigations will be carried out in the next few years.

The Nongraded School
in the Educational Context

The first edition of *The Nongraded Elementary School* was published just as the school reform movement of the late 1950s and 1960s was beginning. The launching of Sputnik (1957) had served as the catalyst, just as publication of *A Nation at Risk* served as the catalyst for reform 26 years later. At the outset, the two reform movements paralleled each other in their emphasis on tightening up and toughening up a school system that presumably had gone soft. They were alike, also, in being stimulated by concern for the role of the United States in world affairs: competition in technology that could be turned to war, in the case of the Soviet Union after Sputnik, and competition in the world's economic system, in the case of Japan, in the 1980s and beyond.

Following *A Nation at Risk* (1983), there were literally dozens of reports recommending improvement in the schools; some estimates put the number released between 1983 and 1985 at 175. Following Sputnik, one report caught national attention: James B. Conant's *The American High School Today* (1959). There is an interesting parallel between many of Conant's recommendations and those of the various commissions a quarter of a century later. Both recommended, among other things, a core of the "harder subjects," particularly mathematics and science, with studies in technology being an addition to the reports of the 1980s.

But there is also an interesting difference. In the more recent period of school reform, many states—often responding to their own study commissions—set common graduation requirements for all high school students that specified more courses in English, mathematics, the sciences, and the social studies: the fields also most frequently stated in college and university entrance requirements. Conant, on the other hand, had been deeply influenced by the work of a committee that he had appointed while President of Harvard University, *General Education in a Free Society* (1945). He translated the committee's "five fingers of knowledge" into a common core of English, social studies, mathematics and science; art and music for all (but with electives from which to choose); advanced studies in core subjects for the college bound; and the opportunity for some electives beyond the common core in general education subjects and vocational education. The specifics became a check list for school boards all across the country.

Conant, in spite of, or perhaps because of, his elitist educational background, shared with the Harvard Committee a keen sense of "the claims of a common culture, citizenship, and standard of human good" and the role of a common K–12 school in meeting them. Clearly, he saw the need for all students to secure the best secondary school education of which they were capable, which meant, for him, creating some carefully planned alternatives to meet individual differences. The committees of the 1980s might have benefited from such thinking!

At the time this reprinting is going to press, evidence is growing to the effect that many students are not being served well in the aftermath of *A Nation at Risk*. Approximately one in four is opting out of high school a year or two before completion. The growing suicide rate among able students is of deep concern in some of our most affluent communities. The thesis coming more and more to the forefront is that these occurrences are to a considerable degree correlated with tougher requirements not only for graduating high school but also for passing courses and grades. One of the most disturbing questions concerns the degree to which the onus has been placed on students rather than on the enterprise called school, especially the lock-step curriculum and graded structure that continue to defy most efforts to ameliorate them.

We turn now to another parallel between post-Sputnik and post-1983 school reform. During the early years, both were driven by lay groups—primarily school boards, in the case of the first, and legislatures, in the case of the second. Both were guided by assumptions of rightness and goodness regarding the basic functioning of schools. They needed mostly a tightening up; more time for more of what they were viewed as doing best over the years. Indeed, proposals for reform were geared much more to "the good old days" than to either changed circumstances in the context of schooling, a changing school population, or earlier proposals that challenged existing patterns and programs. Much of the reform rhetoric of the 1980s put down the reforms of the 1960s as an embarrassing failure not to be repeated anew.

This brings us to perhaps the most important parallel. At the time of Sputnik, a set of interests in schooling quite different from those making the headlines was quietly at work. These were interests of researchers and educators and took at least three forms.

First, the evidence regarding individual differences among learners was becoming compelling. This raised serious questions about the Procrustean graded structure of schooling which, instead of accommodating these differences, unfairly discriminated against both the least and the most able. Over the years, creative practicing educators had become aware of these differences and had experimented with a variety of ways, including "ungrading," to deal constructively with them.

Second, studies of cognition increasingly were demonstrating the extraordinary ability of young children to learn complex matters if only they were rendered accessible—by creative curriculum planners and teachers, for instance. Early in the 1960s, the Bruner dictum provided both the synthesis of this idea and the challenge: ". . . any subject can be taught in some intellectually honest form to any child at any stage of development" (1960).

The third strand of reforms found expression in efforts to revitalize and restructure the school subjects. Layers of minor revisions had been pasted upon previous layers of minor revisions until school subjects had lost whatever coherence they might have once possessed. The work of the University of Illinois Committee on School Mathematics, for example, began in 1951, with its roots going back to the late 1940s. Similar work in physics and biology undoubtedly was stimulated by Sputnik but did not fit the pattern of post-Sputnik reform rhetoric.

We see, then, that by 1959, when Conant's report on the American high school appeared, there were two major reform movements under way: one driven by Sputnik, which did not challenge the fundamental regularities of schooling, and another, which did. The Conant Report (as it is most commonly identified) fit the former pattern. Our book, *The Nongraded Elementary School*, published in the same year; Bruner's *The Process of Education* (1960); and the curriculum study groups, most well under way by 1961, fit the latter. These represented the three sets of interests that, with several related ones, soon were to relegate to history the kinds of reforms that were in the news during the years immediately following Sputnik. By the mid-1960s, these strands dominated the school reform movement, which now looked not at all like what had been recommended in the late 1950s. Furthermore, this second wave of reform was driven primarily by educators in both the universities and the schools, with substantial federal support.

An anecdote will help dramatize what had occurred. After publishing another influential report in 1963, *The Education of American Teachers*, James B. Conant returned to West Berlin where previously he had represented the United States and Allied interests as High Commissioner. In a conversation later, when Conant was once more back in the United States, he confided to John Goodlad (who had worked with him on the teacher-education study) that he simply would not know where to start any attempt to study once more the conditions and needs of schooling. The nature and directions of proposed innovation and reconstruction, Conant said, had changed so much during his absence as to be almost unrecognizable.

Now, let us pick up the parallel with more recent times. A resurgence of concern about the schools comparable to that preceding Sputnik had been building in the United States prior to the release of *A Nation at Risk*. Changing priorities at the federal level and taxing pressures at the local level together were increasing both state financing of schools and state authority for schooling. These developments, in turn, were directing state attention to what the schools were doing and to the determination of priorities for state support. *A Nation at Risk* provided a timely stimulus for intensified interest on the part of governors and legislators. Also, it provided the kinds of recommendations that accorded with states' desires for cost-effectiveness but that did not challenge the established regularities of schooling.

At the same time, there were growing concerns in other quarters that the back-to-basics movement of the 1970s represented an oversimplification of school problems and needs, that the schools were not adapting to changing conditions in the larger social and world context. Instead of a narrower, more rigid curriculum and pedagogy, the schools needed an opening up, with greater attention to general education, students' problem-solving and creative potential, alienation of youth both in and out of school, the needs of an increasingly diverse student population, and so on. Major inquiries into these and other aspects of schooling were well under way prior to 1983.

Three of these, published in the immediate aftermath of *A Nation at Risk*, received nationwide attention: Boyer's *High School* (1983), Goodlad's *A Place Called School* (1984), and Sizer's *Horace's Compromise* (1984). All three differed from the commission reports then on the scene in diagnosing certain chronic problems of schooling and in making recommendations calling for fundamental reconstruction of schools. Their more modest observations and suggestions often were cited to support similar recommendations in the growing number of commission reports; however, those calling for deeper, structural changes usually were passed over—a fact that many reviewers of the reform literature did not miss.

By 1986, three years beyond *A Nation at Risk*, several developments were apparent:

1. Many of the highly touted reforms, such as markedly higher pay for teachers coupled with career-ladder plans, greater emphasis on writing essays, and use of technology for instructional purposes had fizzled out or were operating in only a limited number of instances.
2. The kinds of teaching practices fostering student passivity that Goodlad, in particular, had criticized were on the rise. As one critic put the matter: The patient is getting more of what made him sick in the first place.

3. Testing—for both students and teachers—as a means of assuring "excellence" was very much on the increase.
4. As noted earlier, students were showing some clear signs of negative reactions to increased school pressure for achievement.
5. Large numbers of students (particularly from minority groups), whose secondary school curricula had appeared to meet college and university requirements, were doing poorly and dropping out.
6. The search for better answers to continuing school problems was shifting to a search for the problems behind the problems—for example, the education of teachers; the persistence of traditional modes of teaching; organizational arrangements (such as tracking) that denied some groups of students access to first-rate subject matter; enactments and mandates that tied the hands of principals and teachers at the level of school and classroom; cluttered curricula seeking to cover too much factual material, and the like.
7. There was a growing use of words and phrases such as empowering teachers, site-based management, the principal as educational leader, greater decentralization of authority, and so on, suggesting a shift from conventional to alternative models of change and improvement.
8. There were clear signs that an initially suspicious and defensive teaching profession that had seen itself as maligned and unappreciated was catching a reform fever differing substantially from the one generated by *A Nation at Risk*, a fever to which persons not close to and familiar with schools had been highly susceptible.

And so, it seems, a cycle that began in the 1950s, rose to its peak in the 1960s, and then faded in the 1970s is in the second stage of repeating itself in the 1980s. The critical question is whether it will follow the same curve in peaking late in the '80s and fading in the '90s. For progress to be made, we must assume that the only parallel between the current educational reform movement and the one that preceded it is to be found in the early years but not later.

Earlier in this Introduction, we raised and sought to answer the question of why nongradedness is still alive as a concept and, in some form, in practice. Using both Pavan's conceptualization and research findings, we argued that nongrading accommodates a philosophy that values developing individual potentialities to the maximum possible. Conversely, we argued that the graded structure of schooling does not; that it cannot stand up to either promoting sound educational values or the goals of schooling—especially those goals that speak to access to knowledge and the other attributes of schooling for all.

In the 1960s, when some of the most useful reforms generated by

Sputnik had been assimilated into the schools, educators took advantage of national interest by seeking changes in long-standing practices that were challenged by new knowledge about individual differences, students' ability to learn, how best to make knowledge accessible for learners, and like matters. Contrary to the attacks of critics, the ideas and concepts were sound; the new research confirmed many heuristic principles of education that have stood the test of time but require careful nurturing in practice. In the 1960s, as in earlier periods, the shortfall was in implementation. The fate of nongrading was tied to that of the related reforms, which were being talked about a great deal but which were implemented only a little.

Nongrading challenged the structure of schooling that had grown up with the nation itself, conveniently classifying every schoolchild with a grade number that was easily recorded and remembered and that was erroneously interpreted as having the same fixed meaning. Topics to be taught, textbooks, tests, and even the taking of class pictures were tied to the grade level. The larger the schooling enterprise became, the more accepted and intractable the graded system became.

The 1950s constituted a period of phenomenal growth in school enrollments. It was necessary, over several of those years, for the Los Angeles Unified School District to find space every Monday morning for the equivalent of an elementary school enrollment of 500 children. These pupils needed teachers. Whatever thin requirements for a teaching credential then prevailing were largely waived in the search for adult bodies. Imagine the readiness of large segments of the teaching force then in place for the onslaught of reform in the late 1950s and early 1960s! Most were just well enough prepared to lose confidence in what they knew about teaching in the face of proposals for individualizing learning, team teaching, modular scheduling, programmed instruction, nongrading, set theory, discovery methods, teaching the structure of the discipline, and all the rest. The reform story of the 1960s, contrary to much popular belief, is not what went on behind classroom doors but what was blunted against them.

What did most to jettison the cargo of ideas carried by the second wave were the extant views of the change process. First, the vehicles of change were viewed to be teachers: Teach teachers new skills and give them new materials and the rest would follow. Second, these same teachers were viewed by change agents as passively awaiting better ideas and materials. One had only to devise an effective delivery system, with appropriate feedback loops, focused squarely on the intended recipients (rather crudely referred to as "targets").

It was 1971 when Seymour Sarason laid bare the shortcomings of the first view. Not only did the culture of the school function to screen out what did not fit with present regularities, he said, but also this culture established for the school ways of behaving that made it possible for the school to maintain a sense of stability in the face of threatening inroads from the outside. Expose teachers to alternative ways, particularly ways that transcend classrooms, and cultural forces will blunt or twist these ways so that the school remains as before. In 1974, Ernest House demonstrated the folly of the second view in his book, *The Politics of Educational Innovation.* His arguments meshed nicely with Sarason's in pointing to the general failure of elaborate, expensive efforts to research, develop, and disseminate innovations that did not take into account teachers' present ways of working and the school context of their work.

The idea of the school—in contrast to the student or teacher—as the key unit in effecting fundamental improvement was taking shape. By the early 1970s, ideas pertaining to the restructuring of schools were being built into both the Wisconsin and /I/D/E/A/ improvement strategies (IGE). At that time, the latter were infused with studies begun in 1966 by the Research Division of /I/D/E/A/ in Los Angeles of the school as the unit of change. This work advanced the notion that the very culture of the school that so effectively blocked change could be used as the vehicle to promote it. Necessary to the process, however, are an infrastructure that supported the school (a district office, a network, and so forth), a principal who empowered teachers, and opportunities for teachers to plan and work together in creating a renewing— not just a surviving—culture. By the time the six books reporting this work were published (1973 through 1975), the nation was deeply into a back-to-basics movement and "change" was almost a dirty word: The second wave of reform following Sputnik spent itself on a deserted beach.

However, few periods in American educational history are without significant developments. It became apparent to some concerned educators and lay citizens that the educational needs of minority children could not await changed attitudes and housing patterns. Social and educational reform are both desirable, said Ronald Edmonds (1979), but the immediate agenda is to give minority children, wherever enrolled, the best education of which they are capable. Thus the effective schools movement was born.

By 1986, many of the most easily implemented reforms generated by *A Nation at Risk* were being assimilated into the schools. By 1986, teachers and administrators in more than a few communities scattered across the nation, who had felt dumped upon by mandates and enactments, were beginning to become *pro*active rather than *re*active. Some universities and school districts were beginning to join in partnerships designed to support joint efforts addressed to areas of mutual self-interest. As after Sputnik, a second wave of educational reform was building, once again driven primarily by educators.

How is fundamental change such as nongrading likely to fare in these stirrings and their unfoldings? On the negative side are the memories from the '60s of a massive, relatively well-funded effort that failed to satisfy the hopes of its leaders. But it must be remembered that the thrust was more to use the schools as agents of social reform than to reform the schools—an effort almost always doomed to fail in the short run. That it did fail, even in the short run, is a matter for a debate. One might say, again on the negative side, that the lessons of history testify against significant change within the time span of a generation. But one has only to examine the changes in attitudes toward and provisions for handicapped children over the last quarter century to refute this conclusion.

On the positive side, what we have said so far implies the coming together in the late 1980s and early 1990s of at least eight encouraging factors.

First, the data on and the implications of profound differences among students enrolled in schools no longer are new. They are at least as much a part of the conventional wisdom as are the myths regarding individuality. These differences will become more compelling and more difficult to ignore as we become even more a nation of minorities. Nongrading should grow in support as a way of accommodating individuality to a curriculum that necessarily must become more common.

Second, the hypotheses of researchers such as Bruner and Bloom on the ability of *all* children to learn, which were new and startling to most teachers in the 1960s, have been strengthened by further research and validated in school programs like those reported in the literature on effective schools. There are ways to provide for individual differences without dividing the curriculum into varying subject matter for the most and least able, ways not nearly as apparent in Conant's time as they are today. The nongraded structure facilitates one of these ways in particular, namely, providing more time for the slower students. In our own concern for taking care of individual differences through nongrading and other provisions, it did not dawn on us that schools would use high, middle, and low tracks with quite different subject matter in each as a major means of meeting student differences in achievement. For us, this is giving up on individuals in the name of treating individuality. In her book, *Keeping Track: How Schools Structure Inequality* (1985), Jeannie Oakes provides the evidence and reasoned argument for rejecting such practices.

Third, we now have the theoretical and, to a considerable degree, the research underpinnings to support not just the individual student but also the school as the unit of selection in seeking change. Nongrading transcends individual teachers. Earlier in this Introduction we saw how nongrading was corrupted when individual teachers saw it only as a way to differentiate levels of attainment in a reading program. But when several teachers together look for ways to get rid of the unrealistic floors and ceilings imposed by the graded structure, the open-envelope, nongraded approach begins to make sense.

Fourth, we have had time to digest some of the meanings of the school as a culture. To assume that the school is a unit that is the sum total of its classrooms is to assume, erroneously, that the latter drive the former. Research on effective schools; the analysis in Chapter 8 of *A Place Called School* (1984); Lightfoot's *The Good High School* (1983); and, of course, Sarason's *The Culture of the School and the Problem of Change* (1971), suggest precisely the opposite. Consequently, one is more likely to nongrade successfully when an entire faculty becomes increasingly discontented with present arrangements. Just two or three discontented teachers soon are likely to find themselves frustrated by school regularities and isolated by their peers, a development that was not uncommon in the '60s.

Fifth, the idea of the principal as instructional and, more recently, educational leader has gained widespread acceptance in the 1980s. In the past, principals viewed themselves as managers taking care of the building, individual teachers, student discipline, and similar matters. Total staff meetings, particularly rare at the secondary level, primarily took care of procedural matters. For many schools, a staff meeting devoted to substantive issues, let alone a major innovation, would have been a major innovation itself. Although the new role for principals is still one more of rhetoric than reality, at least it conveys the idea of someone concerned about the entire institution and seeking ways to make it better. Related concepts gaining acceptance, such as site-based management and teacher involvement, fit with the notion of the principal as educational leader and, in turn, with ideas pertaining to renewing the school's culture. It is within this framework of ideas and their implementation that modifying the graded school and creating a nongraded school become feasible.

Sixth, nongrading is no longer novel and innovative. It is now part of the lexicon of educational discourse worldwide. Consequently, the word and what it denotes can be considered dispassionately, without the somewhat frightening connotations of innovation and change. Although we deliberately departed from "ungraded" in favor of "nongraded" in *The Nongraded Elementary School*, we built on ideas that were not new. In 1959, the concepts were associated mostly with experimental and laboratory schools cited in the literature or by a few forward-looking, charismatic leaders in public schools. Let us simply say that, now, the word is not at all "precious"; it has been democratized.

Seventh, since change is part of the modern context of schooling and since change, by definition, is movement from what now exists, we can anticipate both a shift in this context and a shift toward a more "soft and tender" philosophy of schooling, away from the "hard and tough." This has been the zigzag course of the country and its schools throughout the century. Just as soon as we get the tough courses and the accompanying tests firmly in place, we will turn our attention once again to the side effects. We have argued (convincingly, we think) above that nongrading is, in fact, a rigorous concept and a structure that provides for and insists on each student working up to capacity. Nonetheless, it also serves to ameliorate progress through a common curriculum by facilitating, for example, more time for slower students. In doing so, nongrading tends to be lumped with other school practices as belonging to the soft and tender side of the two themes William James saw woven into the fabric of American life. Consequently, as we move toward ameliorating the effects of the recent hard and tough reforms, nongrading is sure to find a brighter place in the educational sunlight of coming years.

Eighth, it is somewhat ironic that nongrading is likely to receive a considerable impetus as one way to facilitate some of the major reforms of the post-*Nation at Risk* era that so far are not catching a firm hold on practice. The practical, organizational aspects of nongrading and not the philosophical underpinnings will be what makes it attractive. This is not at all un-American. We always have been both highly philosophical in our aims for education and our goals for schools, while being almost disdainful of philosophy in our search for the practical. "Don't bother me with all that abstraction," says the newspaper reporter, "just tell me what you propose to do and how it's going to work." The problem with some of the potentially most significant recommendations of the commission reports—for example, a rigorous, common curriculum for all students—is that the present circumstances of schooling just won't let them work without serious repercussions that our citizens ultimately will not tolerate. Fundamental changes in the very structure and regularities of schooling are necessary to the implementation of recommendations that erroneously assume no formidable obstacles standing in the way of implementation.

What is the potential of a book written a quarter of a century ago for serving today's schools? To this question we now turn.

A Dialogue about the Book

BOB: John, I'm looking at the 1963 edition with its attractive blue cover and realizing that this reprinting will contain an exact reproduction of every page in it, plus these words we are adding to it in 1987. This makes me wonder, how much of what we said nearly a quarter of a century ago makes sense now?

JOHN: I think the book holds up surprisingly well, especially in the light of the enormous changes that have occurred in schooling, many of which we have reviewed in this Introduction. Both of us probably have made substantial conceptual shifts, and we would like to see these reflected in the book. Since we cannot do that, however, let's just talk about what we would be willing to keep if we were rewriting and what we would feel obliged to change.

BOB: You wrote nearly all of Chapters 1, 2, 3, 5, and 9. My assignment back then was Chapters 4, 6, 7, and 8, and the Bibliography. Let's see if we have, separately or together, any residual pride of authorship.

JOHN: I hope that this does not prove embarrassing . . . but I have been revisiting old Procrustes . . .

BOB: How does Chapter 1 look to you now?

JOHN: I would want to cite a good deal of the enormous body of literature on individual differences that has accumulated during these years. In particular, I would want to draw on the material regarding cognitive styles and the vast body of new material from developmental psychology. The field of special education is particularly rich in its implications for nongradedness. What surprises me, however, is what surprised me then, namely, how little there is still on the nature of individual differences in the classroom and the demands the range places on teachers. Our arraying of the data in the earlier editions was unique at the time, and unfortunately it remains unique today. Surely there is opportunity for researchers to say more about individual differences in ways that will help teachers. I trust that the growing interest in research on classrooms—for example, in connection with cooperative learning—will soon provide a much richer aggregation of data.

BOB: Recently, there has been a spate of research reviews on the pros and cons of hard-nosed promotion policies. These reviews simply do not reach back far enough; they ignore almost all of what you reviewed so thoroughly in coming to your conclusions. However, it is interesting to note that the conclusions of those reviewing the research today are so close to your own. Am I on track with respect to Chapter 2?

JOHN: For sure! It is interesting to note, however, that the researchers and reviewers of researchers then and now missed the point that is the very basis of our proposals to nongrade. Perhaps you recall my own research and my later review of the research—both of which preceded our writing the book—in which I concluded that both promotion and nonpromotion have negative repercussions for many children. To find that promotion is *somewhat* more beneficial than nonpromotion is of negligible significance compared with this earlier conclusion. There is evidence to show that promoting slow-learning children into work with which they have difficulty increases stress and is not good for their mental health. Nonpromotion appears to have a negative impact on the peer relationships of those not promoted and does not produce the achievement gains anticipated. We propose *nongrading*, as you know, so that both promotion and nonpromotion would be eliminated.

BOB: Because it had such a specific historical focus, Chapter 3 probably is one that should be substantially updated and extended. Do you agree?

JOHN: Yes, indeed. When we first wrote the book and even when we revised it four years later, our experience with teachers seeking to nongrade their schools was exceedingly limited. In Chapter 3, I was arguing the case for nongrading over grading, as well as endeavoring to create an image of what a nongraded school would look like. Our experience since then would enrich this part of Chapter 3 immensely. What I would stress now, far more than I did then, would be the philosophy behind nongrading and how this must infuse much more than merely school structure.

BOB: Chapter 4 was my responsibility. The main change we made was to include new material on multiage grouping. I believe that gave us a much better definition of operational elements.

JOHN: Would you still consider this to be a valid description of the nongraded school in operation?

BOB: Valid in one sense, yes, but it's really not a sufficient description. The discussion of admission practices at the time of entry to school, of grouping in general, and especially of multiaging would need beefing up to fit the school scene in 1987. I think I would want to say a lot more about the usefulness of team teaching and multiaging as facilitating-mechanisms, as opposed to seeking levels or groupings based on achievement measures. I'd like to say "Amen" to the complaint that pupil groupings, in spite of the rhetoric used, almost always are much too permanent. I would like to insert, also, reference to some of the newer work on cooperative learning and peer tutoring. In fact, we probably ought to do an entire book on what I was trying to do in Chapter 4. We should at least put that idea on a back burner.

JOHN: I agree, except that my back burner, like yours, already is overcrowded. Much of the same could be said about Chapter 5. In this Introduction, we already have said quite a lot about the ways through which curricula have been differentiated in content for learners of differing learning rates; to me, this is a corruption of the whole idea of individual differences and how to deal with them. Nongrading, in both philosophy and structural implications, provides a major means of meeting individual differences in a common curriculum.

BOB: My Chapter 6 on reporting now seems to me like a period piece.

JOHN: You're unhappy with it?

BOB: No, in fact I still believe in just about every sentence I wrote. But so much more is now available about child growth and development, pupil motivation, the effects of rewards and punishments, and even the legal aspects of pupil record keeping and confidentiality, that a substantial rewrite probably would make sense. I'm puzzled, though, about the very small quantity and the rather uneven quality of research on reporting pupil progress that has been completed since the 1960s. In view of all the national attention about use of tests, pupil labeling, and declining ego-strength in young children, I think it's a scandal that more of our best research people aren't working on the topic. I wonder, for example, about the impact of the new technology, with which there is always the danger of even more impersonalization.

JOHN: Do you still feel as you did about report cards?

BOB: No, I'm even angrier about them now than I was when I wrote the chapter. But I'm still "spitting into the wind" on that topic, and it's discouraging.

JOHN: On page 123 of the 1963 version, at your insistence, we italicized the sentence advocating the face-to-face parent–teacher conference. Did that make you feel somewhat better?

BOB: It sure did! In 1987, I guess I'd rent a skywriting plane and spread that sentence across the sky at least once a week: "The parent–teacher conference . . . is probably the most fruitful and effective single means available [for reporting pupil progress]."

JOHN: So much for Chapter 6! Chapter 7 also was your responsibility. Since 1963, there has been a great deal of research on the broad topic of mental health in children. Have you any second thoughts about what you wrote?

BOB: *What* I said, or rather, the essential concepts I was examining, seems defensible to me years later, but I'm nervous that the figures (on pages 144, 146, and 148) with accompanying prose may convey too mechanical a view of how different types of children can and should progress through the system. I feel, also, that the examples don't sufficiently convey what a multi-age, team-taught environment contributes to smooth, continuous pupil progress.

JOHN: What about the mental health aspect? And motivation in children?

BOB: I believe Chapter 7 holds up very well on both dimensions. Since 1963, the research underscores and elaborates the points we made. Some of it also supports what we said in other chapters about reducing the abrasive, competitive atmosphere and making it possible for youngsters to feel good about themselves and about their school experiences, while each learns to the best of his or her ability. However, in the new material of this Introduction, we do refer to several related studies.

JOHN: Do you feel that we did enough, or can do enough now, to persuade school people that a graded, self-centered, competitive atmosphere is counterproductive? Many teachers seem to rely rather heavily on the threat of nonpromotion and the giving of poor grades as motivators.

BOB: I don't know if any one book can do that. It's a terrible shame that the current national atmosphere is one of turning the screws and requiring more *and* heavier work of boys and girls. I don't question that students can and should do much better— in fact, I rejoice in Ben Bloom's assertion that 95 percent of all children are capable of succeeding at school tasks if a properly supportive environment is created. As we already have stated in this Introduction, my hope is that the highly pressured context of schooling will change in the late 1980s and early 1990s, as has happened before.

JOHN: Now, let's turn to Chapter 8. I think that you and I shared in putting this one together. How does it strike you now?

BOB: It's probably too simplistic for a 1980s audience—at least I hope so. The Max Marshall story may seem dated in light of everything that has been written about the change process, some of which we already have reviewed. What do you think of it?

JOHN: When we wrote the book, we were both terribly naïve about the change process. We believed simply that good ideas would prevail—and over the long haul, they do. The years I spent in studying change during the 1960s and 1970s were motivated in large part by what I learned in seeking to implement nongrading. I am somewhat embarrassed to admit that it has taken me most of my life to come to the conclusion that many things not making much sense persist because they serve too many people too well. The graded system serves well recordkeepers, textbook publishers, administrators oriented to management, many parents and teachers, and others. The fact that it does not serve children and youth well is too often a secondary consideration. In brief, I would want to rewrite the chapter substantially.

BOB: Well, this brings us to your Chapter 9, the look-to-the-future chapter. How does the future look to you now? Is the chapter still somewhat relevant?

JOHN: I hope we have been reasonably objective so far in this Introduction. If this is the case, then the concepts of nongrading stand up well. Also, as we already have said, there are more things going for nongrading today than there were in the '60s. Many of the difficulties of teachers and principals arise out of the ways in which the pupil population in the United States has changed during this century. Indeed, if these changes had not occurred, I doubt that *A Nation at Risk* would have been written and disseminated. There would have been little or no need for it. Ironically, that report says very little about what is rather rapidly emerging as this nation's greatest educational problem, namely, accommodating successfully in schools a diverse student population exceeding anything we have known so far. The changing demographics, more than philosophical arguments, will force us into a search for school practices designed to accommodate these individual differences without loss of educational quality in schools. More than ever before, the search must be for ways to assure both quality and equity. It is my hope and expectation—and yours too, I trust—that nongrading will be found to serve very well this important educational cause.

References and Bibliography

Anderson, Robert H. "Theory and Practice in the Nongraded School." In *Teaching in a World of Change*, pp. 45-70. (See also "Theory and Practice in Team Teaching," pp. 71-108.) New York: Harcourt, Brace & World, 1966.

Anderson, Robert H. *Opting for Openness*. Arlington, VA: National Association of Elementary School Principals, 1973.

Bentzen, Mary M. *Changing Schools: The Magic Feather Principle*. New York: McGraw-Hill, 1974.

Bloom, Benjamin S. *Stability and Change in Human Characteristics*. New York: John Wiley & Sons, 1964.

Bloom, Benjamin S. *All Our Children Learning: A Primer for Parents, Teachers, and Other Educators*. New York: McGraw-Hill, 1981.

Bloom, Benjamin S. (ed.). *Developing Talent in Young People*. New York: Ballantine, 1985.

Bloom, Benjamin S. "Automaticity: The Hands and Feet of Genius." *Educational Leadership* 43 (Feb. 1986), pp. 70-77.

Boyer, Ernest L. *High School*. New York: Harper & Row, 1983.

Bruner, Jerome S. *The Process of Education*. Cambridge, MA.: Harvard Univ. Press, 1960.

Conant, James B. *The American High School Today*. New York: McGraw-Hill, 1959.

Conant, James B. *The Education of American Teachers*. New York: McGraw-Hill, 1963.

Culver, Carmen M. and Gary J. Hoban (eds.). *The Power to Change*. New York: McGraw-Hill, 1973.

DiLorenzo, Louis T. and Ruth Salter. "Co-operative Research on Nongraded Primary." *Elementary School Journal* 65 (Feb. 1965), pp. 269-277.

Edmonds, Ronald R., "Effective Schools for the Urban Poor." *Educational Leadership* 37 (Oct. 1979), pp. 15-27.

Ellison, Alfred. "The Myth Behind Graded Content." *Elementary School Journal* 72 (Jan. 1972), pp. 212-221.

Fazzaro, Charles J. "The Nongraded Junior High School: A Place for the Young Adolescent to Grow." *The North Central Association Quarterly* 49 (Spring 1975), pp. 380-386.

Goodlad, John I. *The Dynamics of Educational Change*. New York: McGraw-Hill, 1975.

Goodlad, John I. *A Place Called School: Prospects for the Future*. New York: McGraw-Hill, 1984.

Harvard Committee. *General Education in a Free Society*. Report of the Harvard Committee. Cambridge, MA: Harvard Univ. Press, 1945.

Harvard Graduate School of Education. "Repeating a Grade: Does It Help?" *The Harvard Education Letter* 2:2 (March 1986).

Heathers, Glen. "School Organization: Nongrading, Dual Progress, and Team Teaching." In John I. Goodlad (ed.), *The Changing American School*. Sixty-fifth Yearbook Part II, National Society for the Study of Education, pp. 110-134. Chicago: Univ. of Chicago Press, 1966.

Holmes, C. Thomas, and Kenneth M. Matthews. "The Effect of Nonpromotion on Elementary and Junior High School Pupils: A Meta-Analysis." *Review of Educational Research* 54 (Summer 1984), pp. 225–236.

House, Ernest R. *The Politics of Educational Innovation.* Berkeley, CA: McCutchan, 1974.

Howe, Harold II. "Giving Equity a Chance in the Excellence Game." In Beatrice Gross and Ronald Gross (eds.), *The Great School Debate: Which Way for American Education?* pp. 281–297. New York: Simon & Schuster, 1985.

Jeter, Jan (ed.). *Approaches to Individualized Education.* Alexandria, VA: Association for Supervision and Curriculum Development, 1980.

Johnson, Roger T. and David W. Johnson. "Cooperative Learning Groups: The Power of Positive Interdependence." *Wingspan* 1 (Jan. 1983), pp. 11–14. Pedamorphosis, Inc., Box 271669, Tampa, FL 33688.

Klausmeier, Herbert J. "The Multi-Unit School and Individually Guided Education." *Phi Delta Kappan* 53 (Nov. 1971), pp. 181–184.

Lewis, James Jr. *A Contemporary Approach to Nongraded Education.* West New York, NY: Parker, 1969.

Lightfoot, Sara Lawrence. *The Good High School.* New York: Basic Books, 1983.

Lindelow, John. "The Grade Retention/Social Promotion Debate." *Research Roundup*, 2 (Nov. 1985), pp. 1–4. Alexandria, VA: National Association of Elementary School Principals.

McLoughlin, William P. *The Nongraded School: A Critical Assessment.* Albany, NY: Office of Research and Evaluation, Univ. of the State of New York, State Education Dept., Sept. 1967.

McLoughlin, William P. *Evaluation of the Nongraded Primary.* Jamaica, NY: St. John's Univ., Apr. 1969.

McLoughlin, William P. "Continuous Pupil Progress in the Nongraded School: Hope or Hoax?" *Elementary School Journal* 71 (Nov. 1970), pp. 90–96.

McLoughlin, William P. "Individualization of Instruction vs. Nongrading." *Phi Delta Kappan* 53 (Feb. 1972), pp. 378–381.

Muzi, Marialise. "What Is Meant by School Environment: 'Team Teaching' and the 'Nongraded School.'" *Western European Education,* 12(Spring 1980), pp. 5–37.

National Association of Secondary School Principals. *Schools in the Middle: A Report on Trends and Practices.* Reston, VA: NASSP, Sept., 1985.

National Commission on Excellence in Education, *A Nation at Risk: The Imperative for Educational Reform.* Washington, DC: United States Dept. of Education, 1983.

Oakes, Jeannie. *Keeping Track: How Schools Structure Inequality.* New Haven, CT: Yale Univ. Press, 1985.

Otto, Henry J. *Nongradedness: An Elementary School Evaluation.* Bureau of Laboratory Schools Monograph No. 21. Austin: Univ. of Texas at Austin, 1969.

Paden, Jon, John M. Bahner, Gilbert L. Johnson, John Rye Kinghorn, and Charles L. Willis. *Reflections for the Future.* Dayton, OH: Institute for Development of Educational Activities, 1978.

Pavan, Barbara Nelson. "Moving Elementary Schools Toward Nongradedness: Commitment, Assessment, and Tactics." Unpublished dissertation, Harvard Univ. Graduate School of Education, 1972.

Pavan, Barbara Nelson. "Nongradedness? One View." *Educational Leadership* 30 (Feb. 1973), pp. 401–403.

Pavan, Barbara Nelson. "Good News: Research on the Nongraded Elementary School." *Elementary School Journal* 73 (Mar. 1973), pp. 233–242.

Pavan, Barbara Nelson. "Good News: Research on the Nongraded Elementary School." *Independent School Bulletin* 33 (Dec. 1973), pp. 16–21.

Pavan, Barbara Nelson. "The Nongraded Elementary School: Research on Academic Achievement and Mental Health." *Texas Tech Journal of Education* 4 (1977), pp. 91–107.

Popkewitz, Thomas S., B. Robert Tabachnick and Gary Wehlage. *The Myth of Educational Reform: A Study of School Responses to a Program of Change.* Madison, WI: Univ. of Wisconsin Press, 1982.

Pratt, David. "Age Segregation in Schools." Paper presented at the Annual Meeting of the American Educational Research Association. Montreal, Quebec, Canada: April 11–15, 1983. [*Note:* A 1986 condensed version, entitled "On the Merits of Multiage Classrooms" is now under journal review.]

Pratt, David. Personal letter to Robert H. Anderson, June 12, 1986.

Purdom, Daniel M. "A Conceptual Model of the Nongraded School." Unpublished dissertation, Univ. of California at Los Angeles, 1967.

Purdom, Daniel M. *Exploring the Nongraded School.* Dayton, OH: Institute for Development of Educational Activities, 1970.

Purdom, Daniel M. "The Ideal Nongraded School." *Orbit*, 3 (Oct. 1972), pp. 4–7.

Romberg, T. A. (ed.). "The Development and Refinement of Prototypic Instructional Systems." Theoretical Paper No. 15. Madison, WI: Research and Development Center for Cognitive Learning, 1968.

Sarason, Seymour B. *The Culture of the School and the Problem of Change.* Boston: Allyn & Bacon, 1971.

Shaplin, Judson T., and Henry F. Olds, Jr., (eds.). *Team Teaching.* New York: Harper & Row, 1964.

Shiman, David A., Carmen M. Culver, and Ann Lieberman (eds.), *Teachers on Individualization.* New York: McGraw-Hill, 1974.

Sizer, Theodore R. *Horace's Compromise: The Dilemma of the American High School.* Boston: Houghton Mifflin, 1984.

Snyder, Karolyn J. and Robert H. Anderson, *Managing Productive Schools: Toward an Ecology* (See pp. 156–209.) Orlando, FL: Academic Press, College Division, 1986.

Spock, Benjamin. "School Reform: Coercion in the Classroom Won't Work." *The Atlantic* 253 (Apr. 1984), pp. 28–36.

Stanton, Henry. "The British Way-V: Vertical Grouping." *Teacher* 90 (Jan. 1973), pp. 106–108.

Steere, Bob J. "Nongradedness: Relevant Research for Decision Making." *Educational Leadership* 29 (May 1972), pp. 709–711.

Taylor, Ruth (comp.). *The Nongraded School: An Annotated Bibliography.* Current Bibliography Series No. 5. Toronto: Ontario Institute for Studies in Education, 1970–1972.

Tye, Kenneth A. and Jerrold M. Novotney. *Schools in Transition.* New York: McGraw-Hill, 1975.

Van Hoven, James B. "Reporting Pupil Progress: A Broad Rationale for New Practices." *Phi Delta Kappan* 53 (Feb. 1972), pp. 365–366.

Walker, N. William, "Elementary-School Grade Retention: Avoiding Abuses Through Systematic Decision-Making." *Journal of Research and Development in Education,* 18 (Fall, 1984), pp. 1–6.

Williams, Richard C., Charles C. Wall, W. Michael Martin, and Arthur Berchin, *Effecting Organizational Renewal in Schools.* New York: McGraw-Hill, 1974.

Wisconsin Center for Education Research. *News.* (Spring 1985) 1025 West Johnson Street, Madison, WI 53706.

Wisconsin Research and Development Center for Cognitive Learning. *1971–1972 Directory of IGE/Multi-unit Elementary Schools in the United States of America.* Madison, WI: Univ. of Wisconsin, 1971.

York, L. Jean. *Team Teaching as a Facilitator of the Nongraded School.* Module V of a Series on Team Teaching. Austin, TX: Research and Development Center for Teacher Education, 1971.

1. THE CHILD AND
PROCRUSTEAN STANDARDS

Introduction

Greek mythology tells us of the cruel robber, Procrustes (the stretcher). When travelers sought his house for shelter, they were tied onto an iron bedstead. If the traveler was shorter than the bed, Procrustes stretched him out until he was the same length as the bed. If he was longer, his limbs were chopped off to make him fit. Procrustes shaped both short and tall until they were equally long and equally dead.

Certain time-honored practices of pupil classification, while perhaps not lethal, trap school-age travelers in much the same fashion as Procrustes' bed trapped the unwary. These practices are concomitants of our graded system of school organization. First, a certain amount of progress is held to be standard for a year's work. Then, the content of the work is laid out within the grade, to be "covered" and, to a degree, "mastered." The slow are pulled and stretched to fit the grade. Sometimes, because their God-given limbs lack enough elasticity, they are "nonpromoted"—left behind, where presumably another year of stretching will do the trick. The quick are compressed and contracted to fit the grade. In time, they learn to adapt to a pace that is slower than their natural one.

In this volume, the authors want to point out the anachronistic nature of graded school structure and many of the practices that inevitably accompany it. They seek, further, to propose and describe an alternative: a nongraded structure and a variety of more enlightened school practices that are related to the absence of grades and lock-step. The incompatibility between Procrustean standards and present insights into child development constitutes the subject matter of this chapter. Chapter 2 analyzes the questionable effec-

1

tiveness of nonpromotion in reducing the discrepancy between grade standards and the realities of pupil attainment in conventional elementary schools. The next chapter describes how the lockstep of graded structure developed and analyzes the emergence of a new vision of what effective school structure might be like. The operation of schools without grades provides the substance of Chapter 4. Chapter 5 examines certain modern theories of curriculum development and their relationship to nongraded structure, with an emphasis on the individual classroom. Chapter 6 discusses home-school reporting, Chapter 7 the relationship between realistic school standards and sound mental health. An eighth chapter offers suggestions for initiating and administering nongraded plans. The concluding chapter presents the available evidence on the worth of nongraded schools in the eyes of the people who supervise them, and analyzes the problems of research and development in this important movement.

The authors' studies suggest that many of those schools which are now nongraded became so not so much because they recognized inadequacies in the graded system, but because they were dissatisfied with the promotion policies, reporting practices, and other immediate concerns. For this reason the authors treat these problems in their own right, as well as in relation to the nongraded school, and supply supplementary readings—especially books and chapters from books—at the end of each chapter. There is also a comprehensive bibliography at the end of the volume. These additional references are mostly primary source materials reporting research findings, exploratory practices, and thoughtful enquiry. No attempt has been made to select only those articles that support the authors' viewpoint. The careful reader will discover for himself in these many papers the overwhelming evidence for the nongraded school which motivated the writing of this book.

Many of the communities with nongraded programs have published mimeographed or printed materials that describe them. These materials have usually been prepared for the use of parents, although some, more detailed, are aimed at the professional audience. Most of these materials may be obtained at no cost or for a reasonable charge. Both the United States Office of Education and the National Education Association Research Divisions are interested in nongrading and may be consulted for further information.

The Central Problem

Most of today's elementary schools classify children by grades. The work of a grade, a year of progress, and a chronological year in a child's life are seen as roughly comparable for school purposes. The expectations for elementary education are viewed in a time span, and the organizing structure is divided into six, seven, or eight grade units of equal length. Textbooks, courses of study, and teacher-parent expectations condition the actual demands of each unit.

Children enter the first unit or grade when they are approximately six years old, perhaps after completing a year of kindergarten. They, their parents, and their teachers view the development of reading skill as a phenomenon that will occur soon after the children cross the school's magic threshold. Their expectations frequently turn to disillusionment. Similar expectations are confronted from level to level of the graded hierarchy. Failure by many children to come up to them may mean frustration for their teachers, disappointment for their parents, and for the children themselves, a loss of self-respect.

The realities of child development defy the rigorous ordering of children's abilities and attainments into conventional graded structure. For example, in the average first grade there is a spread of four years in pupil readiness to learn as suggested by mental age data. As the pupils progress through the grades, the span in readiness widens. Furthermore, a single child does not progress all of a piece: he tends to spurt ahead more rapidly in some areas than in others. Consequently, a difference of one grade between his reading attainment and his arithmetic attainment at the end of the second grade classification may be extended to a three- or four-grade difference by the end of his fifth year in school. The presence of graded structure may disguise or distort such realities but it cannot remove them. In brief, as extensive data presented in this chapter clearly reveal, a fifth-grade teacher, in spite of his designation, is not a teacher of fifth-grade children. At a given time, he teaches third, fourth, fifth, sixth, seventh, eighth, and even ninth grades, as far as learner realities are concerned, even though all the pupils in his room may be labeled "fifth grade." Any attempt to deal with these children as fifth graders can only be Procrustean in its ultimate effects.

Perhaps it is advisable to say a few words here about a common confusion in interpreting mental age as differentiated from intelligence quotient. Mental age (M.A.) like chronological age (C.A.) is an absolute measure in that specific units—years and months—are used. The measuring scale (in this case an intelligence test) may be in error; nonetheless, the results are quantitative and can be dealt with as one deals with pounds, feet, acres, or any other unit of measure. Mental age is an important criterion of ability or readiness to learn. Both a six-year-old and a ten-year-old may be five years old mentally. One, obviously, is much brighter than the other even though both have the same mental age and might well be expected to perform intellectual tasks of equal complexity. Intelligence quotient (I.Q.), on the other hand, shows a relationship between M.A. and C.A. and is thus a relative measure. An I.Q. of more than 100 indicates that the child's mental age is advancing more quickly than his chronological age. A score of, say, 70 tells us nothing about readiness to learn or to profit from a given task, since one child having this I.Q. may be four years old and another eight years old. They would be ready for quite different learning demands. Throughout the volume, the authors infer readiness to learn from mental age rather than I.Q. scores.

Our central problem, then, emerges out of the conflict between long-established graded structure on one hand and increasing awareness of variation in children's abilities and attainments on the other. Our graded structure and parent-teacher-pupil expectations are long established; they represent a certain antique respectability. Our insight into individual differences as a phenomenon to be accounted for is not generally shared, however. The problem of effectively relating individual differences and school structure is of such formidable dimensions that a simple exposition of our dilemma will not dispel it. First, we must see the startling realities of individual differences within a single child and among pupils of a given grade level. Second, we must understand the incompatibility between school grades as applied to ordering pupil progress and these realities of pupil individuality. Next, we must gain insight into the ill effects of certain concomitants of graded structure as, for example, nonpromotion practices. Then, we must propose an alternative structure that does not carry with it the ill effects of graded structure and its concomitants. Lacking extensive empirical evidence regarding the efficacy of an alternative structure, we must determine its potential usefulness from logical analysis and such instances of experimentation as are now available.

Children Through the Grades

Table 1 provides certain achievement data, all collected during January, for five elementary school children. From these figures, it would be difficult to determine the grade levels of the pupils, but one might guess as follows: child 1—fourth grade; child 2—seventh grade; child 3—second grade; child 4—fourth grade; child five—third grade. Such an estimate would be correct in only one instance; child 3 was in the second grade of an urban school. The other estimates were from one to two years in error. Child 1 was in the

Table 1

Achievement data for five school children

PUPIL	paragraph meaning	word meaning	average reading	spelling	arithmetic reasoning	arithmetic computation	average arithmetic
1	4.6	5.3	5.0	4.2	2.7	3.0	2.9
2	9.4	9.4	9.4	7.4	6.1	5.1	5.6
3	2.9	3.1	3.0	1.8	2.3	2.2	2.3
4	3.6	4.2	3.9	5.2	5.6	5.8	5.7
5	4.1	3.5	3.8	3.3	3.4	2.9	3.2

third grade of a small town school; child 2 in the fifth grade of a school in an upper middle class suburb of a large city; child 4 in the sixth grade of a semi-rural unincorporated community; and child 5 was in the same fifth grade as child 2. These children were at the appropriate grade level for their age. But one suspects that the demands being placed upon them were not related to their ability and attainment realities, so effectively obscured by such grade classifications.

An appropriate placement for each child on the basis of scholastic attainment in relation to grade standards would not be easily made. Child 2, for example, belongs in the ninth grade for reading but only in the fifth for arithmetic. Child 4 would be properly placed for reading in the third grade but probably would hold his own for arithmetic if in the fifth. The moment other areas of development and achievement were included, the problem of determining appropriate grade placement would become even more complex.

These children were selected at random from the achievement distributions of four classrooms in four American schools. Even the limited data presented reveal the varied achievement patterns within a single child and the inappropriateness of grade assignments. Thirty or forty children per grade per classroom present a variety of abilities and attainments, most pronounced at the upper elementary grade levels, that must be respected if intelligent classification decisions for instructional purposes are to be made. Data presented on succeeding pages are used to illustrate in single classrooms generalizations about individual differences derived from studies of many classrooms.

Children in the first and second grades

Table 2 presents certain statistics, collected in May of the year, on a first-grade group of children. These children come from homes that are very much like those of most American school children, except that there is some weighting toward the lower middle section of the socioeconomic class scale. Although their parents expect these children to get a reasonably good education, there is relatively little parental understanding regarding the kind of home environment that is needed to support learning and school expectations. Study, reading, and intellectual pursuits are not valued highly in most of the homes from which this particular group of children comes. Two or three of the children are from executive and professional families and a number from the relatively unskilled labor classes.

This group is deliberately chosen in order to illustrate certain realities of the classroom situation with which teachers everywhere are faced. The group might have been chosen so as to skew the distribution upward or downward, but the generalizations drawn from such a sample would not be so applicable to the general school scene.

Deducting eight months from each chronological age takes us back to the beginning of September when these children, lacking kindergarten experience, first entered school. At that time, the range in chronological age was from five years and nine months (children 19 and 23) to seven years and four months (child 24). This last child was the only repeater in the group. Deducting eight months from each mental age does not give the exact mental age for the beginning of school because some children are advancing more and some less than a mental age month for each month of chronological age advancement. However, such a procedure is sufficiently accurate for our purposes. The range in mental age, then, in September was from approximately three years ten months to approximately eight years four months—a spread of four and one-half years.

This last statistic supports our first major generalization about the pupil realities with which teachers must deal: *Children entering the first grade differ in mental age by approximately four full years.* If what children are to learn, then, is to be classified by grades, some children obviously are not ready to profit from whatever might appropriately be laid out for a year of work, while others are ready to profit from work pitched at a significantly higher level. Any realistic attempt to approximate the readiness of these individuals for school work must assume a four-year range in difficulty for what various children are to do: work levels must be geared for two years below first-grade expectancies as well as for two years above.

Table 2
Data for a first-grade class (May)

CHILD	C.A.	M.A.	I.Q.	paragraph meaning	word meaning	spelling	arithmetic reasoning	arithmetic computation	battery median
1	6-6	7-9	119	1.9	2.4	3.0	3.1	2.3	2.4
2	6-8	7-4	110	1.8	1.7	2.7	2.4	2.3	2.3
3	7-2	7-0	98	2.2	2.0	2.3	2.2	2.3	2.2
4	7-2	8-9	122	1.5	2.2	2.8	2.1	2.3	2.2
5	7-0	8-0	114	1.7	1.6	2.8	2.2	2.3	2.2
6	6-8	6-8	100	1.9	1.7	2.3	2.2	2.3	2.2
7	7-1	8-2	115	1.9	1.5	2.6	2.2	2.2	2.2
8	6-11	7-5	107	1.7	2.3	2.9	1.8	2.2	2.2
9	6-11	6-0	87	1.6	2.1	2.6	1.7	2.2	2.1
10	7-3	7-11	109	2.1	2.3	2.5	1.6	1.7	2.1
11	6-10	7-10	115	2.9	1.9	2.8	2.1	2.0	2.0
12	6-10	6-5	94	1.7	2.0	2.0	1.8	2.0	2.0
13	7-0	9-0	129	1.9	1.4	2.7	1.7	2.0	1.9
14	7-5	5-8	76	1.6	2.0	2.7	1.7	1.7	1.7
15	6-10	7-1	104	1.1	1.1	1.6	1.8	2.3	1.6
16	6-9	7-5	110	1.2	1.2	2.3	1.6	1.8	1.6
17	7-2	6-10	95	1.1	1.6	1.6	1.6	1.7	1.6
18	6-6	6-11	106	1.0	1.5	1.0	1.5	2.0	1.5
19	6-5	6-0	94	1.0	1.5	1.2	1.3	1.4	1.3
20	6-8	6-1	91	1.3	1.4	2.0	1.2	1.3	1.3
21	6-8	7-4	110	1.0	1.0	1.3	1.6	1.3	1.3
22	7-1	6-6	92	1.2	2.2	1.3	1.2	1.6	1.3
23	6-5	5-6	86	1.2	2.2	1.0	1.2	1.2	1.2
24	8-0	7-0	88	1.3	1.1	1.1	1.2	1.0	1.1
25	6-7	4-6	68	1.2	1.2	1.0	1.0	1.0	1.0
26	7-5	7-3	98	1.0	1.0	1.0	1.7	1.4	1.0
27	6-11	6-1	88	1.0	1.0	1.0	1.0	1.0	1.0

This group is very much like other entering first-grade groups. Most of the children represent the modal pattern in chronological and mental age in that they cluster from slightly below to slightly above six years. The intelligence quotient range of from 68 to 129, with an arithmetic mean of 101, is about as close to normal as one could get in selecting an illustrative class.

The achievement test data call for some interpretation. The overall range, represented by the battery median for each child, and the ranges in specific achievement areas are somewhat less than the range in "assumed readiness to learn" as computed from the mental age data. There are several explanations for this. It will be remembered that these children come predominantly from homes that do not emphasize learnings of the sort promoted by the school. Consequently, it is not to be expected that the more able youngsters will be utilizing their full capacities by the time they have completed eight months of schooling. At the bottom end of the scale, on the other hand, the test instruments simply did not permit computation of scores at lower than the beginning first-grade level. Achievement tests are designed, ordinarily, to test accomplishment in school learning tasks and so, by definition, do not permit scores of less than 1.0 even though a given youngster may be years away from doing first-grade work.

Even with the limitations noted, the range within the group is startling. It is three years or more in spelling and arithmetic reasoning and just short of three years in paragraph meaning. These statistics support a second major generalization about the pupil realities with which teachers must deal: *The achievement range begins to approximate the range in intellectual readiness to learn soon after first-grade children are exposed to reasonably normal school instruction.*

Further analysis of Table 2 reveals some interesting aspects of the individual child's progress. While children at the top and children at the bottom of the general achievement distribution tend, respectively, to do consistently well and consistently poorly in the several specific areas, there are some notable exceptions. Child 1 is a full year behind child 11 in paragraph meaning, and the latter, interestingly enough, is top achiever in this field even though only slightly above the median for general achievement. The range between high and low scores for child 1 is more than a full year even though he has attended school only eight months. Likewise, at the lower end of the group's general achievement, child 23 ranks well up with the first half-dozen children in word meaning even though his paragraph meaning score lags a full year behind.

These data support still a third generalization about the pupil realities facing teachers: *Individual children's achievement patterns differ markedly from learning area to learning area.* Before a given child completes the first grade, his achievement scores frequently vary by more than a full grade from subject to subject. Likewise, children who tend to be generally slow or rapid learners usually reveal at least one major inconsistency in scoring a full grade above or below their general achievement profiles in at least one learning area.

The wide range in abilities and attainments among children and within a given child, constituting the pupil realities with which schools and teachers must deal, increases and grows at an accelerating pace as children advance through the grades. Table 3 presents data for the same group depicted in Table 2, the statistics this time compiled eleven months later. This, then, is the same class with the same teacher almost one full grade later. Only 22 of the original 27 remained, although the group had increased in size from 27 to 39 pupils. So as not to confuse the comparison of tables, data for only the continuing 22 are presented here.

Intelligence tests were not repeated, on the assumption that I.Q. remains relatively constant, and so both mental age and I.Q. are estimated from the first-grade scores. This is not an entirely accurate procedure but, again, the procedure is appropriate for the kinds of broad generalizations we wish to make.

Several observations about the group are pertinent here. First, as would be anticipated when the rate of development is more rapid for some children than for others, the spread in mental age is now somewhat greater than it was eleven months previously. The achievement range in the language areas has moved proportionately closer to the mental age range than was true the previous year. While there is a considerable range in arithmetic, it does not reflect the mental age range to the degree that the language areas do. The spread in the mathematical areas, while growing steadily greater, will not advance as rapidly as will the spread in either mental age or language achievement. This is partly due to the naturally high correlation between language facility and mental age and partly because number activities of young children are confined primarily to the classroom. Children do not continue these activities at home to the degree that they talk, listen, and read, thus extending their language and writing facility.

These data suggest two other major generalizations describing the pupil realities with which teachers must deal: *First, the initial spread among pupils in intellectual readiness to learn (as determined by the M.A. factor) grows still greater as children advance through their second year of school.* Those already out in front and traveling at a greater speed merely pull farther and farther away from their slower-paced classmates. *Second, the spread in achievement in the various subject areas also grows greater, closely approximating the spread in mental age.*

Observations about individual children also are pertinent to the problems that concern us. The child of the highest I.Q. (13) still

Table 3
Data for a second-grade class (April) *

CHILD	C.A.	(estimated) M.A.	(estimated) I.Q.	paragraph meaning	word meaning	spelling	arithmetic reasoning	arithmetic computation	battery median
1	7-5	8-10	119	3.7	4.7	4.2	3.9	2.5	3.9
2	7-7	8-4	110	4.2	3.7	4.5	3.5	2.5	3.7
3	8-1	7-11	98	3.5	3.1	3.7	3.9	2.3	3.5
4	8-1	9-10	122	4.8	4.9	4.5	3.9	2.5	4.5
5	. . . .	. . . .	. . .	. . .	. . .	. . .	. . .	. . .	. . .
6	7-7	7-7	100	2.5	2.2	3.2	2.8	2.2	2.5
7	8-0	9-2	115	3.7	3.2	4.3	3.9	2.5	3.7
8	7-10	8-5	107	3.5	3.5	4.3	3.5	2.2	3.5
9	. . . .	. . . .	. . .	. . .	. . .	. . .	. . .	. . .	. . .
10	8-2	9-0	110	3.0	2.4	3.2	2.8	2.3	2.8
11	7-9	8-11	115	4.2	4.2	4.6	4.1	2.5	4.2
12	7-9	7-3	94	3.5	3.2	3.4	2.8	2.4	3.3
13	7-11	10-2	128	3.9	2.8	3.7	3.1	2.4	3.1
14	8-4	6-4	76	2.7	2.8	3.7	1.9	2.2	2.7
15	7-9	8-1	104	2.0	2.4	2.7	2.6	2.3	2.4
16	7-8	8-5	110	2.5	2.3	2.7	2.8	2.3	2.5
17	. . . .	. . . .	. . .	. . .	. . .	. . .	. . .	. . .	. . .
18	7-5	7-10	106	1.3	1.4	1.7	2.3	2.3	1.7
19	7-4	6-11	94	1.9	1.9	2.5	2.2	1.3	1.9
20	7-7	6-11	91	3.3	3.5	3.2	2.2	2.1	3.2
21	. . . .	. . . .	. . .	. . .	. . .	. . .	. . .	. . .	. . .
22	8-0	7-4	92	1.9	1.9	1.7	1.9	1.8	1.9
23	7-4	6-4	86	1.5	1.2	1.6	2.1	1.8	1.6
24	8-11	7-10	88	1.3	1.9	1.4	1.8	1.6	1.6
25	7-6	5-1	68	1.5	1.7	1.5	1.5	1.3	1.5
26	8-4	8-2	98	1.8	2.2	1.6	2.2	2.3	2.2
27	. . . .	. . . .	. . .	. . .	. . .	. . .	. . .	. . .	. . .

* This is the same group depicted in Table 2, one grade and eleven months later.

has not established himself in the forefront of the group so far as achievement is concerned, having changed his relative position only slightly. When it is noted that he is one of the older children in the group and that a high M.A. (10 years and 2 months) was therefore necessary to produce the relatively high I.Q., it becomes apparent that this child really is operating significantly below expectancy. Had he been grouped on the basis of high I.Q. in a top ability group, he obviously would have been over his depth. Child 4, on the other hand, also one of the high C.A. and high M.A. children, has clearly established himself where these factors suggest that he belongs.

Child 24, the first-grade repeater referred to in discussing Table 2, still lags close to the bottom in achievement. Obviously, nonpromotion for this child did not change his learning rate and did not significantly advance his achievement.

Again, the differences among subject areas for a given child are great. A spread of more than two years separates word meaning achievement from arithmetic computation for child 1. An equally great spread from area to area may be noted for children 2, 4, 8, and 11, and a spread of one year from subject area to subject area is the rule rather than the exception. Such a condition is of particular significance when we realize that these children had not yet completed their second year of schooling. Obviously, attempts to group these children homogeneously in relation to an overall concept of homogeneity (such as ability to do school tasks as revealed by I.Q. or M.A.) or in relation to some fixed standard of normality (such as grade level) are doomed. Nonetheless, we go on acting in many quarters as though the kind of reality presented here were nonexistent.

Children in the third and fourth grades

There is really very little need to carry this analysis further. The points we seek to make should now be obvious. But, for the sake of readers who teach at still higher grade levels, we proceed farther in the graded hierarchy.

Tables 4 and 5 present data for 24 children from the third grade who continued as a group into the fourth. The class actually was much larger each year but data for only those children who continued through the two years are presented here. These pupils are from the same school as were the children used to illustrate the first and second grade distributions (Tables 2 and 3) and, again, the teacher went with her third-grade group into the fourth grade. There is merit here in continuing to use examples from a single school. Moving from school to school would distort the picture of a steadily spreading range of individual differences normally to be expected as children move through the grades.

The ability distribution for the third-grade group shown in Table 4 is quite similar to that of the second-grade group in

Table 4

Data for a third-grade class (April)

CHILD	C.A.	M.A.	I.Q.	paragraph meaning	word meaning	spelling	arithmetic reasoning	arithmetic computation	battery median
1	8-6	11-1	130	4.7	6.0	4.5	4.8	3.9	4.7
2	9-0	9-2	102	6.0	4.7	4.5	4.2	4.0	4.5
3	8-10	10-1	114	4.0	4.7	4.5	4.8	4.2	4.5
4	9-1	8-11	98	4.1	3.6	4.3	4.5	3.7	4.1
5	8-7	8-9	102	3.8	3.7	4.0	4.8	4.0	4.0
6	8-2	8-8	106	3.9	4.0	4.5	3.5	3.3	3.9
7	8-4	8-11	107	4.1	3.7	3.1	4.8	3.5	3.7
8	8-4	7-11	95	2.7	2.6	3.4	3.5	3.8	3.4
9	8-6	7-9	91	3.4	2.9	3.7	3.3	3.1	3.3
10	8-5	8-5	100	3.5	3.3	3.8	3.1	3.3	3.3
11	8-7	7-4	85	2.7	2.5	3.4	3.3	3.6	3.3
12	8-6	8-6	100	3.4	2.8	3.1	3.9	3.3	3.3
13	8-8	9-1	105	3.2	3.2	3.2	3.1	3.3	3.2
14	8-4	8-6	102	3.1	3.1	3.8	2.8	3.1	3.1
15	8-9	8-3	94	3.1	3.1	2.9	3.5	3.2	3.1
16	8-3	7-1	86	3.3	2.6	3.5	2.8	3.1	3.1
17	8-2	6-10	84	2.9	3.1	3.1	3.1	3.1	3.1
18	9-3	6-10	74	2.3	2.7	3.2	2.8	3.6	2.8
19	8-2	6-9	83	2.1	2.8	2.9	2.2	2.8	2.8
20	8-7	9-0	105	2.5	1.7	3.0	2.6	4.1	2.6
21	8-10	8-5	95	2.5	2.5	3.1	2.4	2.8	2.5
22	9-4	7-2	77	2.2	2.0	1.8	2.2	2.8	2.2
23	9-9	7-7	78	2.2	2.3	2.0	2.1	2.7	2.2
24	9-11	7-10	79	1.6	1.7	2.2	2.4	2.9	2.2

Table 3. Since, however, no child in the former group is as low on the ability scale, the overall third-grade range in mental age of four years four months is somewhat less than might otherwise be anticipated. The range in overall achievement is three and one-half years but in paragraph meaning and word meaning it is almost identical with the mental age spread. Again, the range from subject to subject for individual children is great, being two or more years for children 1, 2, and 20, and a year or more for children 5, 6, 7, 8, 11, 12, 14, 18, 22, and 24.

Table 5 depicts the same group eleven months later, now near

Table 5
Data for a fourth-grade class (March) *

CHILD	C.A.	(estimated) M.A.	(estimated) I.Q.	paragraph meaning	word meaning	spelling	arithmetic reasoning	arithmetic computation	battery median
1	9-5	12-3	130	5.9	6.5	6.1	6.1	5.9	6.1
2	9-11	10-1	102	7.2	5.0	5.5	5.9	5.5	5.5
3	9-9	11-2	114	6.7	5.7	5.3	6.5	5.8	5.8
4	10-0	9-10	98	5.9	5.7	6.4	5.0	3.9	5.7
5	9-6	9-8	102	5.7	4.1	4.3	4.1	4.8	4.3
6	9-1	9-8	106	4.7	5.2	3.9	5.1	5.0	5.0
7	9-3	9-11	107	5.9	3.8	4.2	5.9	4.9	4.9
8	9-3	8-9	95	3.7	2.7	4.0	4.6	4.9	4.0
9	9-5	8-7	91	4.5	3.8	4.3	4.7	4.7	4.5
10	9-4	9-4	100	5.2	4.4	5.0	4.5	4.9	4.9
11	9-6	8-1	85	3.8	3.3	3.4	4.7	5.0	3.8
12	9-5	9-5	100	5.0	3.7	4.0	4.7	4.9	4.7
13	9-7	10-1	105	4.3	4.0	4.0	4.9	4.8	4.3
14	9-3	9-5	102	4.4	4.4	4.3	4.6	4.9	4.4
15	9-8	9-1	94	3.3	3.4	3.8	4.0	4.5	3.8
16	9-2	7-11	86	4.3	3.6	3.9	4.9	4.7	4.3
17	9-1	7-8	84	2.9	2.5	3.4	3.3	4.0	3.3
18	10-2	7-6	74	3.1	3.3	3.9	4.2	4.7	3.9
19	9-1	7-6	83	3.1	3.2	3.5	4.6	5.9	3.5
20	9-6	10-0	105	4.1	3.7	3.7	5.4	5.2	4.1
21	9-9	9-3	95	3.2	3.5	3.7	4.1	3.6	3.6
22	10-3	7-11	77	3.2	2.6	2.1	3.3	3.8	3.3
23	10-8	8-4	78	2.7	2.8	2.3	2.1	4.2	2.7
24	10-10	8-7	79	1.7	2.4	2.2	2.1	4.1	2.2

* This is the same group depicted in Table 4, eleven months later.

the end of the fourth grade. The range in all areas but arithmetic computation is four or more years, and in paragraph meaning is more than five and one-half years. Still another generalization about the pupil realities with which teachers must deal is pertinent: *By the time children complete the fourth grade, the range in readiness to learn (as suggested by the M.A.) and in most areas of achievement is approximately the same as the number designating the grade level.* In other words, pupils in the fourth grade differ by as much as four years in mental age and achievement; in the fifth, by five

years; in the sixth, by six years. In reality, then, the grade
level designation means little. A fourth-grade teacher who troubles
to look back of the grade-level label realizes that, to be honest with
himself and his pupils, he really must teach grades one through six
or higher.

Grade groups and individual pupils in profile

To reinforce the major points of previous pages, certain data
from Tables 2, 3, 4, and 5 have been drawn together into Figure 1.
The bar graphs reveal at a glance the overall spread in each class
previously analyzed. A vertical bar for each grade shows the spread
from top to bottom for pupils in each of the seven progress categories. The number at the lower end of each bar indicates the grade
level. Bars 1 and 2 in each category represent the first and second
grade spread for one group of pupils (taken from the raw data in
Tables 2 and 3). Bars 3 and 4 in each category represent the third
and fourth grade spread for the second group of pupils (taken from
the raw data in Tables 4 and 5). The left side of the figure is

Figure 1

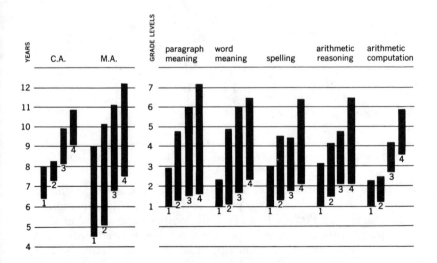

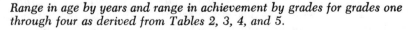

*Range in age by years and range in achievement by grades for grades one
through four as derived from Tables 2, 3, 4, and 5.*

calibrated for age and should be consulted for determining the spread in M.A. and C.A. The right side is calibrated for grades and should be consulted for determining the spread in achievement for the five remaining categories. From Figure 1, one may quickly review the generalizations about pupil individuality and grade variation as stated previously in these pages.

In Figure 2, three children have been selected from each of the four grades presented in Tables 2, 3, 4, and 5. Placing the bar graphs for these children side by side reveals not only the striking differences between selected children from any one grade but also the variation within a given child. Each child presented, with the exception of the first-graders, varies two or more years from his highest to his lowest achievement area. Some children cut across as many as four different grades. Child 20 in grade 3, for example, ranges from the high first grade in word meaning to the low fourth grade in arithmetic computation. Not only is the spread from child to child as great as four grades but such a range is occasionally represented in a single child. The prospect of applying grade standards to such unique and varying organisms as elementary-school children comes to seem more and more ludicrous.

Admittedly, the children shown in Figure 2 are twelve of those for whom the range from achievement area to achievement area is greatest. Nonetheless, about as many more with such varying ranges might have been selected. Ironically, only two children (13 and 14) in the "fourth-grade class" scored consistently within fourth-grade norms when tests were administered in April.

Once again, it is noted that the greatest variation occurs, usually, for children at the top and bottom of the achievement continuum. And yet, paradoxically, when grouping by ability levels is proposed in educational circles, invariably it is the gifted or the slow pupils who are to be segregated into "homogeneous" groups. When will we start paying at least some attention to the facts, to the realities of the human material with which we deal?

Inter-Class Grouping for Increased Homogeneity

The tremendous variation in pupil abilities and attainments at given grade levels has long been recognized. Even before the close of the nineteenth century and before the graded structure had fully crystallized, educators of insight were observing that the grading of pupils, as then practiced, ignored uniqueness and pupil individuality. During several decades spanning the old age of one century and the early childhood of another, various experimental structures were designed at least to modify graded structure. (See Chapter 3.)

Figure 2

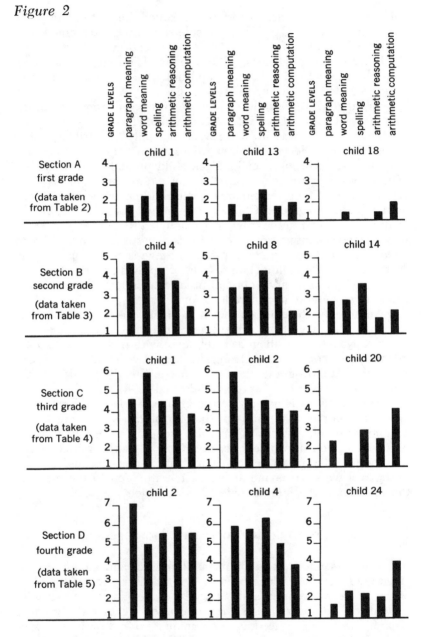

Achievement profiles for twelve children from four grades, each section showing three children from the same grade level.

But the drive behind these efforts soon dissipated itself against the mass rigidity of the graded elementary schools. Nonetheless, through the years the hope has remained that some technique might be developed for inter-class grouping of pupils resulting in increased homogeneity. The notion that pupils of like ability should be placed together for more effective learning seems always to have its proponents. The aspect of this notion concerning us here is whether such grouping expedites the application of grade standards.

For many teachers, a group of thirty pupils grouped homogeneously would be a teaching Utopia. Some admit that they would be willing to teach larger classes under such conditions. But what do we mean by "grouped homogeneously"? Applied to humans, the term "homogeneous" is a relative one. Were we to examine the chronological age spread of the class groups which were presented earlier in this chapter, we would see considerable homogeneity as contrasted with the comparative heterogeneity in all other areas. But, were we to divide each of these class groups into three smaller groups on the basis of reading attainment, there still would be considerable heterogeneity in reading within any one small group. There would also be heterogeneity in other areas, such as arithmetic. Grouping children "homogeneously" on the basis of a single criterion does not produce a group that is homogeneous to the same degree judged by other criteria.

The most widely advocated criterion for securing class-to-class pupil homogeneity is general ability. First-grade classes frequently are established initially by dividing entering pupils into A, B, and C groups on the basis of data from tests of such ability. There seems to be a growing interest in reducing group variability by screening off pupils who are either high or low on the ability continuum. Thus, the top four or five and bottom four or five pupils from each of a half-dozen classes of a single grade-level might be selected to make up two more "homogeneous" classes. The top group would then be given an enriched or accelerated program, or both, and the bottom group a so-called remedial one. The heterogeneity of the remaining classes presumably would thus be substantially reduced. Before examining the extent of reduced homogeneity in the other classes, it is desirable to point out that the variability among pupils remains considerable even in the two segregated "homogeneous" groups. We have already demonstrated earlier in this chapter (page 15) that there tends to be a greater area-to-area range in attainment within single pupils who are in the upper and lower levels of any general ability scale than within single pupils more closely approximating average ability. Consequently, teachers who proceed as though their class of gifted or retarded pupils were homogeneous are fooling themselves and cheating their pupils.

Using the illustrative data of Table 6, let us examine the grade-level variation in a fifth-grade class from which the most and least able pupils have been removed. The setting is a relatively large elementary school in an upper middle class residential section of a major city. All children with I.Q. of more than 120 have been grouped into a small class of gifted pupils. All children with I.Q. under 90 have been grouped into another small class of retarded pupils. The remaining fifth-grade classes are somewhat larger than they would otherwise have been but, happily, are presumed to be considerably reduced in heterogeneity. The question is: Did this inter-class grouping create a situation in which grade standards might now be reasonably applied? The answer, obviously, is that it did not.

Earlier, it was pointed out that the range in both readiness to learn (as suggested by M.A.) and in general achievement is approximately the same as the number designating the grade level by the time children complete the fourth grade. As would be expected, since the children of very high and low I.Q. have been removed, the range in M.A. is only three years—from nine years to twelve years. But the range in over-all attainment is five grades, the grade level designation—from 3.5 grades to 8.4. In specific attainment areas, the range is, of course, much greater. It is more than eight grades in paragraph meaning and language, for example. The total profile is so much like the profile of the fourth grade presented earlier (except that it is extended upward a year and represents the generally superior work of a higher socio-economic group with a mean I.Q. of 105), one would not perceive that an attempt had been made to increase homogeneity. Any instructional application of grade standards here obviously would be meaningless, as in the situations previously presented.

Several other observations, based on these and previous data, are pertinent here. Chronological age tells little about other variables to be found in a given class group and is a worthless base for the application of grade standards, however useful it may be for classifying pupils otherwise. Likewise, I.Q. is a poor basis for estimating achievement. In Table 6, for example, the two children of highest I.Q. are well down on the achievement scale. An overall achievement score (battery median) is more accurate than I.Q. or M.A. as a basis for securing scholastic homogeneity, but even here the application of grade standards calls for weird distortions. Many of the individual pupils in Table 6 vary by five or more grades from achievement area to achievement area.

The more we divide general development into specific traits, the easier it is to group pupils homogeneously on a single trait but the harder it becomes to group them homogeneously on all traits

Table 6
Data for a fifth-grade class in an upper middle class community

CHILD	M.A.	C.A.	I.Q.	paragraph meaning	word meaning	spelling	language	arithmetic reasoning	arithmetic computation	battery median.
1	11-3	10-3	110	9.4	9.4	7.4	10.6	6.1	5.1	8.4
2	11-3	10-2	111	7.7	10.0	8.8	11.2	6.9	5.7	8.3
3	11-0	10-6	105	10.4	9.4	6.7	9.0	6.1	5.0	7.9
4	11-4	9-11	114	7.1	6.9	6.7	8.6	5.7	5.3	6.8
5	11-1	10-7	105	10.8	8.6	6.6	4.8	6.7	6.4	6.7
6	11-4	10-4	110	7.4	8.2	5.6	6.0	7.7	5.8	6.7
7	11-3	9-9	115	4.8	8.0	6.5	7.0	6.9	5.2	6.7
8	10-11	10-4	106	7.1	7.5	7.2	5.2	5.5	5.8	6.5
9	10-11	10-7	103	6.1	8.2	5.2	8.9	6.9	5.0	6.5
10	11-2	10-1	111	8.6	9.4	7.0	5.4	5.8	5.7	6.4
11	11-5	10-9	114	7.4	7.1	5.6	4.8	7.3	5.6	6.4
12	11-4	10-8	106	9.0	6.3	4.3	8.0	6.5	5.4	6.4
13	11-5	10-7	108	7.7	7.3	4.6	10.4	5.5	5.3	6.4
14	11-7	10-4	112	7.4	6.9	5.6	5.8	6.7	5.1	6.3
15	11-7	9-11	117	7.1	7.5	5.5	6.0	6.3	6.3	6.3
16	11-10	9-10	120	5.6	7.3	5.0	7.0	5.5	4.5	6.1
17	11-1	10-8	104	6.1	8.2	5.8	5.4	5.8	4.0	5.8
18	11-11	10-5	114	5.2	6.9	5.7	8.6	5.5	5.4	5.6
19	11-7	9-10	118	5.6	7.5	4.8	8.1	5.4	4.0	5.5
20	11-1	10-0	111	5.6	6.5	5.1	7.9	4.9	3.9	5.4
21	10-11	10-1	108	5.2	5.9	5.7	5.0	5.3	5.1	5.3
22	11-2	10-2	110	5.2	5.7	5.9	4.0	5.4	5.3	5.3
23	10-5	10-3	102	4.4	5.5	5.2	5.2	5.1	4.8	5.2
24	12-0	10-0	120	6.8	8.6	5.0	5.2	5.1	4.5	5.1
25	9-10	10-2	97	5.4	5.4	4.6	5.8	4.8	4.3	5.1
26	10-8	10-5	102	4.8	5.0	5.1	6.5	5.0	4.1	5.0
27	9-10	10-8	92	4.4	4.5	5.2	3.7	5.0	5.3	4.8
28	9-8	10-8	91	6.1	4.9	4.2	3.3	5.0	4.6	4.8
29	10-4	10-7	98	6.1	4.6	5.3	4.2	4.7	3.7	4.7
30	10-1	10-5	97	6.3	4.8	4.8	4.9	4.7	4.6	4.7
31	9-11	10-9	92	5.2	4.8	3.9	4.1	4.8	3.7	4.5
32	10-3	10-1	102	4.3	4.0	4.0	4.5	4.6	5.0	4.4
33	9-8	10-7	91	4.6	3.2	3.6	5.1	3.9	4.8	4.3
34	9-8	10-1	96	2.7	3.2	4.6	3.7	5.0	5.3	4.2
35	10-0	10-10	92	4.0	4.6	3.4	7.0	3.9	4.1	4.1
36	9-0	10-0	90	4.1	5.0	3.3	2.9	5.3	3.7	3.9
37	10-7	10-1	105	3.3	3.4	4.8	7.0	3.9	3.7	3.8
38	9-2	9-10	93	4.1	3.5	3.3	4.4	3.4	2.9	3.5

and, hence, to apply a single classification scale such as grade level. One of the authors once found himself in a teaching situation that offered promise of considerable homogeneity. The institution was a specialized one in that it received only boys committed for delinquent acts. The pupils were relatively homogeneous on a criterion supposedly related to learning in that almost all of them fell in a low I.Q. range of 70 to 110, with a mean of 85. But, after six weeks of teaching them, he found himself wishing for a "special" specialized school down the road that might receive those who deviated most markedly from the others on various significant traits! To search for a teaching Utopia where homogeneous grouping will solve the problems raised by the graded system is to search for a will-o'-the-wisp.

Other Types of Variation

Many readers will protest our emphasis on academic variation or differences. The emphasis is deliberate. Too often, proponents of new procedures in elementary education defend them on the grounds that their proposals will be conducive to improved social adjustment or mental health. We believe such ends to be important; so important in fact that we have devoted a chapter to the mental health concomitants of nongrading. But the learning of certain fundamental academic skills is regarded by many as a central function, if not *the* function, of elementary education. Any proposal for

Figure 3

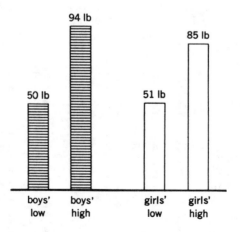

Extremes in weight in a third-grade class.

20

reorganization that side-steps the question of how such learnings will be affected is unlikely to receive wholehearted support. Therefore, we argue the case for the nongraded elementary school first on academic grounds. We believe that abolition of grade barriers frees each child, whatever his ability, to move forward in his learnings as rapidly and as smoothly as possible. But we also believe that such structure is in harmony with his social and emotional well-being.

Figures 3, 4, 5, and 6 illustrate several physical and social differences in a third-grade class. Figure 3 shows the startling range in weight. The heaviest boy is 90 per cent heavier than the lightest; the heaviest girl 75 per cent heavier than the lightest. Figure 4 reveals the extremes among the children in performing five activities requiring speed, agility, and general physical coordination. The nature of each task is quite clear with the possible exception of the vertical jump and the target throw. In the first, the children stand beside a wall and jump upward. The distance is the difference between the highest spot touched without jumping and the spot

Figure 4

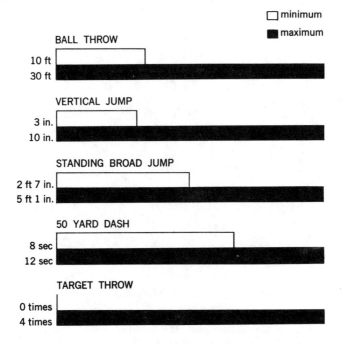

Extremes in physical skills among third-grade children.

touched at the height of the jump. In the target throw, each child had ten trials at throwing an eight-inch ball into a can.

As in the rest of conventional school life, there are grade standards for such activities. The teacher of this class followed the guides offered by the Philadelphia Board of Education.[1] There is no need for us to go into what minimum standards are suggested for each grade level. Let it suffice that this class, like other classes, spread out far above and far below them.

Figures 5 and 6 present some sociometric data for the same group. The data for Figure 5 were compiled by asking the question: In our class, which person would you like to have as your best friend? Seventeen of the 33 children received all the choices, one of these garnering the disproportionate total of six. It is interesting to note that eight of the 16 children not chosen had been nonpromoted at least once in their short school careers. (For further documentation of the social rejection pattern for nonpromoted children, see Chapter 2).

The data for Figure 6 were compiled by asking the question: In another class, which person would you like to have work with you on a problem? The children reached far afield: all the way up to the seventh grade and all the way down to the first, the full gamut

Figure 5

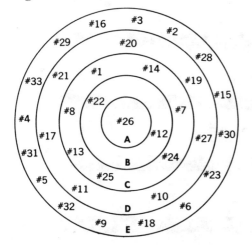

A 1 child received 6 choices

B 2 children received 3 choices

C 7 children received 2 choices

D 7 children received 1 choice

E 16 children received 0 choices

"Best Friend" sociogram for a third-grade class.

[1] School District of Philadelphia, the Board of Public Instruction, *Course of Study in Physical Education: Grades 3 and 4* (Philadelphia, Philadelphia Public Schools, 1950), pp. 164-69.

Figure 6

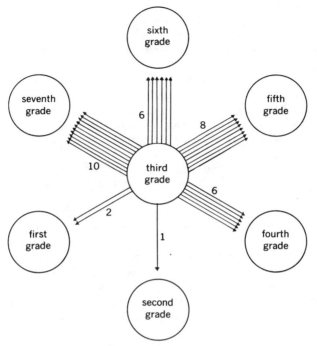

Preferences of 33 third-grade children for a partner from another grade.

of grades housed in the school. Like the other classes described earlier, this one varied widely in ability and academic accomplishments: from 7 years to 10 years 8 months in M.A. and from 74 to 129 in I.Q.; from 1.7 to 5.0 grades in reading; from 0 to 4.2 grades in spelling; and from 1.3 to 3.3 in arithmetic. The grade range from subject to subject within a given child was considerable: from 2.7 in arithmetic reasoning to 5.3 in word meaning for one; from 1.7 in arithmetic computation to 3.9 in spelling for another.

In order to avoid loading the statistics in favor of a startling picture of heterogeneity, the class described briefly on the preceding pages was chosen because it had been a rather slow-moving group. Few youngsters had spurted ahead to increase the overall attainment spread. It would have been difficult to choose anywhere a randomly structured third-grade class of less heterogeneity. Yet, even in this conservative selection, the results are startling. The youngsters differ widely on every criterion. Individual children differ widely within themselves from criterion to criterion. If the top or bottom child on any trait were checked throughout on all traits—academic, social, physical, and so on—a jagged, irregular profile would result. What a complex picture of variability is presented by a class of elementary-school pupils! What a pitifully erroneous connotation is conveyed by the hopeful label, "third grade"!

But even graphing these several components does not portray the total variety within a given child. The parts add up to much less than the whole. There was a time, not too long ago, when we believed that school accomplishment was the product of I.Q. and motivation. The work of Haggard [2] and others is showing us how naïve we were. Even youngsters of unusually high ability often do less than mediocre school work, perhaps because of sensitivity to environmental pressures to learn. At any rate, children vary in the amount of anxiety that they bring to learning tasks from other situations or that arises out of the learning task. Vague or specific anxiety in children is a powerful determinant of learning efficiency.[3] There is no way of knowing the degree of such anxiety from intelligence test scores, socio-economic status, or similar data and, therefore, of knowing how a child's ability to do the work of a given grade level will be affected. Graded school structure had settled into place long before we had such insights. Must we retain this structure now that our perspective of learner realities has achieved new dimensions?

The Transition to High School

The American high school is being increasingly caught in a squeeze of an intensity that it has not known before. The physical burdens of a rapidly expanding population may be seen quite readily. But the ideological burdens, while perhaps not so visible, may well prove more troublesome.

One aspect of the ideological squeeze—the impact of conflicting viewpoints on what the secondary school is for—is somewhat outside our present purposes. One other is not. The elementary school gradually has been developing the philosophy that it should take each child as far as he can go. The implementation of such a philosophy in practice has been frustrated by the presence of grade

---

[2] Ernest A. Haggard, "Socialization, Personality, and Academic Achievement in Gifted Children," *School Review*, 65 (December 1957), pp. 388-414.

[3] See, for example, William H. Stavsky, "Using the Insights of Psychotherapy in Teaching," *Elementary School Journal*, 58 (October 1957), pp. 28-35.

standards and the various pressures to conform to them. These pressures, however, have forced persons connected with elementary education to examine the effects of enforcing grade standards through such practices as nonpromotion. As a result, it has been found that rigorous nonpromotion policies (see Chapter 2) neither improve the child's readiness to learn nor augment his learning increments. Sending most pupils into high school with achievement at grade level could be accomplished only by Procrustean methods: lopping off the heads of the most advanced and grotesquely stretching the slow. Any expectation on the part of the high school that there will be anything but wide variation in attainment among its entering freshmen is unrealistic. And yet, at the other end of the educational hierarchy, colleges and universities increasingly are demanding (and able to hold out for) higher standards on the part of their entering freshmen. From take-them-from-where-they-are to arbitrary standards is a broad ideological gulf. The few years of high school provide only a short bridge for spanning it.

The secondary school, then, unlikely to be granted still more years for doing its job and, therefore, for lengthening its bridge, understandably looks downward to the elementary school for a means of reducing the gulf. The look is unlikely to be encouraging, as a glance at Figure 7 will reveal. Here are mid-term data in one achievement area for the eighth-grade classes of two elementary schools in a large city. Most of the children from both schools will move on into the secondary school the following year. Although achievement scores are skewed toward the lower end of the scale for school A and the upper end for school B, the spread for both groups is tremendous and only slightly greater for B than for A. About half the pupils in school A and a quarter of those in school B would be retained in their present grade were grade-level in reading demanded for admission to the high school. Furthermore, some of those in school A would be old men with their beards draped into the inkwells were admission to high school delayed until eighth-grade reading standards had been met. Likewise, some of the advanced pupils in school B would meet these standards when only babes.

Analysis of similar data for these two schools would reveal large spreads in other areas of achievement. The troublesome and yet very significant point, however, is that *pupils advanced or retarded in one learning area are not necessarily similarly advanced or retarded in other areas.* Pupils at twelfth-grade standard for reading might well be at tenth-, ninth-, and seventh-grade levels for other subjects. For the secondary school to demand grade-level standards of entering freshmen is for it to serve as the child's

Figure 7

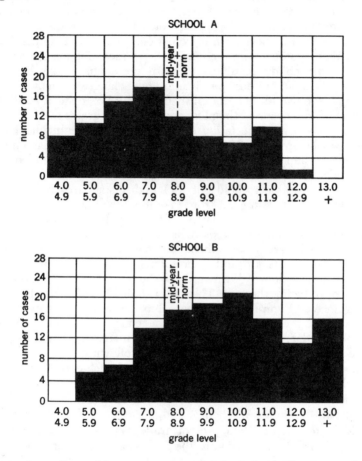

Range in reading achievement among eighth-grade pupils of two schools in a large city.

Procrustes and the elementary school's executioner. For the secondary school to expect (and, if need be, demand) a profile for each child admitted, a profile showing progress that may be interpreted for individual pupils, is quite another matter. With such data, the high school may then plan programs appropriate to the realities of individual differences rather than appropriate to the mythical, nonexistent grade standard.

The American secondary school faces grave ideological and crushing physical burdens. From above and below and from all sides it is being subjected to tremendous pressure.[4] Elementary-school policies of acceleration, retardation, or both, do not materially reduce the variation in achievement among those millions of young people moving up to the higher unit. But this fact is not always clear to secondary-school teachers. Meanwhile, from above, comes the cry that the high schools are not adequately preparing their graduates for college. Intensification of the squeeze will result in the high school increasingly turning critical attention to the standards of the elementary school. Unless the latter is able to point convincingly to the inappropriateness of grade standards as a basis for judging its effectiveness, the elementary school will be forced into the completely untenable position of striving for closer approximation of such standards by its pupils. This unhappy prospect increases the urgency for examining the graded lock-step of elementary-school organization and for developing structure more compatible with the realities of pupil variation.

The structure recommended here is the nongraded elementary school. Such a school is not devoid of standards. Rather, it is more rigorous in the quality of learning it promotes. The nongraded pupil is encouraged, in a setting conducive to individual pacing, to move forward in the various aspects of his development at rates appropriate to his unique traits. If this be abdication of standards then we have, indeed, stepped through the looking-glass into a world stranger by far than any perceived by Alice.

In Conclusion

Several important generalizations about the pupil realities with which elementary-school teachers must deal have been brought into sharp focus through the analysis of classes at several grade levels:

1. Children enter the first grade with a range of from three to four years in their readiness to profit from a "graded minimum essentials" concept of schooling.
2. This initial spread in abilities increases over the years so that it is approximately double this amount by the time children approach the end of the elementary school.
3. The achievement range among pupils begins to approximate the range in intellectual readiness to learn soon after first-grade children are exposed to reasonably normal school instruction.
4. Differing abilities, interests, and opportunities among children

---

[4] For a comprehensive analysis of this pressure, see Francis S. Chase and Harold A. Anderson, eds., *The High School in a New Era* (Chicago, University of Chicago Press, 1958).

cause the range in certain specific attainments to surpass the range in general achievement.

5. Individual children's achievement patterns differ markedly from learning area to learning area.

6. By the time children reach the intermediate elementary grades, the range in intellectual readiness to learn and in most areas of achievement is as great as or greater than the number designating the grade level.

By the fourth or fifth year of school, more than half the achievement scores in a class are above and below the grade level attached to the group. There is, then, no such thing as a fourth-grade class or a fifth-grade teacher, regardless of the labels within our conventional graded structure.

In spite of pupil realities, however, expectations for applying grade norms and standards are many and compelling. Test results must be converted to grade norms. Parents understand grade norms; they and their parents grew up with them. They expect their children to be at "grade level" (or, preferably, above). Parents feel comfortable with reporting practices that reveal progress in relation to grade standards and, frequently, are interested in some kind of grade-level comparison of their children with other children. Parents and children alike take for granted assignment to a grade level and hope for promotion to the next.

All these expectations would be reasonable and appropriate if only children would be more "reasonable" in their developmental patterns. If only children would be all of a size, all of a kind, all of a common ability, all of a common attainment, they would fit neatly into the concept of a grade for a year. But they are not like this and we really would not want them to be. Our very social order is founded on the premise that human individuality is to be fostered and that our organizational practices are to be judged by how adequately they promote both group and individual welfare.

To expect two children who begin their school careers several years apart in readiness for school tasks to be at the same place several years hence is to do injustice to both. Not only is one child initially far ahead but, in addition, he is traveling at an accelerated rate. Imagine for a moment two cars setting out to race over an uninterrupted freeway to Miami, Florida, the Chevrolet starting at Chicago and the Cadillac at Atlanta, Georgia. Simultaneous arrival in Miami could result only if the Cadillac suffered a delaying breakdown. The job of elementary education is not to convert the low horsepower child into a high horsepower machine, nor is it to promote senseless races between the two. The real job is to keep both tuned and operating at top-level efficiency and then to clear the road blocks so that each may proceed at his unique and appropriate pace.

For Further Reading

Beck, Robert H., Walter W. Cook, and Nolan C. Kearney. *Curriculum in the Modern Elementary School*. Englewood Cliffs, N. J., Prentice-Hall, Inc., 1953. Chapter 2.

Here is found one of the relatively few discussions of individual and trait differences related to a variety of elementary-school practices. The statements and charts of pages 27 through 33 covering ability and achievement distributions are particularly to the point.

Henry, Nelson B. (ed.). *Individualizing Instruction*. Sixty-first Yearbook of the National Society for the Study of Education, Part I. Chicago, University of Chicago Press, 1962.

Following a series of chapters on theoretical issues, five chapters present illustrations of individual differences. In another section school practices are examined. The final chapters deal with implications.

Prescott, Daniel A. *The Child in the Educative Process*. New York, McGraw-Hill Book Co., 1957.

This entire volume is virtually dedicated to pupils as individual, developing persons. It is difficult to isolate specific chapters as having more pertinence than others to our purposes. Chapters 10 and 11, however, are focused directly upon human development, with particular reference to the shaping of individual personality.

Russell, David H. *Children's Thinking*. Boston, Ginn and Co., 1956.

This volume provides a breadth of viewpoint toward intellectual development based on an analysis of about one thousand research references. Chapter 2 serves as an overview of material covered in detail in subsequent chapters.

Williams, Roger J. *Biochemical Individuality*. New York, John Wiley and Sons, Inc., 1956.

A comprehensive treatment of an aspect of individuality seldom considered by educators appears in this book. For a brief summary of the evidence submitted in the complete volume, see Roger J. Williams, "Individuality and Education," *Educational Leadership*, **15** (December 1957), 144-48.

2. TO PROMOTE

OR NOT TO PROMOTE

Introduction

The pressures on teachers to apply grade standards vary, as do their reactions to these pressures. Studies conducted over several decades have revealed nonpromotion rates varying from zero in some school districts to 34 per cent in others.[1] The variation from grade to grade within a school and from school to school within a system is almost as great as the variation among systems.

In one large suburban school system in the South, Goodlad was easily able to separate a half-dozen schools with primary level nonpromotion rates of less than 5 per cent from a half-dozen schools with primary nonpromotion rates of more than 10 per cent.[2] In one county school, in fact, there were no first-grade retentions while, in another, 28 of 56 first-grade children were retained! Consistently, in all of the more than thirty schools with some incidence of nonpromotion, the rates were highest in the first grade. And, at all levels, boy retentions outnumbered girl retentions approximately three to two.[3] Furthermore, in this school system, the range in ability levels

---

[1] See, for example, Leonard P. Ayres, *Laggards in Our Schools* (New York, Russell Sage Foundation, 1909); Arch O. Heck, *Administration of Pupil Personnel* (Boston, Ginn and Co., 1929), pp. 357-60; Hollis L. Caswell, *Non-Promotion in Elementary Schools* (Nashville, Tennessee, Division of Surveys and Field Studies, George Peabody College for Teachers, 1933), pp. 24-25; Carleton M. Saunders, *Promotion or Failure for the Elementary School Pupil?* (New York, Teachers College, Columbia University, 1941), pp. 7-15.

[2] See John I. Goodlad, "Some Effects of Promotion and Nonpromotion upon the Social and Personal Adjustment of Children" (unpublished doctoral dissertation, University of Chicago, 1949).

[3] For a comprehensive treatment of some pertinent nonpromotion statistics, see Hollis L. Caswell and Arthur W. Foshay, *Education in the Elementary School*, 3rd ed. (New York, American Book Co., 1957), pp. 364-70.

among children retained county-wide came close to approximating the overall ability range in many classrooms. The usual I.Q. range found in an elementary-school classroom was from below 70 to slightly more than 130, whereas the range among nonpromoted children was from below 70 to 124. Nonetheless, lack of scholastic aptitude obviously was a significant factor in decisions to retain children, since the average I.Q. among nonpromoted children was close to 90. As Troyer has pointed out, most of the failing and unsatisfactory grades on homework, special papers, projects, class recitations, examinations, and, finally, report cards go to the children in the lower one-fourth of the ability distribution.[4]

Parents probably would be shocked to know how much the promotion careers of their children depend upon factors over which these children have little or no control. Whether or not a child is promoted appears to depend more upon biological, economic, and social chance than upon sound educational design or how hard he works. In fact, whether or not a child is promoted depends on where he happens to go to school. Susan, in school A and classroom X, with I.Q. of 110 and achievement substantially below what one might anticipate for her, and Sam, in school B and classroom Y, with I.Q. of 80 and achievement equally low, might well be retained in their present grade for another year. Meanwhile, Jean and Bill, with similar ability-accomplishment patterns, in school C and classroom Z, might well be promoted. By carefully studying school policies and statistics, the parents of Susan and Sam might change their children's school careers from failure to success stories (outwardly, at least) simply by changing their place of abode. Ironically, it would not be necessary, under such circumstances, for Susan and Sam to change their work habits or ability-accomplishment profiles in the slightest!

Parents reading the above might understandably turn their wrath upon their local school, but their fury would be ill-directed. They are as much of the pressure picture as the teachers. Many parents, as evidence presented later shows, are reluctant to see the familiar graded structure and its accompaniments disappear. Parents view teachers as sympathetic with school as it is. Teachers view parents as having certain time-honored expectations that coincide pretty much with the *status quo*. Could this be another of those educational practices being continued, not because teachers and parents have studied it together, but because both believe the other expects it? Perhaps an analysis of the pressures teachers face and

---

[4] Maurice E. Troyer, *Accuracy and Validity in Evaluation Are Not Enough*, The J. Richard Street Lecture for 1947 (Syracuse, Syracuse University Press, 1947), p. 5.

the validity of the decisions they make under pressure will provide a basis for truly professional judgment and the development of consistent practices understood and endorsed by both teachers and parents.

The Pro and Con of Nonpromotion

The most consistent factor among nonpromoted children is that they are low achievers. And yet, many low achievers are promoted. Apparently, some teachers react to the failure of children to reach grade standards by retaining them; others by promoting these slow learners. The operation of two such diametrically opposed practices, under comparable conditions and in the name of pupil welfare, presents an educational mystery worth investigating.

The authors have investigated it with groups of teachers in many sections of the country. Each time, the stage for investigation was set somewhat as follows. First, the inconsistency in promotion practices was pointed out much as demonstrated in the preceding pages. Then, the issue was sharpened: "Apparently, thousands of teachers in all parts of the country retain each year a million or so elementary-school youngsters in their present grades. Meanwhile, other teachers promote children who closely resemble their nonpromoted peers. Let us take a look at why some well-meaning teachers retained children and then at why other equally well-meaning teachers promoted very similar children. Think, first, of the reasons teachers like yourselves might use to justify acts of nonpromotion."

Not to promote

Time after time, the reasons put forth by teachers to explain the incidence of nonpromotion are these: [5]

1. Certain children do not make sufficient academic progress during the year to profit from the work of the grade above. (This reason, the most commonly presented, often is expressed simply as "lack of achievement.")
2. We cannot go on indefinitely pushing children up. Let's face it: some upper grades and certainly our high schools expect children to measure up. If we don't insist on certain standards now, children will be unprepared for what must inevitably come later.

---

[5] For further analysis see John I. Goodlad, "To Promote or Not to Promote?" *Toward Effective Grouping* (Washington, D.C., Association for Childhood Education International, 1962), pp. 34-38.

3. The teacher in the grade immediately above expects children to come prepared; it's just too bad for the children if they are sent up unprepared.
4. Continued inability to do the work of the grade is discouraging and frustrating to children. They are better off if retained in a grade level where they can gain some success and satisfaction.
5. The presence of slow learners in the class presents a hindrance both to children and to teachers who already are badly overloaded. Retaining slow learners will reduce this problem.
6. Immature children, by repeating the grade, will find more suitable playmates and work companions.
7. Promotion of all is unfair to those who have come up to grade standards. These more able students come to resent equal reward for obviously inferior performance.

To promote

When the question is reversed and teachers are asked to explain why many teachers apparently decide on promotion as the better alternative, the following reasons come forth:

1. If the teacher and child have already failed to make the hoped-for progress, the child might just as well move on to another grade and another teacher. (Sometimes, this is stated that the slow-learning child will achieve just as much in the grade ahead as he will by having to repeat the present one.)
2. From the beginning, first-grade teachers must deal with a wide range of individual differences. They cannot reduce the range, and so teachers in higher grades must anticipate dealing also with the range as it exists.
3. Grade failure is itself more devastating to the child's adjustment than are his difficulties with the work at hand. Slow learners will have enough problems in school without adding the shame and humiliation of nonpromotion.
4. Since good teaching increases rather than reduces the range of abilities with which a teacher must deal, retaining a few children at the bottom end is not likely to reduce materially the next teacher's problem of dealing with individual differences. Besides, if each grade retains some children, each grade will carry these into the next year, thus assuring the presence of these slow learners in any case.
5. Chronological age is the best single criterion for determining the placement of a child with other children. Consequently, keeping children of the same age together (therefore promoting them), is the best way to assure appropriate work and play companions for all.

6. Class size and the cost of education are increased when even a small percentage of children is retained.[6]
7. At elementary-school levels, where children are called upon to compete regardless of their desire or readiness to do so, educational practices must be adapted to the welfare of the individual, not the child to arbitrary grade standards. Promotion is aligned with such a point of view.

Both sets of arguments contest the same points but from different positions which, in turn, are used to support directly opposed educational practices. Children learn more if they are promoted; they learn more if retained. Children get along better socially if promoted; they establish better social relations if nonpromoted. Either there is no basis for choosing between these arguments or the available evidence has not affected the thinking and acting of teachers using them. Actually, there is a considerable amount of research that could be used in resolving such arguments on quite rational grounds.[7]

A look at the evidence

NONPROMOTION AND ACHIEVEMENT. Regardless of whatever other evidence may be found to support promotion or nonpromotion, the respective influence of these two practices on pupil achievement is still of fundamental concern to teachers. Early studies (1911-1941) [8] of the effects of nonpromotion on achievement agree closely in their findings: children do not learn more by repeating a grade but experience less growth in subject-matter achievement than they do when promoted. Coffield, seeking to assure himself that more recent instructional procedures had not changed the generally negative

---

[6] Fifty years ago, Ayres worked out a formula for determining the cost of pupil failure to taxpayers. See Leonard P. Ayres, *op. cit.*

[7] For a rather detailed analysis of many studies conducted before 1950, see John I. Goodlad, "Research and Theory Regarding Promotion and Nonpromotion," *Elementary School Journal*, 53 (November 1952), pp. 150-55.

[8] For example, see Charles H. Keyes, *Progress through the Grades of City Schools* (New York, Bureau of Publications, Teachers College, Columbia University, 1911); Vivian Klene and Ernest P. Branson, "Trial Promotion versus Failure," *Educational Research Bulletin*, Los Angeles City Schools, 8 (January 1929), pp. 6-11; *Report of the Division of Educational Research and Results for the Year Ended June 30, 1933* (Board of Education, School District of Philadelphia, 1933); Grace Arthur, "A Study of the Achievement of Sixty Grade 1 Repeaters as Compared with That of Nonrepeaters of the Same Mental Age," *Journal of Experimental Education*, 5 (December 1936), pp. 203-05; Carleton M. Saunders, *Promotion or Failure for the Elementary School Pupil?* (New York, Bureau of Publications, Teachers College, Columbia University, 1941).

effects of nonpromotion, reopened the question for intensive examination at all elementary-school levels. His findings agree with those of the earlier studies. At all grade levels, promoted low achievers generally do better in school work than their nonpromoted counterparts.[9]

In all these studies, a number of nonpromoted children did show reasonable growth in achievement during the repeated year. But, to offset this, a much larger percentage actually did worse on achievement tests after a year of repetition than they had done when tested just before the impact of failure or the subsequent deadening effect of repetition, or both, destroyed the will to learn and impaired some of the learning that already had occurred. The argument that nonpromotion may be justified because it usually raises achievement must be rejected.

A phase of the achievement argument against promotion of slow learners is that too extensive practice of promotion lowers standards and achievement levels in higher grades. Cook has effectively exploded this "day-of-reckoning argument." He compared a high nonpromotion rate district in Minnesota with a neighboring low nonpromotion rate district. He found upper-grade achievement levels in the high nonpromotion schools to be lower than upper-grade achievement levels in the schools with significantly lower rates of nonpromotion.[10] On the basis of evidence regarding the effect of nonpromotion on achievement cited above, one might well anticipate such a finding. With children actually learning less under conditions of high failure rates, the attainment rate gradually is slowed down until the accumulation of under-grade achievement becomes considerable in upper elementary grades. One of the authors fell victim to such circumstances in his own elementary-school teaching. More than half the young people in his seventh-grade class had repeated a grade at least once, several having repeated two or even three times throughout their short school careers. As a result, the average age of the group was well over fifteen by mid-year, but average achievement was a full year retarded. But poor motivation for schooling and low achievement were really the least troublesome of the many vexing problems that had developed over years of pressure to maintain grade standards.

NONPROMOTION AND PUPIL ATTITUDE. Disagreement over the advantages and disadvantages of promotion and nonpromotion in-

---

[9] William H. Coffield, "A Longitudinal Study of the Effects of Nonpromotion on Educational Achievement in the Elementary School" (unpublished doctoral dissertation, State University of Iowa, 1954).

[10] Walter W. Cook, *Grouping and Promotion in the Elementary Schools.* Series on Individualization of Instruction No. 2 (Minneapolis, University of Minnesota Press, 1941).

cludes differing assumptions about the effects of these practices on pupil attitudes toward school and learning. This area has been less carefully explored. Nonetheless, there is a considerable body of psychological evidence showing that failure is a deterrent to the development of sound attitudes. Caswell and Foshay analyzed this evidence carefully [11] and concluded that nonpromotion often results in emotional depression and discouragement, in the pupil's distrust of his own ability and ultimately in his expectation of further failure. Caught up in a situation where he does not succeed and where continued striving does not lead to accomplishment and satisfaction, the child tends to rationalize his failure and to build up explanatory defense mechanisms.[12]

A cyclical relationship between school failure, discouragement, decrease of interest in school work, aggressive and attention-getting behavior, and delinquent acts is revealed frequently enough in case studies to give cause for concern.

In one study, Goodlad discovered that nonpromotion, low level of school achievement, lethargic school habits, and often intensely negative attitudes towards school and schooling are common among delinquent boys.[13] In another, teachers and principals who assisted in the collection of data reported more occurrences of stealing, more incidents demanding disciplinary action, and greater resistance to the schools' civic efforts among nonpromoted children.[14] Sandin reported similar findings.[15] From an analysis of data collected from all grade levels of elementary education, he concluded that the attitude of retarded-progress children toward school and school life was less favorable than that of their regular-progress peers. A large proportion of the nonpromoted children wanted to quit school just as soon as the first opportunity to do so presented itself.

It becomes apparent that nonpromotion is not conducive to the development of pupil feelings of satisfaction and well-being. Promotion offers greater hope that pupils will develop a sense of personal worth, that they will take pleasure from school life, and that they will want to continue with their schooling.

---

[11] For documentation of their findings, see Hollis L. Caswell and Arthur W. Foshay, *op. cit.*, pp. 387-94.

[12] *Ibid.*, p. 392.

[13] John I. Goodlad, "The Male Institutional Juvenile Delinquent" (unpublished master's thesis, University of British Columbia, 1946).

[14] John I. Goodlad, "Some Effects of Promotion and Nonpromotion upon the Social and Personal Adjustment of Children." (See footnote 2 of this chapter.)

[15] Adolph Sandin, *Social and Emotional Adjustments of Regularly Promoted and Non-Promoted Pupils,* Child Development Monographs No. 32 (New York, Bureau of Publications, Teachers College, Columbia University, 1944).

NONPROMOTION AND PERSONAL-SOCIAL ADJUSTMENT. What is the relationship between promotion practices and the children's personal-social adjustment? How do nonpromoted children get along with their peers as compared with regular-progress pupils? How do they feel about the adequacy of their self-development? Today's elementary schools are deeply concerned with such questions, on the assumption that they are important in themselves and that they have a direct bearing upon other areas of learning.

Sandin explored these questions extensively, comparing nonpromoted pupils through the grades with the general population of regularly promoted children.[16] Some findings pertinent to the questions raised were these:

1. Repeaters more frequently preferred to associate with companions from upper grades.
2. Repeaters, generally speaking, did not receive the social approval or acceptance of the regularly promoted.
3. Repeaters received significantly more ratings as being unfriendly, cruel, and bullying to classmates.
4. As pointed out in the previous section, intensive analysis of selected nonpromoted children revealed them to be lacking to an alarming degree in self-confidence, self-respect, and general feelings of well-being.

Sandin compared repeaters with the general population of regular-progress pupils. He did not attempt to match a nonpromoted group with a promoted group. Consequently, he was forced to ask himself whether the generally undesirable conditions associated with nonpromotion might be a cause rather than a result of school failure. To test this possibility, Goodlad equated a group of promoted with a group of nonpromoted children and compared the progress of the groups over a period of one year.[17] On the assumption that the effects of early grade failure might be more effectively isolated from the general picture of adjustment, a group of first-grade repeaters was equated with a group of children promoted to the second grade. Factors equated were chronological age, mental age, and achievement. Considerable preliminary work was done to secure equivalent conditions regarding the teaching setting, classroom enrollment, urban-rural location of schools, physical normality of the selected children, and socio-economic status of their families. The gross grade-to-grade and school-to-school differences in promotion practices, described earlier, made it possible to select children who were enrolled in the same school system. The equated

---

[16] *Ibid.*

[17] John I. Goodlad, "Some Effects of Promotion and Nonpromotion on the Social and Personal Adjustment of Children." (See footnote 2 of this chapter.)

groups were selected from eleven schools and twenty-three class-rooms. Two null hypotheses were tested:

1. There are no differences in personal adjustment between non-promoted first-graders and an equated group of promoted second-graders.
2. There are no differences in social adjustment between nonpro-moted first-graders and an equated group of promoted second-graders.

Sociometric techniques, personality inventories, and controlled teacher ratings were used to compare the two groups at the beginning and end of a school year. A regression technique was used to predict the desired performance of the nonpromoted children from the actual growth of the promoted group. The results of these comparisons substantially reinforced the general conclusion supported by the other studies cited.

The study revealed the sharpest group differences in the area of peer-group relationships. The nonpromoted children, at a high level of statistical significance (consistently better than 1 per cent), showed up poorly on all three types of inventories used. Taken together, self-ratings, peer-ratings, and teacher-ratings revealed an alarming picture of social inadequacy among the nonpromoted group. At the beginning of the year, their classmates selected the nonpromoted children more frequently as children they wanted for friends—but also rejected them as friends more frequently. This, at first glance, appears to be a strange contradiction but there seems to be a logical explanation. At the beginning of the year, the nonpromoted children were old-timers; they "knew the ropes." Doubtless, some beginners were impressed with this and sought out the veterans as leaders. Contrariwise, some aggressive children may have seen the older, nonpromoted children as threats to their own developing leadership abilities, with resulting clashes. The nonpromoted children received a high rating for bullying which perhaps resulted from clashes with established leaders among the incoming group, as did their initial rejection as friends by many of the beginners.

Meanwhile, at the beginning of the year, the group promoted to the second grade the previous year was not making a significantly noticeable entry into classroom society. They were neither accepted nor rejected by their peers at a level that might be considered normal. They appeared not to be noticed by their classmates.

Significant changes had occurred by the end of the year. The nonpromoted children no longer were wanted, even by one another. A tight mutual acceptance circle present initially among the nonpromoted group had broken down completely. But the rejection pattern persisted; nonpromoted children, initially unwanted by many, were even more unwanted by year's end. The promoted group, meanwhile, grew in acceptance to a level of normal expectancy by the end of the year. Their very low level of rejection did not change.

In brief, a year of experience as nonpromoted members of first-grade classes had devastating effects on the social acceptance of the children involved. The null hypothesis that there are no differences between promoted and nonpromoted children in regard to social adjustment must be emphatically rejected.

The rejection by their peers increased the nonpromoted children's feelings of inadequacy. More consistently than promoted children, they rated themselves as unwanted and unliked by their peers and as the unhappy victims of quarrels and fights. They seemed, in many instances, to have resigned themselves to lack of success in school and expressed little fear of failure in school work. Could it be that school failure of their children the previous June prompted the parents to confer with the teacher, with the consequence that they expected less of their children? By contrast, the promoted children worried about their school work and feared that their parents were also concerned. Furthermore, the promoted children cheated considerably more. Did the parents of promoted slow learners, not having had this traumatic experience of school failure, still hope for their children's success in school and therefore put pressure on them? At any rate, promoted slow learners resorted to cheating in order to appear to be progressing.

Except for this area of tension over school work, the promoted children felt much better about themselves as people, and the hypothesis that there are no differences in personal adjustment between nonpromoted first-graders and their promoted counterparts must be rejected.

Toward a Sound Educational Position

During the second half of the nineteenth century and the first decades of the twentieth, the elementary school came to be viewed as a series of graded hurdles to be cleared one after the other by participants in a common race. The child who failed to clear a hurdle simply waited, presumably to muster the ability to clear it on his second try a year later. The next chapter describes how such a viewpoint developed and became well established in American life. More recently, the elementary school has been viewed by some as an institution that receives children of approximately the same age but of varying abilities; that provides six, seven, or eight years of schooling to all; and that guides every child to function to the best of his ability throughout the time that he is enrolled. Grade standards, "minimum essentials," and higher rates of nonpromotion usually have been associated with the first of these two viewpoints. De-emphasized grade standards, flexible concepts of adequacy, and lower nonpromotion rates increasingly are being associated with the second. Exponents of this second viewpoint frequently have resorted to "automatic" or "social promotion" as a device for supporting their position in practice.

Analysis of the evidence that promotion for most children is preferable to nonpromotion does not solve our problem. Social or automatic promotion does not change children's learning rates. It does not automatically provide conditions conducive to individual growth. Teachers are still faced with the fact that, at a given grade level, less than half the children approximate the standards of that grade in their various areas of attainment. Merely promoting a child actually may lull the teacher into thinking the act of promotion will produce learning and satisfactory pupil adjustment. No administrative or organizational decision by itself automatically solves any instructional problem.

Teachers often observe that some promoted youngsters encounter grave learning and adjustment problems the subsequent year. Careful program modification for nonpromoted children, on the other hand, often results in quite satisfactory progress for many of them.[18] As long as graded structure is with us, certain burdens peculiar to it must be provided for. In the face of a decision to be made regarding the grade placement of a given child, the body of research into the effects of nonpromotion must be heeded. The policy emerging from this evidence is, "When in doubt, promote." A teacher who decides to retain a child does so in the face of evidence that children usually do better when promoted. He must have good reason to believe that, through retention, this particular child will be placed in an environment conducive to pupil growth and satisfaction. Another year in the grade must provide not repetition, but the best possible opportunity to grow steadily along lines of personal fulfillment and individual unfolding. Likewise, the teachers who promote and receive slow-learning children have a responsibility to see that these children are carried forward from where they now are instead of being frustrated by unrealistic grade expectations. By forgetting grades and grade standards, it is possible

---

[18] For a description of one such modified program, see Lawrence O. Lobdell, "Results of a Nonpromotion Policy in One School District," *Elementary School Journal, 54* (February 1954), pp. 333-37.

to provide educational habitats suited to the wide range of individuals who live in them.

It is unfortunate, however, that appropriate attention to individual learners must be accomplished by circumventing structures once created to expedite the educational process. When the need for circumvention has developed to this degree, the time has come to ask whether organization exists for instruction or whether instruction must be ruled by the demands of structure. The answer is clear: administration and organization exist only to expedite the processes of learning. The authors seriously question the usefulness of graded structure as a device for furthering the learning of elementary-school children. They believe that the adaptations and adjustments its continuation now demands will become even more burdensome as more teachers recognize the conflict between graded structure and the ends they seek to promote. In fact, as the next chapter suggests, our graded system of elementary-school organization soon may be regarded as an anachronism.

In Summary

Early pages of this chapter revealed that whether or not a child is regularly promoted depends more upon where he goes to school than upon his ability, present achievement, or how hard he works. Teachers apparently differ among themselves regarding the relative merits of promotion and nonpromotion, work under differing degrees of pressure regarding the importance of grade standards, and react quite differently to these pressures. The arguments favoring promotion or nonpromotion fit into four major categories: pupil achievement, pupil attitudes toward school and schooling, pupil social-personal adjustment, and the teacher's view of the school's function. The evidence from research comparing nonpromoted pupils with promoted pupils in these first three areas is overwhelming. Promoted slow-learning children achieve at higher levels, are involved less often in aggressive acts toward school and schooling, get along better with their peers, and appear to have more wholesome feelings of personal worth. Upper grade achievement levels are higher in schools that have low nonpromotion rates. A major area of tension among promoted slow-learners appears to be associated with fear of failure. They express worry over their school progress, believe their parents to be similarly concerned, and frequently resort to cheating as a way of assuring higher achievement.

However, neither promotion nor nonpromotion by itself takes care of pupils' nonlearning or the teachers' problems of individualizing instruction. The increasing spread of attainment as pupils advance through the grades is the natural concomitant of the increasing spread in the pupils' abilities. Pupils more and more achieve above or below grade levels with the result that these levels become increasingly burdensome to teachers who see the conflict between grade standards and the realities of pupil development. When teachers recognize this conflict, it may be best simply to pull the grade barriers away.

For Further Reading

Caswell, Hollis L., and Arthur W. Foshay. *Education in the Elementary School,* 2nd ed. New York, American Book Co., 1950. Chapter 13.

Caswell and Foshay do an unusually good job of showing the practical differences of applying a theory of "grade standards" as contrasted to a theory of "equalization of educational opportunity." Using research evidence, they examine the assumptions underlying nonpromotion.

Goodlad, John I. "Some Effects of Promotion and Nonpromotion Upon the Social and Personal Adjustment of Children," *Journal of Experimental Education,* **22** (June 1954), 301-28.

This is one of the few inquiries into personal and social aspects that uses equated groups. An experimental group of nonpromoted first-grade children was compared with a control group of promoted second-grade children.

Herrick, Virgil E. "Elementary Education—Programs," *Encyclopedia of Educational Research* (C. W. Harris, ed.), third edition, New York, The Macmillan Co., 1960. Pages 430-42.

Pages 438-39, on "Promoting and Reporting Practices," review the research on nonpromotion and related studies of the reporting systems used in the schools.

Sandin, Adolph. *Social and Emotional Adjustments of Regularly Promoted and Non-Promoted Pupils.* New York, Bureau of Publications, Teachers College, Columbia University, 1944.

This volume reports Sandin's research into the differences between promoted and nonpromoted pupils at all elementary-school grade levels. Sandin's conclusions pointed to the need for studies of matched groups, such as the study conducted several years later by Goodlad.

Saunders, Carleton M. *Promotion or Failure for the Elementary School*

Pupil? New York, Bureau of Publications, Teachers College, Columbia University, 1941.

This older volume summarizes studies into the effects of nonpromotion on pupil achievement. The most definitive study since the volume's publication probably is that of William H. Coffield, "A Longitudinal Study of the Effects of Nonpromotion on Educational Achievement in the Elementary School," unpublished doctoral dissertation, State University of Iowa, 1954.

Spain, Charles R., Harold D. Drummond, and John I. Goodlad. *Educational Leadership and the Elementary School Principal.* New York, Rinehart and Co., 1956. Chapter 8.

On pages 197 through 202, the authors present the arguments usually used by teachers to defend either promotion or nonpromotion. They then use research findings in analyzing the validity of the two sets of arguments.

3. TODAY'S NONGRADED
SCHOOL EMERGES

When the Quincy Grammar School opened its doors to pupils in 1848, certain enthusiastic citizens predicted that its new organization would set the pattern for fifty years to come. More than one hundred years later, the basic pattern is scarcely changed! The Quincy school was graded.

Our schools, then, were not always graded. Both the "district" schools of the eighteenth century and the dame schools of the seventeenth were without grade classifications. In the former, children attended only when teacher and school moved to their district,[1] picking up after a long time lapse where they had left off in their studies. In the dame school, children as young as three associated with children as old as ten, each child receiving twenty minutes or so of individualized instruction perhaps twice daily. Since all teaching was on a definitely individual basis, children spent the balance of their time listening to others recite, talking and whispering, or getting into mischief.[2] By the beginning of the eighteenth century, the dame school was a town institution, the source of all "formal" education for most girls and for boys not moving on to the town grammar school.

Although these early institutions of learning must have been dreary and boring beyond belief, it is interesting to note that instruction was highly individualized. Usually, groups were small: eight or nine youngsters frequently constituted an entire class and, hence, the school. The teachers were poorly prepared and so the curriculum consisted of whatever reading and ciphering they were

---

[1] For a description of a school's itinerary, see Sarah L. Bailey, *Historical Sketches of Andover* (Boston, Houghton Mifflin Co., 1880), p. 318.

[2] For further description, see William H. Small, *Early New England Schools* (Boston, Ginn and Co., 1914), pp. 178-79.

able to teach. Attendance was at best sporadic and the teacher and child began at the point where learning and instruction were last interrupted. There were no principals, no supervisors, no courses of study as we know them today, no graded series of texts, no grades. All these were yet to come.

The Emergence of Graded Structure

The Quincy Grammar School did not "just happen." Movements toward grading were clearly in evidence during the preceding century. In the eighteenth century, the selectmen of Boston developed separate reading and writing schools. Boys attended one and girls the other, changing at midday. New buildings provided reading schools on the upper floor and writing schools on the lower. A certain ordering of instruction began to appear: arithmetic was to be learned at the age of eleven; ten lines were to be written from copybooks in a single session, and ciphering done every other day.[3] Certain accomplishments were deemed appropriate for specific levels, and the emphasis was on subject matter and skills.[4] In fact, grade "norms" were being introduced.

The ordering and regimentation of which graded structure came to be a part were substantially advanced by the monitorial system. Meyer provides us with a colorful description of the arrangement, launched separately but almost simultaneously in England by Bell and Lancaster:

> The monitorial system was so named because of its monitors. Under it a master would teach a lesson to a number of older and—when he was lucky—brighter boys, each of whom would then seek to lodge his knowledge in a small squad of comrades. Monitors were put to work not only as junior henchmen, but as academic bus boys whose chores were of an inordinate variety. Thus there was a monitor to check attendance, another to rule paper, and yet another to safeguard books and slates. There was a monitor to keep the wardrobe under watch, and a *monitor to examine and promote the pupils* (italics ours).[5]

It is difficult to separate a specific movement from the general character of the times. There is no apparent cause-and-effect rela-

---

[3] Ellwood P. Cubberly, *Readings in the History of Education* (Cambridge, The Riverside Press, 1920), pp. 543-44.

[4] Lowry W. Harding, "Influence of Commissions, Committees, and Organizations upon the Development of Elementary Education," *The American Elementary School*, Harold G. Shane, ed. (New York, Harper and Brothers, 1953), p. 160.

[5] Adolphe E. Meyer, *An Educational History of the American People* (New York, McGraw-Hill Book Co., 1957), p. 126.

tionship between the development of graded-school structure and broader educational, social, political, and economic conditions of the nineteenth century. And yet, there is a compatibility between the graded system and the setting in which it germinated and grew. The low cost of the monitorial system (Lancaster put the annual pupil cost at $1.06 in his school and Bell at an even dollar [6]) spurred the movement toward free public education. Likewise, the monitorial system exposed the wastefulness of individual tutoring and focused attention both upon certain merits and certain problems of large group instruction. The factory system superseded the craftsman, bringing to industry the mass production of the assembly line. Meanwhile, growing confidence in the capacity of the human race for unending progress, the diffusion of religious humanitarianism, the beginning of the labor movement, and growing nationalism created a *milieu* that was receptive to the revolutionary idea of education for all. In such a setting, the ideas of educational spokesmen like Mann, Stowe, and Barnard, while controversial, struck many receptive ears. Each section of the country had its nineteenth-century leaders who attacked the dogma that education is the privilege of the few who can afford tutor, grammar school, or academy and not the business of government. The graded system was to provide an orderly means of classifying the many young people who were to come to school as a result of increased public interest in schooling.

In this changing American culture, the reports of school reformers who had studied German education, particularly during the third and fourth decades, received some favorable attention. Admittedly, state lawmakers merely listened, but at least they heard, even though they did not act until increasing pressure was brought to bear. Mann, who visited Germany in 1843, did not view everything he saw there with favor, but he felt that much of it was good and could be adapted to fit the American scene. The employment of the school for national ends, its operational efficiency, the trained teachers, centralized control, modern methods, and the organization of the German schools, all had their appeal.

During the previous century, teacher training had become rather firmly established among the Germans, although the first state-conducted normal school (actually in Prussia) did not come into being until 1809. The idea that teachers might benefit from training arose in America late in the eighteenth century. Eloquent pleas for normal schools early in the nineteenth century were answered by Samuel Hall and James G. Carter, whose normal schools

---

[6] *Ibid.*, p. 128.

opened in 1823 and 1827, respectively.[7] Then, in 1838, Massachusetts launched the first public normal school of the Republic. Impoverished, derided by academicians (and even by the schoolmasters, who regarded the schools as a slur on their competence), and scarcely more than elementary schools, the normal schools languished for decades. Nonetheless, they were to become a powerful instrument for unifying educational practices, ordering the content of instruction, and hence for spreading graded structure during the last half of the nineteenth century.

Still another development, already mentioned, had its own considerable influence on the movement toward graded structure. This was the appearance of new textbooks. Speller, reader, grammar, and geography texts made their appearance in the eighteenth century. The remarkably modern arithmetic texts of Warren Colburn made their appearance in 1821. Then, in 1836, the first works that were to become *The McGuffey Eclectic Readers*, graded through six levels and glamorized with abundant illustrations, began their fifty-year domination of juvenile (and adult) literary life.[8] The phenomenal sales of these early works inspired others to produce them and the textbooks poured in upon the schoolmaster. Persuasive salesmen and uninformed teachers together compounded a situation of complete confusion that only gradually cleared when uniform textbooks ultimately were selected from recommended lists.

Textbooks series—first in reading and arithmetic and later in science, social studies, health, and so on—came to be rigorously ordered by grades. The work considered appropriate for a given grade level determined the content of the textbook, and then the content of the textbook came to be regarded as appropriate for the grade. In time, more fundamental procedures for determining the curriculum were scarcely considered. Teachers and parents alike came to equate adequacy of pupil performance with ability to use the book designated for the child's grade level. It is understandable that new procedures which threatened or sought to circumvent this concept of the graded textbook also threatened security-giving patterns and were often viewed with suspicion.

The concept of progressively more difficult instructional materials is sound. We will always need them and we will require, too, some symbols for denoting vocabulary difficulty, concept level, and so on. The sequence of difficulty, however, must be internal to the materials. To relate such difficulty to a concept of "average"

---

[7] *Ibid.*, pp. 204-05.

[8] See Alice McGuffey Ruggles, *The Story of the McGuffeys* (New York, American Book Co., 1950).

for a given grade level is to run counter to the pupil realities described in Chapter 1.

Five major developments, each bearing upon graded structure, may now be placed in close juxtaposition: (1) the movement toward public, state-supported education; (2) the practical success and astonishing economy of the monitorial system; (3) the several appeals of German education as interpreted by American spokesmen; (4) the call for trained teachers, answered in part by the founding of state-supported normal schools; and (5) the appearance of graded schoolbooks in all areas of instruction.[9]

In this setting, the graded concept had its own emerging pattern. Comenius urged the notion of graded instruction in the seventeenth century. In America, we see glimmerings of the point of view underlying grading when, in 1818, the citizens of Boston proposed a three-year school for teaching the fundamentals required by the grammar schools. Between the ages of four and seven, children in these primary schools presumably would be taught simple arithmetic and some little reading.[10] Then, to the horizontal structure of the reading and writing schools (see page 45) a vertical organization was added: the reading unit was further subdivided into four classes. The beginning age, organization, and over-all length of school varied from place to place. One early pattern of elementary-school organization, for example, provided primary, secondary, intermediate, and grammar divisions, each of two years' duration. The problem of ordering numbers forced some form of grading on the monitorial schools. Then, in 1843, Horace Mann extolled the virtues of Prussian graded schools. According to Meyer, "Classifying pupils in accordance with their years and their scholastic accomplishment, and arranging them in grades, each with its own master, had become familiar enough in the cities by the forties."[11]

The Quincy Grammar School should be regarded, then, not as the first graded structure but as a milestone in an evolutionary process. This milestone does, indeed, mark the emergence of the full-fledged graded school. The building was four stories high, in contrast to the two-story reading and writing schools (the latter being three stories whenever they also housed primary schools). But the Quincy Grammar School was perhaps more remarkable inside than out:

> The essential features consisted, first, in giving a separate room to each teacher; second, in grouping a sufficient number of these

---

[9] For further reading, see Frederick Eby and Charles Flinn Arrowood, *The Development of Modern Education* (New York, Prentice-Hall, Inc., 1934).

[10] See Joseph M. Wightman, *Annals of the Boston Primary School Committee* (Boston, George C. Rand and Avery, City Printers, 1860), pp. 33-34.

[11] Adolph E. Meyer, *op. cit.*, p. 188.

rooms in the same building to accommodate pupils enough for a good classification; third, in the provision of an assembly hall spacious enough to seat all the pupils accommodated in the building.[12]

Teachers no longer administered to the entire age and achievement range. Pupils were sorted out into "grades" of like achievement and pupils either "passed" or "failed" at the end of the year. The school was *unified*, as well as *graded*, with a principal in charge of the entire building.

By 1860, the graded system had been widely adopted, especially in the cities,[13] and, by 1870, in the words of Shearer, "the pendulum had swung from no system to nothing but system." [14] With increasingly large numbers of children to be classified and accounted for, rapid standardization of textbooks, ordering of subject matter, and teacher education to provide training in the new patterns, the elementary school had crystallized into a structure remarkably like that predominating today.

The faults and weaknesses already pointed out and to be further emphasized here, must be regarded as shortcomings not for their day but in terms of twentieth-century insights and data such as are presented in Chapter 1. The graded elementary school was a part of its time, just as present questioning of it results from our new insights into the continuous progress of the individual. School organization can never be more than a means of expediting the best education visualized at a given period in time.

Early Questioning of Graded Structure

Some educators became vocal in their questioning of graded schools soon after such structure appeared in the cities and before its establishment in rural areas. In 1868, W. T. Harris introduced into St. Louis a plan of frequent promotion and reclassification. He thus maintained graded structure but reduced rigidity by regrouping at six-week intervals those pupils who varied markedly from the rest of the group. By the 1870's, Francis W. Parker was attacking the grade-to-grade organization of textbooks.[15] At the turn of the century, President Charles W. Eliot of Harvard and President Wil-

---

[12] John D. Philbrick, *City School Systems in the United States* (Washington, D.C., U. S. Government Printing Office, 1885), p. 158.

[13] Freeman Butts and Lawrence A. Cremin, *A History of Education in American Culture* (New York, Henry Holt and Co., 1953), p. 275.

[14] William J. Shearer, *The Grading of Schools* (New York, H. P. Smith Publishing Co., 1899), p. 21.

[15] H. S. Good, *A History of Western Education* (New York, The Macmillan Co., 1947), pp. 480-81.

liam R. Harper of the University of Chicago lamented the neglect of personal and social needs. In calling for flexible school organization to support unique abilities, they presaged a later voice: "The stereotyped pattern of the graded school system demands a stereotyped individual as learner." [16]

John Dewey's work at the Laboratory Schools of the University of Chicago challenged established practices of his time. Seeking to clarify a philosophy of bettering society through liberating individuals, he supported rather than minimized the variations among children in a group. His school eliminated arbitrary classification of grades, textbooks, and subject matter, and encouraged both the use and enrichment of children's daily experience in and out of the classroom.[17]

The closing years of the nineteenth century and early years of the twentieth were marked by a number of experimental efforts to break down established patterns of elementary-school organization.[18] Study of these attempts is still standard fare in many college classes on school organization. We choose only a few samples here. The Pueblo Plan (Colorado), instigated by Superintendent Preston W. Search in 1888, encouraged individual progress, each pupil following a differentiated channel of a "multiple track" system. The Batavia Plan (New York), introduced by John P. Kennedy, employed additional teachers to give special assistance to slow learners so that they might not become unduly retarded. In North Denver, Colorado, on the other hand, the brighter pupils were singled out for such help. Burk's work at the San Francisco Normal School extended the earlier Pueblo Plan. Grades were retained but the work was divided into units. Successful test performance signified completion of the unit's specified subject matter. There were no grade failures. Children moved forward on an irregular front, subject by subject, according to the number of units satisfactorily completed.

Of more recent vintage, the Winnetka and Dalton Plans used an individualized task approach. In the former, Carleton Washburne abolished grade promotion and failure as such. Studies were divided into individual and group activities, the former being further

[16] Alice V. Keliher, *A Critical Study of Homogeneous Grouping*, Contributions to Education, No. 452 (New York, Bureau of Publications, Teachers College, Columbia University, 1936), pp. 9-10.

[17] See William Boyd, *The History of Western Education* (London, A. & C. Black, 1921), pp. 418-27.

[18] For description and analysis, see Newton S. Edwards and Herman G. Richey, *The School in the Social Order* (Boston, Houghton Mifflin Co., 1947), pp. 826-28; John S. Brubacher, *A History of the Problems of Education* (New York, McGraw-Hill Book Co., 1947), pp. 398-400; John D. Russell and Charles H. Judd, *The American Educational System* (Boston, Houghton Mifflin Co., 1940), pp. 247-60.

divided into tasks. Pupils spent about half their time in individual work and half in social activities. In the Dalton Plan, Helen Parkhurst replaced formal recitation with the conference. The rooms were laboratories, each child having his own "contract" and seeking help from several teachers rather than from a single home-room teacher. The so-called nonacademic learnings were dealt with on a total class basis, however.

These and various other schemes are not always readily seen as attempts to break down graded structure. But they were indeed designed to modify the ill effects of grades and to help pupils of varying abilities move ahead unhampered by uniform grade expectations. They were a product of the creative thinking of their time and paved the way for a later large-scale attack upon strict grading. Regrettably, the fading of the moving spirit behind these innovations frequently left only the form, not the motivating idea. One structure was, in effect, replaced by another. In our passion for order, we tend now to look back at the structures that ultimately collapsed instead of at their intent. As we view, then, the emergence of nongraded structure, we must be mindful of the wrongs it seeks to right and never become idolatrous of the encompassing shell.

Twentieth-century philosophical and psychological thought, together with the new century's espousal of educational experimentation, provided the environment for questioning established educational practice. Practice in school organization must be viewed against four sweeping movements of widespread influence. First, Dewey's method of systematic inquiry and reflection, little read in the original by either laymen or schoolmen, received widespread popularization through, for example, the teachings of William Heard Kilpatrick at Teachers College, Columbia, and Boyd Bode at the Ohio State University. Educational objectives were viewed in broader perspective: concern for children's health, personality, and social adjustment was added to the long-established intellectual and moral aspects of education. Instruction designed to educate young people to promote a better social order, with social problems as its subject matter and problem-solving as its method, was not readily adaptable to patterned grades and content.

Second, attention given to human development, expressed by schoolmen through intensive study of children, revealed that children differ not only physically, emotionally, and socially, but also intellectually. The wide range among the children who were classified at a given grade level is documented in Chapter 1. Third, research into child development was paralleled by research into the effects of many school practices. One branch of such research focused upon promotion and retention of pupils, concomitants of graded structure. The substantial body of evidence pointing to the negative effects of nonpromotion is summarized in Chapter 2. Fourth, learning theory suggested that improvements could be made on the classic view that subject matter be organized for its own preservation and for uncovering new knowledge. If instruction is the purpose, the newer theory indicated that content should be reorganized for the development of inductive and deductive thinking without reference to its structuring as a man-made subject. Prepackaged bodies of content to be digested curb rather than promote such thinking. A way of examining and arranging the content of learning and instruction to be more useful in teaching pupils of varying abilities found in the elementary school is discussed in Chapter 5.

These four developments, placed in juxtaposition, indicate certain classroom conditions for effective learning. They do not dictate one particular structure, but they do force us to question the efficacy of a structure that encourages consideration of problems along grade lines, imposes uniform standards, gives rise to destructive nonpromotion practices, and compartmentalizes content. These twentieth-century viewpoints necessitate our examining alternative structures that appear to be more compatible with them. Nongraded structure may have its disadvantages but, screened through the educational movements of our time, it comes out amazingly well.

School organization is only one of several major aspects of education, all of which must be kept in balance. To change structure alone may be to create a structure that will now be out of step with everything with which it should be coordinated. In proposing something new, we must recognize both the relation of any proposal to its educational era and the functions new structure must, therefore, serve. If we are successful in maintaining perspective, we will not seek in change a convenient panacea for all educational ills. The bumpy road to educational betterment is littered with the remains of sound educational ideas that perished under the burden of impossible expectations for them.

Nongrading in Modern Dress

The nongraded school is designed to implement a theory of continuous pupil progress: since the differences among children are great and since these differences cannot be substantially modified, school structure must facilitate the continuous educational progress of each pupil. Some pupils, therefore, will require a longer period of time than others for achieving certain learnings and attaining certain developmental levels. This theory of continuous progress differs markedly from two other prevailing theories of pupil progress: the theory of grade standards and the theory of "social" promotion. The authors reject both of these conflicting theories. In Chapter 1, we pointed out that pupil realities and grade standards are irreconcilable. In Chapter 2, we pointed out that "promotion" exists only in relation to grades. Having rejected the desirability of grades, we automatically reject the desirability of any kind of grade-to-grade promotion system.

Arbitrarily separating the matter of grades from that of pupil progress for a moment, we want to reject emphatically the notion of "social promotion" and disclaim any possible association of this idea with what we are proposing in this volume. Social promotion implies a single criterion for pupil progress and denies the breadth of objectives with which elementary education is concerned. Continuous progress implies the advancement of pupils along a broken front in all significant areas of development. *To remove grades without first understanding and accepting this theory of continuous pupil progress is to court local disaster and to discredit the nongraded school movement.*

Since the removal of grade barriers is tied in closely, then, with an encompassing theory that stimulated many different attempts to break lock-step, some of which loosened up grade structure to a degree, it is difficult to pin down a chronology for the emergence of the modern nongraded school. The literature reveals a plan in operation at Western Springs, Illinois, in 1934.[19] It has since been discontinued. It appears that the plan begun in 1942 in Milwaukee is the oldest of those now in effect.[20] Lowell Goodrich, superintendent at the time, had experimented with the plan elsewhere in Wisconsin before endorsing it in Milwaukee. Except for these few early efforts, chronicled attempts at nongrading have been in existence only since World War II. Most of the thirty-one centers with active nongraded units identified by Austin in 1957 started between 1947 and 1950.[21]

The modern nongraded school was born at the primary level. Of sixteen centers identified by Goodlad in 1955,[22] ten were clearly

---

[19] Leonard B. Wheat, "The Flexible Progress Group System," *Elementary School Journal,* 38 (November 1937), pp. 175-83; "Flexible Primary School," *The Nation's Schools,* 22 (October 1938), pp. 26-28.

[20] Florence C. Kelly, "The Primary School in Milwaukee," *Childhood Education,* 24 (January 1948), p. 236.

[21] Kent C. Austin, "The Ungraded Primary Unit in Public Elementary Schools of the United States" (unpublished doctoral thesis, University of Colorado, 1957).

[22] John I. Goodlad, "Ungrading the Elementary Grades," *NEA Journal,* 44 (March 1955), pp. 170-71.

in the primary-unit pattern. Such a plan embraces what are normally the first three grades of the elementary school plus the kindergarten, if the latter exists as part of the public-school system. Thus, a three-year or a four-year continuous-progress ungraded unit is created. In schools in which the plan is continued upward, a three-year intermediate or upper elementary unit is almost invariably superimposed. Rarely (if at all) do intermediate units exist without the undergirding provided by a nongraded primary unit.

The situation regarding nongraded programs throughout the United States is so dynamic that it is virtually impossible to describe the present picture with accuracy. All efforts by research workers, government agencies, and others to compile up-to-date lists and descriptions of existing nongraded schools have thus far fallen short of their goal, sometimes because of failure to discover the less-known (or the newer) programs and sometimes because inaccurate or faulty data are received from questionnaire respondents. Increasingly, however, students of the nongraded school are finding within the literature the historical and descriptive evidence that is badly needed to present a full-scale view of the movement over the country.

One of the difficulties in this matter is that of assessing the position of the rural school, long the citadel of practices rather closely associated with the present tendency to overlook grade barriers. At its best, and under the management of an excellent teacher, the small rural school with its wide age range and limited enrollment has had certain real advantages insofar as grouping and other organizational practices are concerned. A bulletin by Bathurst and Franseth,[23] aimed at helping teachers to organize classrooms containing children from grades one through six or eight by cutting across grade lines, illustrates this claim. Although for excellent reasons the small rural school is disappearing from the American scene, hundreds of rural teachers have in effect operated a "nongraded classroom" over the years without any recognition of the fact, perhaps even on their own part.

Another difficulty is that many existing nongraded schools are operated in very small, semi-rural communities where the principal or teachers or both have imported the idea from places like Milwaukee or have developed it from the literature, and where the operation is too small to warrant much fanfare or publicity. It seems entirely possible that the movement is spreading most rapidly in the "hinterlands," where the Geiger counters of educational investiga-

---

[23] Effie G. Bathurst and Jane Franseth, *Modern Ways in One- and Two-Teacher Schools.* Bulletin 1951, No. 18 (Washington, D.C., U. S. Office of Education), pp. 8-10.

tion are perhaps less likely to probe, and least rapidly in the big cities.

In order to determine the present status of the nongraded movement, the authors followed up every lead that came to their attention. We surveyed approximately 134 communities in 40 states regarding some form of nongraded organization believed to be in operation there as of the 1957-58 school year. In a covering letter, it was explained that the investigation was seeking to compile a listing of school districts operating one or more nongraded elementary schools. The nongraded school was defined as one where the *grade labels* ("first grade," "second grade," "third grade," etc.) *have been entirely removed* from a minimum of two grade levels.

Two questionnaires were enclosed in each letter, one of which constituted an alphabetical listing of all schools presumed to have nongraded programs in existence. Respondents were asked to confirm those plans satisfying the definition of a nongraded program, to cross out those that did not, and to add the names of other communities known or assumed to have nongraded plans. The second questionnaire, applicable only to those places with bona fide nongraded plans, requested details of the plans and opinions regarding them.

Questionnaire studies are inevitably less accurate and useful than studies involving thorough first-hand investigation of existing situations or data. Despite the investigators' efforts to provide a clear and limited definition of the word "nongraded," it appears that some of the respondents claimed to have nongraded plans that do not completely satisfy that definition. Although a high percentage of the questionnaires was returned, a few of the communities reported by Austin and other investigators could not be verified. Nonetheless, it was possible to confirm that a substantial number of communities had committed themselves to nongrading in one way or another.

In the school year 1957-58 some forty-four communities reported the operation of nongraded schools. Leading the list by states were California and Illinois with six each. The next largest number, five, was found in Wisconsin. Georgia and Michigan reported three each, and two nongraded programs were located in each of the states of Massachusetts, Missouri, New York, Ohio, and Washington. States reporting one nongraded program were Colorado, Florida, Kansas, Minnesota, Montana, Nevada, Pennsylvania, Rhode Island, South Carolina, Texas, and Vermont.

In addition to the forty-four mentioned above, another half dozen or so reported programs similar in significant respects. We conclude, therefore, that about fifty communities were operating nongraded schools at that time.

While these are not impressive figures in relation to national school population statistics, it is nevertheless clear that the movement is gaining a foothold. The patterns developing within this movement are described in Chapter 4.

The Nongraded Concept Appraised

As late as 1949 the nongraded school concept was virtually a professional secret. Even today it is unknown to thousands of teachers and little understood by thousands more. Pioneering schools have been so busy preparing for and initiating their nongraded plans that they have not established a framework within which data might be collected and the effectiveness of new schemes evaluated. But so it has been in regard to all new educational movements. A scheme of school organization emerges and stands because of its appropriateness to the general educational thought of its time. The setting was right for graded structure and so schools were graded and remained graded. During the past sixty years, however, educational thought has been shifting, and graded structure appears much less appropriate than it once did.

Graded structure served as an efficient device for classifying the thousands upon thousands of children who poured into the elementary schools during more than one hundred years of rapid educational expansion. It is convenient to use grades still as a ready means of accounting for tremendous numbers of children—so convenient, in fact, that any new system will have difficulty replacing the old, however well the new may reflect current educational thought. But efficiency takes on proper meaning only in relation to the job that *should* be done. To recognize that something is easy does not justify our doing it. Nongrading will grow because of its appropriateness to an accepted educational viewpoint. For this reason, we have gone to considerable pains to point out that the appropriateness of school organization must be judged against the major educational movements of which it is a part.

Nonetheless, we would be disturbed were we to discover that the nongraded school appears to achieve less well those educational ends to which the graded elementary school traditionally has been committed. But there is no evidence to suggest such a deficiency.[24]

---

[24] The research findings are conflicting and inadequate. One or two studies have reported negative findings for the nongraded school, but the techniques used and the data obtained are probably inadequate. See Chapter 9 for further discussion of the research question.

Perhaps one would be closer to the truth if he were to say that there is no evidence to suggest anything. We have little more than inadequate first-hand impressions to go on. Goodlad, in his survey of sixteen centers conducting nongraded plans, was able to collect only information that had to do with school atmosphere, not pupil accomplishment.[25] The centers surveyed reported reduced tensions in children, increased teacher awareness of pupil individuality, and increased parental understanding of the school. Of course, any intensive and successful school-community effort to get a new scheme on the road probably would result in this last benefit. Substantially comparable findings were reported by Austin.[26] Kennedy, in her survey of nongraded schools, gave some special attention to the advantages for bright children. She found greater encouragement for these children to move forward vertically with more stimulating tasks. Teachers had no fear of encroaching on "material reserved for the next grade." [27]

Both Milwaukee and Appleton Schools, Wisconsin, have collected a little comparative test data in regard to their nongraded schools. In Milwaukee, children of the sixth or last semester of the primary unit in four nongraded schools were compared with children of the last semester of the third grade in four graded schools.[28] Ninety-nine nongraded and 123 graded children comprised the samples. Test data in reading and personality adjustment, the only areas reported, slightly favored the nongraded group, even though these children were slightly younger and tested a little lower in mental maturity. These advantages may well have resulted from the fact that three of the nongraded classes were somewhat smaller than the graded classes. However, most studies of class size show no significant advantages of small classes over large classes in regard to academic achievement. During the 1955-56 school year, eleven fifth-grade rooms in Appleton, Wisconsin, were compared with three intermediate nongraded rooms in the Franklin School. The median chronological age and median mental age of all pupils tested were ten years six months and ten years eleven months, respectively. Pupils were compared in reading and spelling and results favored the nongraded rooms. Median grade placement scores for non-

25 John I. Goodlad, "More About the Ungraded Unit Plan," *NEA Journal,* 44 (May 1955), pp. 295-96.

26 Kent C. Austin, *op. cit.*

27 Dora F. Kennedy, "Does the Nongraded School Better Meet the Aims of Elementary Education?" (unpublished master's seminar paper, College of Education, University of Maryland, 1957).

28 "A Study of Primary School Organization and Regular Class Organization at Primary 6 and 3A in Eight Schools" (Milwaukee Public Schools, 1952). Mimeographed.

graded children in reading and spelling were 6.1 and 6.0, respectively, in contrast to 5.85 in both areas for the graded groups.

These data are too limited to permit general conclusions, but it is gratifying to note that the nongraded school appears to hold its own firmly. It is to be hoped that experimental schools will feel that they have an obligation to provide data which will permit better appraisal of their accomplishments in the future.

Another way of appraising nongraded structure is to compare it with graded structure on the basis of what might be called "internal criteria"; that is, according to characteristics initially built into each and thus differentiating one from the other. In some instances, the differences will be seen to be merely differences in basic assumptions.

GRADED STRUCTURE	NONGRADED STRUCTURE
A year of progress in subject matter seen as roughly comparable with a child's year in school.	A year of school life may mean much more or much less than a year of progress in subject matter.
Each successive year of progress seen as comparable to each past year or each year to come.	Progress seen as irregular; a child may progress much more rapidly in one year and quite slowly in another.
A child's progress seen as unified: advancing in rather regular fashion in all areas of development; probably working close to grade level in most subject areas.	A child's progress seen as not unified: he spurts ahead in one area of progress and lags behind in others; may be working at three or four levels in as many subjects.
Specific bodies of content seen as appropriate for successive grade levels and so labeled: subject matter packaged grade-by-grade.	Bodies of content seen as appropriate over a wide span of years: learnings viewed vertically or longitudinally rather than horizontally.
Adequacy of progress determined by comparing child's attainment to coverage deemed appropriate to the grade.	Adequacy of progress determined by comparing child's attainment to his ability and both to long-term view of ultimate accomplishment desired.
Inadequate progress made up by repeating the work of a given grade: grade failure the ultimate penalty for slow progress.	Slow progress provided for by permitting longer time to do given blocks of work: no repetitions but recognition of basic differences in learning rate.

Rapid progress provided for through enrichment: encouragement of horizontal expansion rather than vertical advancement in work; attempt to avoid moving to domain of teacher above.	Rapid progress provided for both vertically and horizontally: bright children encouraged to move ahead regardless of the grade label of the work; no fear of encroaching on work of next teacher.
Rather inflexible grade-to-grade movement of pupils, usually at end of year.	Flexible pupil movement: pupil may shift to another class at almost any time: some trend toward controlling shifts on a quarter or semester basis.

The above list is far from complete but to go farther would be to run beyond the background developed so far in these three chapters. There is enough here, however, to reveal clearly that the values underlying the nongraded plan often differ markedly from and cannot be equated with values inherent in grading.

In Conclusion

It should be clear by now that the nongraded plan is a system of organization and nothing more. Reorganization in and of itself will resolve only organizational problems. Nongraded structure is, therefore, no panacea for problems of curriculum and instruction. The teacher who suddenly finds himself teaching in a nongraded school will not necessarily experience any metamorphosis in his teaching. Until he understands what nongrading permits him to do, he will teach no differently from the way he taught before.

But when he does understand what nongrading permits him to do, a door to more creative teaching in line with pupil realities will have opened to him. Now he need not worry about encroaching on the work of a higher grade. Now he may select a range of books without concern for their grade level. Now he may work without the crippling fear of having to fail all children who do not come up to grade standard at the end of the year. Now he need not worry about the fact that Tommy's reading is so far in advance of his arithmetic. But now he has a new set of responsibilities, too. Now he must collect and analyze the kinds of data that will permit the comparison of a child's progress with the child's ability and thus determine the adequacy of progress. Now he must rigorously determine what children should be grouped for instruction in each area of learning. There is no need to enumerate these problems here. We look at them more intensively in Chapter 5. Suffice it to say that the elimination of grades is only the beginning; it merely opens the door to instructional possibilities that must be accounted for and dealt with in their own right.

For Further Reading

Anderson, Robert H., and John I. Goodlad. "Self-Appraisal in Nongraded Schools: A Survey of Findings and Perceptions," *Elementary School Journal,* **62** (February 1962), 261-69.

The first of two articles summarizing a 1960 survey in which eighty-nine communities reported their experiences with nongrading.

Austin, Kent C. "The Ungraded Primary Unit in Public Elementary Schools of the United States." Unpublished doctoral dissertation, University of Colorado, 1957.

This study surveys the status of nongrading and identifies problems likely to be encountered in moving to nongraded structure.

Goodlad, John I. "Individual Differences and Vertical Organization of the School," *Individualizing Instruction,* Sixty-first Yearbook of the National Society for the Study of Education, Part I. Chicago, University of Chicago Press, 1962. Pages 209-38.

Included in this comprehensive examination of vertical school organization is a review of various continuous progress plans and a description and appraisal of nongraded plans.

Goodlad, John I., and Robert H. Anderson. "Educational Practices in Nongraded Schools: A Survey of Perceptions," *Elementary School Journal,* **63** (October 1962), 33-40.

The second article reporting a 1960 survey study. Prominent among the conclusions drawn by the authors is that greater zeal needs to be exhibited toward resolving fundamental questions of school function, curriculum design, teaching, and evaluation.

Shearer, William J. *The Grading of Schools.* New York, H. P. Smith Publishing Co., 1899.

This old volume provides documentation of the growth of the graded school system in the nineteenth century. It describes the systemization of texts and subject matter and practices related to grading.

Wood, Hugh B. (ed.). "The Ungraded Primary School," *Curriculum Bulletin,* **16** (November-December 1960).

Includes an extensive bibliography which the reader will find useful.

4. THE NONGRADED SCHOOL
IN OPERATION

Introduction

In the previous chapters, the theoretical and practical justifications for a nongraded school organization have been explored within the setting of American public education. In this chapter the operation of the nongraded school is described, with particular reference to some of the administrative considerations involved. Examples are taken from several communities with nongraded programs. The ensuing chapter continues the discussion with emphasis upon curriculum considerations.

Every child's experience in school is the result of many things in combination: the general philosophy and aims of the school system; the rules, regulations, and operational procedures whereby these aims are translated into a program; the background and the calibre of the instructional staff and its leaders; the environment from which the child comes to the school; the child's own nature and interests; and other factors.

It is the function of the school, among other things, to accept and enroll the child, to classify and assign him to a teacher and group, to take stock of his growth, and to regulate his progress month by month and year by year. In discharging these functions, the school either profits or suffers from the kind of administrative machinery that exists to govern each child's advancement.

The graded school reflects certain theories of education, or learning, as well as theories of organization. Each *grade* is essentially an administrative device based upon certain notions about the typical learning capacity and the typical needs and interests of children within a prescribed age group. The concept of typical, or normal, or average performance is basic to the administrative decisions which are made. Conversely, the administrative decisions become basic, over a period of time, to the concept of typical, or normal, or average performance. If the foregoing seems paradoxical, let it be said that the establishment of grade-level-expectancy standards over the past century appears to have been a story of continuous compromise between the need for workable rules and the efforts of the staff to see children in broader focus. This is of course an oversimplification of the relationship between administration and teaching, but for the moment it serves to illustrate a major policy problem of our time.

For the fact is that the administrative structure that evolved over the years, in response to a great educational need, was at first able to adjust to changing definitions of that need but eventually crystallized into a pattern which no longer permitted logical compromise. Such compromise as has been made since 1920 or so has been, in effect, illogical. It is illogical to continue to use the terminology and administrative characteristics of a "graded" school despite the virtual abandonment of the classical concepts of promotion and failure. How confused, indeed, must be the children and the teachers in schools where "continuous promotion" (an anachronistic phrase) is practiced but where, at the same time, all the symbols of the graded system remain in use and their outmoded meaning comes at least now and then to the surface of the operation! "Welcome to our graded school," one imagines the teachers saying, "by which we mean that the children are grouped by approximate age levels. Although we promote the children at the end of the year, what we mean is that we move them along with their age group. Although they are *called* fourth graders we don't exactly mean 'fourth grade' the way other people use the phrase. Unfortunately, of course, some of us *do* mean it that way. All this makes us uncomfortably uncertain as to what we actually believe."

The uncertainty of teachers regarding grade standards and the meaning of promotion is the source of much cynicism both within the profession and without. Among its most ugly manifestations is the carping of college personnel against the public schools, of secondary teachers against elementary teachers, and of upper grade teachers against those in lower grades, usually with respect to the loss of standards and the uncertain meaning of a diploma or a promotion. The failure of administration to prevent these unpleasant conditions through the invention of more flexible arrangements for the classification and progress of children, and through helping the entire school organization to cope more adequately with changed conditions, has intensified the problem. As a result, uncertainty and frustration are frequently felt by teachers and administrators as they attempt to explain to themselves and to others what is best for child X or child Y at various points along the graded trail to a high school or college diploma.

Admission to School

At the very start of this trail there are problems in the graded school. Policies governing admission or entrance to school are inevitably based upon the concept of grades, and geared to the established definitions of "typical," "normal," or "average." The kindergarten, which in most communities is relatively free of academic requirements *per se*, offers an excellent opportunity for the school staff to estimate a child's academic potentialities in a relaxed and informal atmosphere. This in turn gives the school at least some opportunity to delay or to advance, as appropriate, the moment when grade-level-expectancy standards will begin to dominate his school life. When kindergarten services are offered, therefore, the admissions procedure is a more natural and pleasant one for a child than when they are not. Since roughly two out of three American children are denied the privilege of attending a tax-supported public kindergarten, however, most children face the prospect of having a "first grade" label attached to their very first school experience, whether the label is an appropriate one or not.

As will be discussed more fully in Chapter 8, the overwhelming majority of communities operating ungraded classes have kindergarten programs as well. In all cases, the regulations governing admission to the first primary year (or whatever the equivalent of first grade is called) are applied to kindergarten admission, with the obvious exception that the age requirement is one year less. In other words, if a child is required to be six years old by September 1 (or October 1, or some other date) [1] of a particular year in order to be admitted to the first primary year that fall, he may enter kindergarten in September of the previous year. In many states the age requirement is spelled out by law, in such a way that no local option exists. In other states, the law may specify minima and maxima but leave the local community with power to adopt its own requirements within that framework. A few communities have adopted admission policies that establish automatic eligibility for children of a prescribed age, and leave to the local school authorities the power of admitting certain younger children who meet the

---

[1] The trend is toward raising the minimum age requirement to six years by September 1. The authors are wholeheartedly in sympathy with this trend.

qualifying standards (such as academic readiness as measured by tests and observations).

There remain a number of places, chiefly in the largest cities, where children are admitted to kindergarten or the first primary year at the beginning of the February-June semester. In such cases, the requirement is usually the attainment of age five or six by February 1 or a date within several months of February 1. In the majority of communities, and all but a few of those operating nongraded schools, the so-called "annual admission" plan is followed and children enter school only in September.

There are no basic differences in the ways that nongraded and graded schools handle the admission of children entering school for the first time, except in the terminology employed. When it comes to admitting children who have previously attended school and who have transferred to the school in question, however, there are some minor differences in procedure. In the graded school, the usual practice is to accept the previous school's grade-classification information at face value and to assign the child to the same grade in which he would have been placed in the former school if he had not transferred. If the graded school has a particular basis for *class* assignment (within the same grade), such as grouping by ability in reading, the class assignment may depend on the previous school's evaluation or upon placement tests administered at the time of entrance. Sometimes class assignments are understood to be tentative and change may be made after a reasonable trial period.

In the nongraded school the records from the previous school will also be consulted. Their relevance is not as automatically apparent, however, since the various nongraded class groups are unlikely to be following the same progress pattern used by the previous school. It therefore becomes a matter of consulting class progress records and the teachers involved, preferably with the help of the child and his parents, to determine which of the classes is most likely to fit the child's present needs.

All such discussions will of course take into account the various ways that it is possible to bring children together in a single class for instructional purposes.

Grouping Children in the Nongraded School

Existing nongraded programs do not follow any uniform pattern with respect to grouping practices, although it is quite clear that progress in *reading* is one of the major factors in making most decisions about grouping. In a number of "ungraded primary" plans, for example, the children are grouped according to reading-achievement levels, usually for the purpose of reducing the range of abilities with which the teacher must cope in language-arts instruction. Here it is assumed that reading achievement is approximately correlated with achievement in other curriculum areas, and that some degree of homogeneity is obtained by using reading as the yardstick when assigning children to classes. This implies that some groups will include children who are considerably older or younger than the average child in the group; it implies, further, that older children whose pace in reading is slower than "normal" may experience some repetition of subject matter in other curriculum areas when they are transferred eventually to a younger group whose reading level corresponds with theirs. This of course depends upon the extent to which teachers are able to individualize the instructional program in all content areas. Proponents of this modified form of homogeneous grouping (one-dimensional homogeneity) argue that children's overall needs are better served when teachers deal with a limited range of problems in the skill generally regarded as the most important of all the child learns in his early school years, namely reading.

This argument is rejected by others who feel that a wide spread of reading abilities and reading problems within the same class is not necessarily as problematical as the implications of homogeneous grouping. Many schools therefore assign children to class groups on a relatively random or chance basis, within age classifications roughly comparable with those of graded schools. Others group children on the basis of more carefully delimited age classifications, for example dividing 50 first-year-primary children into two class groups with those over six years six months in one class and those under six years six months in the other. Still another approach is to constitute class groups on a rough social-unity basis, attempting to combine those children in one class whose interests, personalities, and backgrounds are well balanced with respect to each other. This latter approach is difficult to describe and difficult to employ, because many subjective judgments go into any conclusion that children X, Y, and Z are compatible with each other. Nonetheless, administrators and teachers frequently feel justified in approaching the grouping of an entire class along these lines, just as they feel confident that it is justifiable to separate children who appear to be enemies, or who are twins, or who have extraordinary tendencies toward mischief when together, both for the good of the individuals concerned and for the good of the classes of which they are members.

A description of one graded school's efforts to achieve desirable groupings of children is presented by Rosella Roff, referring to practices in the McMicken Heights School in the Seattle area.[2] Here each group is planned so that there is a full range of reading abilities and of reading levels; an average range of personality problems; balance of boys and girls; and recognition of the effects of friendships and other peer relations. There is also an effort to alternate children between men and women teachers above the primary level. In this school there is a "divided reading program," which calls for half the class to report at nine o'clock and engage in one hour of skill teaching in reading until ten o'clock when the other half of the class arrives. In the afternoon, the first group leaves an hour earlier than the others, and the remaining hour is used for reading skills by the second group. It is argued that this system allows for the provision of individual attention in a relaxed atmosphere.[3]

To return to the nongraded school, progress in reading is given more emphasis as a basis for administrative decisions than seems to be desirable. As a general rule, class grouping based primarily upon reading achievement suffers from two limitations: (a) it reflects a continuing tendency toward "grade-mindedness" in teachers and administrators, at the less dangerous level of reading-progress alone; (b) it tempts parents to think in terms of "fast-average-slow," and to harbor resentments against having their children in the slower groups. On the other hand, it is perhaps less difficult for teachers to work with such groups, since there may be fewer sub-groups to deal with in the reading program. Another advantage, presumed or real, is that children at either end of the achievement continuum may eventually become clustered together in appreciable numbers. Therefore the group of children whose chances of eventually gaining a year's time are good may find themselves comprising a social entity within the same homeroom and thus derive psychological and intellectual support from each other. Similarly, the children who may require an additional year before entering the first graded year (the 4th grade, or the 7th grade), will share many experiences in common. The acceleration or time-extension of the elementary training of either group of children is believed to be more difficult when the individuals are grouped separately in a number of homerooms.

Frequently the teacher-cycling plan is associated with the nongraded school, apparently creating a fairly general impression that the two practices belong inseparably together. This is not the case,

---

[2] Rosella Roff, "Grouping and Individualizing in the Elementary Classroom," *Educational Leadership,* 15 (December 1957), pp. 171-5.

[3] *Ibid.*

although it is undoubtedly true that teacher cycling has occurred more commonly in nongraded than in graded schools.

Briefly, teacher cycling means keeping the teacher with the same group of children over a period of more than one year. In some communities, teacher X will remain with a group through grades one and two; teacher Y, through grades three and four; teacher Z, through grades five and six. Such practices are of course more common in small schools and in growing communities than in large and stable communities where administrative manipulation of staff assignments is less flexible. At least one obstacle to the introduction of cycling is the tendency of teachers, probably because of grade-mindedness and the crystallization of habits, to settle down more or less permanently into a specific grade level. This in turn is one of the major reasons that administrators attempt to introduce cycling, since cycling is seen as a way of opening new horizons for teachers and breaking them loose from their "ruts." As a result, the cycling question has stimulated much argument within the profession, with the more conservative teachers tending to oppose it.

Parents, too, tend to question the cycling plan, but for a discouraging reason. While parents agree that there are benefits in having their children with a strong teacher for more than a single year, they abhor the thought of exposing their children to two or more successive years of contact with a weak teacher. As most parents read the present situation, any general policy of cycling would pose too great a risk for their children in this respect.

Recently, too, antagonists of teacher cycling have appeared in other camps. A number of experiments are currently underway, in which classroom groups and their teachers are being combined into a larger total group than is usual, and in which the "team" approach to staff organization is being attempted. Underlying such experiments, at least in part, is an assumption that children can adjust to (and profit from) learning situations involving several teachers with whom they work. These experiments challenge certain widely held theories about the bases of pupil security and the ways children adjust to different adult personalities. These latter theories, which have received almost no support from research over the years, are now open to serious question as a more optimistic view of children's adaptability and "emotional toughness" emerges.

Proponents of teacher cycling tend to argue that children benefit when they and their parents deal with the same professional person over a longer period of time. They point out that in many cases the teacher is just beginning to understand the child and to develop effective ways of helping him with his problems, when the year comes to an end and a new, strange teacher takes over. Usually, parents and teachers in their contacts with each other (*e.g.*, in progress-reporting conferences) barely get acquainted in one year's time; it is believed that better communication is possible when the relationship extends into a second or third year. The phrase "loss of investment" is frequently used to describe the central problem involved.

Whether the opportunity to build upon the investment of a previous year's work, as afforded by cycling, is more important than the advantages of entrusting children to different personalities continues to be debated both within the profession and without. One viewpoint on this problem was recently offered by an anthropologist. Speaking on the transmission of culture in American schools, George D. Spindler offered the opinion that the potential negative effects of imposing a teacher's value system and cultural biases upon children can be such that teacher cycling might be harmful to them.[4] Clearly this is a problem that calls for further experimentation. The answer may lie in organizational devices such as team-teaching, which permits long-term relationships of children with teachers while also allowing a variety of adults to be involved.

In the old-fashioned country school, to which reference has been made elsewhere in this volume, it was customary for a teacher to remain with each group of children for a number of years. Inevitably children at various age levels and achievement levels worked alongside each other in the one-room schoolhouse. At its best, such a school may well have had some of the characteristics now desired for the nongraded program. Of interest is the fact that some recent proposals for school reorganization have the effect of recapturing some of the potential advantages of the multi-graded one-room school. No discussion of the nongraded school, or of arrangements that are conducive to nongradedness, would be complete without some mention of the multi-graded or multi-age pattern which has been instituted in a number of communities.

Multi-age grouping, or interage grouping as some have called it, has been of interest to educators for many years, yet relatively little basic research on it has been completed. Before the advent of graded organization multi-age groupings were common, and they still are in sparsely populated rural areas. Pupils were grouped this way, however, out of sheer necessity rather than for some logical or theoretical reason. Only as graded practice has come into disrepute, with educators seeking alternative patterns of class organization, has an interest emerged in the multi-age group as a possible educational arrangement. In spite of this recent upsurge of interest, only a few studies have been reported.

---

[4] George D. Spindler, *The Transmission of American Culture,* the 1957 Burton Lecture (distributed for the Graduate School of Education by Harvard University Press, Cambridge, Massachusetts, 1959), p. 51.

Several doctoral dissertations have been completed in this field, beginning with Foshay in 1948.[5] Probably the most widely discussed study is that conducted in Torrance, California, by Rehwoldt and Hamilton.[6] Foshay's study uncovered some social advantages for the experimental multi-graded group, but most of the other findings were essentially in favor of the control graded group. The researchers concluded that the social advantages they observed could be duplicated in any graded group by using interage grouping for certain purposes.[7] The Torrance study, on the other hand, pointed out a number of significant gains in both the social and the academic areas by students in multi-grade classes. Noting the contradictions in these previous studies, Chace approached the same questions in an investigation reported in 1961.[8] Chace's data, "relative to academic and social development, tend slightly to support the findings of Rehwoldt that students in multiple-grade groups do better."[9] However, the data also support Foshay's conclusions that more flexible grouping might enable the single-grade classroom to realize some of the advantages found for the multi-grade organization.[10]

Perhaps to be especially noted in the preliminary data from multi-age classes are the references to social benefits. Sometimes lost in the discussion of graded organization is the fact that an artificial and unnatural homogeneity of chronological age and academic experience is engendered by the arrangement of one-grade-per-class. In many ways this homogeneity encourages an unhealthy attitude within each age group toward other age groups, especially those who are younger and hence have less status. It also causes each group to lose some of its perspective on human experience by narrowing the social atmosphere within which the children live. One is tempted to wonder whether the resulting ingrownness of each graded class does not accumulate in various antisocial ways, especially when the pupils reach the more volatile teen-age stage.

---

[5] Arthur W. Foshay, "Interage Grouping in the Elementary School," unpublished doctoral dissertation (Teachers College, Columbia University, New York, 1948).

[6] Walter Rehwoldt and Warren W. Hamilton, "An Analysis of Some of the Effects of Interage and Intergrade Grouping in an Elementary School," mimeographed final chapters of doctoral dissertation (University of Southern California, 1956). Available from the authors. See also the same authors, "By Their Differences They Learn," *The National Elementary Principal*, 37 (December 1957), pp. 27-29.

[7] Foshay, *op. cit.*, p. 237.

[8] E. Stanley Chace. "An Analysis of Some Effects of Multiple-Grade Grouping in an Elementary School," unpublished doctoral dissertation (University of Tennessee, August 1961).

[9] *Op. cit.*, p. 166.

[10] *Ibid.*

Lane and Beauchamp have recommended that class groups be established with a wide range of ages, cutting across several grade lines, so that classes will more nearly resemble the groups in which people usually find themselves and in which many levels of maturity are usually represented.[11] The Torrance Plan makes essentially the same suggestion. Many of the team-teaching plans now being developed also involve the deliberate use of multi-age arrangements. In fact it now seems to a number of theorists, including the authors, that the most desirable pattern of class organization is one in which both the nongraded concept and the multi-age grouping concept are central.[12]

In summary of this brief discussion on grouping, there are various ways of grouping children in a nongraded school, just as there are in a graded school. There is no necessary connection between the grouping used and the nongraded idea. While so-called homogeneous groupings based upon reading achievement are found quite frequently in nongraded schools, there are many where groupings are based simply upon age, random selection, social relationships, or similar factors. It is natural for teachers in a nongraded school to want to continue with their class for more than one year, but there is no direct relationship between this arrangement and the nongraded plan. Some schools are deliberately establishing class groups that cut across a number of grade lines, while others are experimenting with teams of teachers working with classroom groups that have been combined, at least in part, into a larger unit. Therefore there is no established pattern in the grouping of children in nongraded schools, and in fact there probably should not be. Once grade-mindedness has been shattered and teachers begin to deal with children within a more flexible frame of reference, many possible solutions to age-old problems are likely to come to mind.

Illustrative Programs

As the literature attests, there are a great many communities throughout the United States in which some form of nongraded organization has been attempted over a number of years. Probably the best known, and certainly one of the oldest because its incep-

---

[11] Howard Lane and Mary Beauchamp, *Human Relations in Teaching* (Englewood Cliffs, New Jersey, Prentice-Hall, Inc., 1955), pp. 298-303; see also pp. 297-319.

[12] See further discussion in Chapter 9 and also pp. 260-62 of *Individualizing Instruction,* Sixty-first Yearbook of the National Society for the Study of Education, Part I (Chicago, University of Chicago Press, 1962).

tion dates to 1942, is the Primary School Plan in Milwaukee, Wisconsin.[13] Another well-known primary program is the one in Park Forest, Illinois.[14] A community which has attempted to extend the nongraded idea into the upper elementary and junior-high school years is Appleton, Wisconsin.[15] These and other pioneer programs, which are in general organized as reading-levels programs, have attracted much national interest. Probably many of the newer programs have followed their general pattern.

The authors believed, therefore, that it would be of interest to use as an example in this volume a plan which differs from the reading-levels-oriented plans which are already so well known.

Englewood Elementary School, Sarasota County, Florida [16]

Englewood is a small, semitropical community which lies directly on the coastline of southwestern Florida. Between September 1957 and June 1961 the school grew from approximately 240 pupils and 9 professional staff members to more than 400 pupils and 15 professional staff members. During this time a nongraded organizational structure was adopted, cooperative-teaching practices were developed, and major curriculum revisions were undertaken. Below we describe the school's transition from a traditional graded structure to a nongraded structure, the effect of the new structure on individual pupils, and the advantages which the teachers discovered as they undertook the change to the new structure.

It had become apparent to the staff of 8 teachers and a principal that the grade-level distribution of the 240 pupils in the school would require the organization of at least one combination class. The easiest apparent solution was to divide the fourth grade into two sections, to create a second-third grade combination class, and to have one class each for grades one, two, three, five, and six. As Christmas approached, the fifth and sixth grades had each grown

---

[13] See Florence C. Kelly, "Ungraded Primary School," *Educational Leadership, 18* (November 1960), pp. 79-81. See also the handbook for parents, "The Primary School" (Milwaukee Public Schools, 1960).

[14] See Kent C. Austin, "The Ungraded Primary School," *Childhood Education, 33* (February 1957), pp. 260-63. See also mimeographed brochure, *The Primary School in Park Forest* (issued annually by School District 163, Park Forest, Illinois).

[15] See Arthur D. Morse, *Schools of Tomorrow—Today* (Albany, New York State Education Department; also Doubleday and Company, Inc., Garden City, New York, 1960), Chapter 2.

[16] The Englewood illustration was written by John M. Bahner, now of Harvard University but formerly principal of the Englewood Elementary School.

to over forty-five pupils. With the Florida tourist season soon to begin, the staff expected an influx of additional children. It became obvious that another combination class would have to be created for the fifth- and sixth-grade levels. This was done in January.

Then, toward the end of that year, the staff evaluated its grade structure. With the help of its curriculum consultant, the faculty began to examine its knowledge of the developmental growth of children in a formal learning situation and to formulate possible ways of grouping pupils based on this knowledge rather than on tradition. Throughout their experience, these staff members had observed that individual pupils and groups of pupils had a range of abilities that extended over at least several years. It became clear that a single grade designation could never adequately describe the achievement level of either the class or each separate pupil. A third-grade teacher, for instance, could never say that her entire class was performing at a typical third-grade level in all areas; nor could she say that more than one or two pupils were performing at a third-grade level in every area. A child in her third grade might be "at grade level" in his understandings of his environment, but be capable of reading on a fourth-grade level and of handling arithmetic computations on only a second-grade level.

The teachers had already adjusted their methods of teaching somewhat to allow for these individual differences as well as they could, but they began to wonder if some adjustments were not needed in the organization of classes. To them it seemed obvious that some children needed more than six years to achieve the goals of an elementary-school program, and, conversely, some children could pursue the elementary school program with sufficient quality and maturity to enter the junior high school after spending only five years (above kindergarten) in the elementary school. The staff was aware of the research on pupils who repeated grades, or who "skipped" grades, and was eager to find an arrangement which would have none of the disadvantages associated with nonpromotion and double-promotion.

The faculty therefore sought a new type of class organization which would ensure that all pupils, fast and slow, could move smoothly through the school at their own rate without skipping or repeating. Both an ungraded structure and an increased use of combination grades were discussed. The two teachers who had combination grades during the year expressed satisfaction with them and reported few difficulties. Since none of the staff had the benefit of any experience in an ungraded system and since it was doubtful that such a plan could have been "sold" to the community overnight, it was decided to organize the classes for the 1958-59 school year as follows:

Kindergarten—two sections. Classes: grades 1, 1, 1-$\underline{2}$, $\overline{2}$-3, $\underline{3}$-4, $\overline{3}$-$\underline{4}$, $\overline{4}$-5, $\underline{5}$, $\overline{5}$-$\underline{6}$, and $\overline{6}$ (ten classes, total).

A line over a number indicates the section where the three or four most advanced pupils of a grade were placed; a line below a number indicates where the three or four most retarded were placed. This grouping kept a teacher from having to work with both the extremely accelerated and the extremely retarded in the same classroom, yet a heterogeneity of pupils was still retained—a condition which the staff felt was important. At the same time, separating the extremely advanced from the extremely retarded reduced the range in each classroom to a point where the teachers with combination classes could see no difference between this range and what they had had the preceding year with only a single grade level. Following this decision to create a new grade organization, everyone on the staff had a share in placing pupils in the home-rooms designated by that organizational structure. Many factors were considered as pupils were placed on class lists: (1) ability, (2) achievement, (3) desirable and undesirable friends, (4) emotional stability, (5) number of years in school, (6) parents' attitudes, (7) physical maturity, (8) pupils' attitudes, (9) social development, and (10) teacher-pupil rapport (due to personality, methods of teaching, or sex).

This variety of factors to be considered gave much concern to the teachers as they found themselves having difficulty weighing the relative values of one factor over another. At the heart of this problem was the faculty's desire to have pupils work with class-mates having a wide variety of talents and backgrounds (heterogeneous grouping), yet to have the faster pupils challenged by association with their academic peers and the slower pupils placed in combination classes with the expectation that they would perhaps take an additional year in the elementary school program (homogeneous grouping). This problem was partially resolved by limiting placements made primarily on the achievement criterion to only the extreme 5 per cent at each end of the achievement range.[17]

In the fall of 1958 the teachers sensed a concern among the parents and pupils about whether or not a child had "failed"—for example, when a fifth-grade child was placed in a 4-5 combination while some of his former classmates were placed in a 5-6 combination. The faculty decided that more study needed to be given to the manner in which parents and children were notified of the next

---

[17] Cooperative and team teaching practices were also employed by the staff as means of alleviating their contradictory desires and of making instruction easier, but an elaboration of these practices is beyond the scope of this illustration.

year's placement on the June report card; they realized that parents and pupils did not fully understand what the school was attempting to do by means of the new class organization. The staff decided that the best methods of telling them were to have special meetings of the parents of each room and to spend some time discussing the problem at the parent-teacher conferences held during the months of November and April.

Another problem brought about by the new grade organization was that of reporting to the next teacher each child's curriculum experiences. In a traditional organization, if everyone in the third grade is given the same third-grade material, then the fourth-grade teacher knows what her pupils were exposed to during the preceding year. Since this was not the case in the Englewood School, teachers realized they needed to discover just where each child was in the development of particular skills and what subjects the child had been exposed to in such areas as social studies and science. Thus, during the 1958-59 school year, the staff recognized the need to keep more appropriate records for each child and to pass detailed information on to the next teacher in order that the latter would not need to spend a large amount of time in collecting or diagnosing perhaps erroneous information from the pupil himself about what books he had read or what topics he had studied.

Most important of all, however, were the discoveries the staff made of the advantages the new organization had for the children. As the staff seized every opportunity through parent-teacher meetings, study groups, and individual conferences to explain the reasons behind the new organization, parents began thinking of the children in each age level as having a wide range of abilities. They began to realize that the reading ability of their child was apt *not* to be at the same level as his arithmetic ability. The new organizational structure helped parents to realize that all pupils in a classroom do not work on the same level in any one area, much less all areas. The realization that it was quite normal for a child to deviate from the average in an area was a great comfort for parents, since their own child did just that. Moreover, it was reassuring for them to know that other parents now realized this same phenomenon and therefore would be more apt not to brag about or degrade such deviations. For the most part, they came to accept as perfectly natural that some children needed longer than six years to move through the elementary-school program.

For example, Johnny, a boy of low scholastic aptitude, was in the class that was designated as a third grade in 1957-58. All the available evidence indicated that Johnny would need seven years beyond kindergarten in Englewood School. During 1958-59 Johnny was placed in the 3-4 class. It was anticipated that the next year he would be placed in a 4-5 class, the following year probably in another 4-5 class, and the year following in a 5-6 class. Thus he would take four years to cover what is typically known as the fourth, fifth, and sixth grades. Of course, if the staff was wrong about Johnny's ability, or if his growth pattern changed to a point where it no longer seemed desirable to have him spend seven years in the elementary program, he could always be placed in the junior high school after another three years and nothing would have been lost. In either event the staff felt confident that no social stigma would be attached to Johnny's slower progress since his deceleration would be gradual, he would not repeat a grade, and he had already made many friends among his younger classmates.

Through a similar use of the combination grades an extremely mature, gifted child could go through a typical three- or four-year span more rapidly.

In the multi-grade classes the size of the group is no longer a matter of chance because of the varying numbers of children at each grade level. With combination grades a principal can if he wishes make every class almost equal in size. Better yet, a teacher (or teachers) can be given a class of a size appropriate to the teacher's ability, the size of the room, or similar criteria, and the remainder of the students can be distributed suitably among the other teachers on the staff.

Another very important advantage of multi-age grouping is the flexibility the principal and the teachers have in placing the pupils during or at the end of each year. In a twelve-classroom school with a traditional grade organization, there is usually a choice between two classes in which to place a pupil at each grade level. With a multi-age organizational structure, the school could choose among at least three classes, and in some cases four classes. With an increased number of classes in which to place a pupil, the staff can take into consideration all eleven factors listed previously and still avoid undesirable placements.

The Englewood staff also discovered that multi-age grouping provided each class with pupils who set an example which increased the social maturity of the younger ones. The fastest pupils of the younger group also were stimulated intellectually by the older pupils. Moreover, both of these good effects took place without any downgrading of the older pupils either socially or intellectually.

In the spring of 1959 the Englewood faculty spent several meetings evaluating their current organizational structure. They rejected a return to traditional grade organization and decided that children would profit most by increasing the use of combination grades for the next year. The organizational structure for the 1959-60 school year was designated as follows:

Kindergarten—two sections. Classes: grades 1, 1, 1-2, 2-3, 2-3, 3-4, 4-5, 4-5, 5-6, 5-6, 6 (eleven classes in all).

The method of reporting pupil placements to parents in June 1959 was decided at the final faculty meeting of the year. While there was agreement that the school would have a completely non-graded structure within a few years, there was disagreement as to what report-card terminology would be best to move parents further along in their understanding and acceptance of a nongraded school. The use of the terms "primary," "intermediate," and "upper" were considered as were designations of triple combinations (that is, 1-2-3, 2-3-4, 3-4-5, etc.). Since no single procedure seemed satisfactory, numerical designations similar to that of previous years were used. In addition, the principal wrote the following note which was stapled to the report cards.

> Most of the parents of Englewood School pupils realize that their own child does not perform at the same level in all subjects. They also realize that within any one classroom there will be students who are achieving in reading, for instance, on several different grade levels. Therefore, calling a group of about 30 children "third graders" does not mean that every child in the room is achieving on a third grade level in all areas.
>
> When these facts are considered, it can be easily understood that there is no such thing as promotion at the end of the year in Englewood School. Our pupils are progressing at various speeds and in several different groups throughout the year. In June we merely re-arrange the pupils into groups which the teacher feels will provide the best stimulation for each individual child and which will allow the child to continue his development at his own speed. As far as "promotion" is concerned, the vacation period between June and September is no different from Christmas vacation —although the period is longer and the children are most likely to have a new teacher upon their return.
>
> The back of the report card shows a placement for next year. Remember that a designation such as "3-4" is not a true picture of the achievement range in that class. There will be some pupils doing first and second grade work on one hand, and at the other extreme in this class will be some who are capable of fifth grade work. This class is *not* composed of the fastest third-year pupils and the slowest fourth-year pupils, but rather is made up of fast, average, and slow students of both age groups who the staff feels will work well together.

During the 1959-60 school year the Englewood faculty found it desirable to elaborate a curriculum structure which reflected among other things their nongraded thinking. Their curriculum work included the development of a complete list of reading skills which they expected each pupil to develop during his stay in the

Englewood School. The list, with the teachers' evaluations of each skill, was placed in each pupil's cumulative folder and in effect constituted the reading curriculum for the entire school as well as a progress record. The list was divided into reading categories (for example, word-attack skills and comprehension skills), but it did not designate grade levels, or even reading levels since the latter designation has the same faults that grade-level designations have.[18] A similar list was devised for the computational skills in arithmetic.

In the areas of social studies and science the staff felt that basic concepts or "big ideas" were the fundamental objectives of the educational program. By rejecting the traditional curriculum outline of having the subject content prescribed for each grade level and by substituting for this those basic understandings in each subject area which serve as the foundation for the entire six-year program, the teachers once again denied grade level as an appropriate category for curriculum determination. The task of the teachers became that of diagnosing the educational needs of individual pupils in every subject area, of planning appropriate classroom experiences for each pupil, and of motivating each pupil to move along the many educational paths at his optimum speed. These educational paths were now defined as six-year paths—six years for the typical students, that is, in each of the subject areas.

In the spring of 1960 the Englewood School faculty decided upon an organization which was completely nongraded. With the exception of kindergarteners (who did not become part of a multiage group until the 1962-63 school year), all pupils were placed in combination classes, including two triple combinations. The organization for the 1960-61 school year was established as follows (for the sake of clarity, only numerical designations are used which correspond to the typical grade-level indications of elementary schools):

> Kindergarten—two sections. Classes: "grades" 1-2, 1-2, 1-2, 1-2-3, 2-3, 3-4, 3-4, 3-4-5, 4-5, 5-6, 5-6 (eleven in all).

Except for the office records which were needed for county and state reports, grade levels were not used. Classes were referred to only by the teacher's name or by the room number.

With two exceptions, the majority of the children within each of the classrooms fell into a two-year chronological age span. But because of triple combinations and individual pupils in the process of being decelerated, all classes had at least a three-year age span and several groups had an age span of four years. Care was taken

---

[18] Reading levels are principally reading vocabulary levels, and pupils who may have the same vocabulary level do not have identical facility with specific skills. Thus, children on the same reading level should not always have identical classroom experiences in reading.

in placing pupils so that no teachers taught classes with wider achievement spans than they would have taught in a school with a traditional graded organization. In June 1960 the report cards again had a note appended to them similar to the one quoted above. However, no numerical grade-level designations were used. In short, the organizational structure had no reference to grades or levels, the curriculum had no reference to grades or levels, and the conversation around the school had no reference to grades or levels (except when the term *grade level* was used as a national achievement norm). The transition to a nongraded school was complete.

For Further Reading

Imhoff, Myrtle M. "The Primary Unit." Selected References, No. 1, Washington 25, D.C., U. S. Department of Health, Education, and Welfare, Office of Education, revised, May 1957, 9 pages.

This brief pamphlet discusses the growth of ungraded plans and provides references to both earlier and more recent written materials describing programs over the United States.

Otto, Henry J. *Elementary-School Organization and Administration.* 3rd ed. New York, Appleton-Century-Crofts, 1954.

In Chapter 5, pages 165-220, Otto presents a thorough and useful discussion of "Grouping Children for Wholesome Development."

Slater, Eva May. *The Primary Unit.* Curriculum Bulletin No. 3. Storrs, Connecticut, Curriculum Center, School of Education, University of Connecticut, 1955, iv + 33.

Included in this useful publication are a review of the history and development of the primary school unit and descriptions of six programs in Wisconsin, Nevada, and California.

Wrightstone, J. Wayne. *Class Organization for Instruction.* What Research Says to the Teacher, No. 13. Washington 6, D.C., National Education Association, May 1957.

This excellent and inexpensive pamphlet reviews the research on class organization and suggests a number of ways in which modern patterns of grouping and of organizing the school program contribute to the welfare of children.

5. MODERN THEORIES OF CURRICULUM AND THE NONGRADED SCHOOL OF TODAY AND TOMORROW

Introduction

The curriculum is the heart of a school's program. It is our contention throughout this volume that school structure must serve instructional ends in expediting the continuous progress of students of widely varying abilities and attainments. The curriculum is more, however, than the learners encompassed by it. It is the scheme whereby an institution fulfills its educational responsibilities to these learners. This scheme includes purpose, content, and mode. In a good curriculum, the relationship among purpose, content, and mode is carefully planned, since all three are interdependent. Decisions about purpose directly affect the selection of content, which in turn bears on method. Increasingly, theories are being developed to guide this planning. In this chapter, certain aspects of these theories are first examined. Then, the implications for elementary-school structure are discussed. The chapter concludes with a discussion of the relationship of these curricular and organizational considerations to classroom practices, particularly the grouping of pupils and the utilization of teachers for various learning activities.

Some Curriculum Considerations

Toward a longitudinal view of the curriculum

The well-planned curriculum gives attention to continuity and sequence: How can present learning be related to previous learning so that a foundation for still further learning may be laid? The simple skills (not necessarily simple for the learner) a child begins to develop in kindergarten should be the ones he will continue to develop in the first grade. These skills should be the components of more complex skills to be developed at a later time. The young child learns to move his eyes from left to right across the page and from right to left down to the next line of print. Later, he uses this development in encompassing clusters of words at a glance. Then, he uses and refines this skill further by reading books on various subjects. Instead of a skill, the learning sought may be a concept having to do with the increasing interdependence of people or a value related to behavior toward others. Be they skills, concepts, or values, the threads constituting the curricular fabric must be identified and specific educational experiences organized around them.

The spread from top to bottom on scales of pupil achievement provides a vertical picture of student progress through the elementary school. Grade-to-grade classifications, likewise, are vertical considerations. Placing these views of pupil progress and school organization side by side with vertical curriculum considerations should give us a longitudinal look at the school program. This longitudinal view is essential to a continuous, unbroken learning process in which what is learned at one point builds on what has gone before and prepares for what is to come. But such a view is difficult to achieve when children are thought of as fifth-graders, when the school is divided into grades, and when what is to be taught is packaged for consumption according to these grade-level demarcations.

The substance of the desired longitudinal view is a set of threads or *organizing elements* running vertically through the curriculum and around which learning activities should be organized. There are two sources for determining organizing elements: the learner *behavior* sought and the areas of *content* to be used in developing such behavior. Both behavior and content normally are identifiable in a good set of educational objectives.

The significance of the *behavioral* type of organizing element becomes clearer when we examine a field like reading which has no content of its own. Here, sequence is planned both by identifying the psychomotor skills that constitute the reading act and by analyzing the complexity of these skills as they should mature in the learner. For years, publishing houses have been determining the sequence of volumes in their reading series on the basis of such analyses. As soon as we seek to classify these skills into the stop-and-go lock step of grades, we block the longitudinal view which their identification is designed to facilitate.

A rather long-term interest among educators in identifying

content threads is receiving increased emphasis.[1] Several decades ago, Parker [2] listed eighteen groups in which most, if not all, of the ideas that geography affords are included. These eighteen groups were further organized into three major categories: descriptive ideas, interpretive ideas, and ideas concerned with map and graph symbolism and with the significance of landscape features and technical terms. While these areas of ideas are not specific organizing elements, they at least provide a framework for selecting the concepts, skills, and values to be developed longitudinally through the school's program.

The Dalton Schools developed a comprehensive list of content organizing elements for the social studies.[3] Included are concepts regarding individual "human nature" (e.g., "human beings are almost infinitely teachable"); regarding man and his physical environment ("climate, land features, and natural resources have profound effects on man"); regarding man and his social environment ("specialization and division of labor make for interdependence"). There are attitudes toward self ("growing from self-love to self-respect"); toward social groups ("willingness to work for an abundance of the good things of life for all peoples in the world"); toward others ("equality of opportunity for all"); and there are intellectual and aesthetic values ("freedom of thought, expression, and worship"). Included also are ten skills, abilities, and habits such as skill in analyzing problems, in organizing and interpreting data, and in presenting the results of study. Several of these are further divided into subcategories.

It is important, then, that a school faculty develop a common view of the behavioral and content threads that are to guide the sequential learning of students moving through the school. The point that children move forward at widely varying rates already has been well established. The question before us now is the determination of the kind of longitudinal curriculum framework that will expedite such individualized progress. This is the kind of problem the Englewood (Florida) Elementary School faculty encountered in seeking to improve the science curriculum. After identifying

---

[1] Ralph W. Tyler, "The Curriculum—Then and Now," *Elementary School Journal*, 57 (April 1957), pp. 364-74.

[2] Edith Putnam Parker, "Investigating the Value of Geographic Offerings," *The Teaching of Geography*, National Society for the Study of Education, Thirty-second Yearbook (Bloomington, Illinois, Public School Publishing Co., 1933), pp. 78-80.

[3] Ralph W. Tyler, "Curriculum Organization," *The Integration of Educational Experiences*, National Society for the Study of Education, Fifty-seventh Yearbook, Part III (Chicago, University of Chicago Press, 1958), pp. 115-19.

Modern Theories of Curriculum   81

objectives for their science program, these teachers proceeded to spell out the "big ideas" (content organizing elements) in this field which should be developed throughout the school's six-year span. They identified such ideas as the following:

1. Space is infinite.
2. Adaptation is a characteristic of all living things.
3. There is constant interaction of the forces in the universe.[4]

But when the Englewood faculty came to examine what studying these ideas meant for the pupils, they found that some identification of what the learners were to derive from studying these ideas was necessary. This observation forced their attention back to the original set of objectives and resulted in the identification of specific pupil behaviors to be sought. Examples such as the following are *behavioral* rather than *content* organizing elements:

1. Ability to understand and accept himself and others.
2. Desire to observe, explore, and question the environment.
3. Ability to locate, organize and use time, materials and information effectively.[5]

By working together in this fashion, teachers may come to see their school as a series of interrelated parts, each dependent upon the other, instead of as a number of mutually exclusive cells. These parts are tied together by the organizing threads of the curriculum —concepts, skills and values—which guide rather than dictate the selection of what shall be taught and when, over the entire length of the school's program. Once identified, these threads then become the relatively fixed components of the curriculum and specific topics are suggested as useful according to both their place in the sequence and the readiness of children to cope with them. From the data presented in Chapter 1, it is obvious that the depth of insight into a given concept and the level of maturity in a given behavior will vary markedly within a class group of pupils, whatever their grade-level demarcation. It is clear, too, that the variety of content used and the kinds of groupings employed by a teacher will vary according to both the range of achievement in the group and the particular *kind* of content being dealt with.

The longitudinal identification of organizing elements unifies the whole learning sequence. There are no stages sufficient unto

---

[4] For the others, see John I. Goodlad, "Illustrative Programs and Procedures in Elementary Schools," *The Integration of Educational Experiences,* National Society for the Study of Education, Fifty-seventh Yearbook, Part III (Chicago, University of Chicago Press, 1958), p. 182.

[5] *Ibid.*

themselves. The graded school concept implies that bodies of content may be identified and labeled for a second or a fourth or a sixth grade. But the data of Table 5, for example, in Chapter 1, reveal only two children—number 13 and number 14—to be at grade level in all their learnings. The other children are spread out above and below in the most diverse array of individual achievement patterns imaginable. Grade levels are a myth. Graded content constitutes a foredoomed attempt to relate one kind of reality to what is only a supposed reality; to something, then, that is in effect nonexistent.

Concepts, skills, and values do not lend themselves to grade packaging any more than pupil realities do. But these organizing threads of the curriculum lend themselves very well to the concept of the nongraded school developed in the preceding chapters. A longitudinal view of pupil development, a longitudinal view of the curriculum, and an organizational structure unbroken by grade-to-grade divisions go hand in hand.

The organizing threads, once identified, become the relatively fixed or constant components of the curriculum. The children who are to deal with them and the content selected for their development become the variables. In much conventional curriculum planning, however, what are proposed here as relative constants tend to be the variables and what are proposed as variables tend to be the constants. Too frequently, when teachers come together to work on school programs, they want to congregate by grade levels, and they ask, "What should be covered in sixth-grade science?" or "When should the history of our state be taught?" Teachers often fret because newcomers to their classes have not studied Egypt or some other topic recently dealt with in their own classes. Such considerations are quite foreign to the longitudinal concept of curriculum development described here. We select given content because it permits the practice of certain desired pupil behavior or it further clarifies an important concept.

With so much knowledge available to us today, we cannot possibly teach everything, or even the smallest fraction of what is known. Furthermore, yesterday's facts often are no longer facts. But the central truths from various fields of knowledge do not change overnight. Rather, they provide the somewhat more stable "truth" to which specific facts may be related. To proceed as though there is and always will be a body of specifics, and that these are the sacred cows of the elementary-school program is to ignore reality. Instead of worrying about whether or not this child has studied Egypt, teachers should seek to discover what he has derived from his study of some other country, Switzerland, perhaps. Is he beginning to see that where and when one lives in large measure determines the specific problems of living which one faces? Is he beginning to see that one must face certain kinds of problems whenever and wherever he lives? If so, he probably is capable of moving with the class into a study of another country, whether he had previously dealt with Egypt or Switzerland or neither. No sequence is provided in placing Egypt before or after Switzerland in the course of studies. The sequence occurs in the child who experiences carefully paced progress in understanding the several important concepts to be derived from such studies. Again, the behavioral change sought and the concepts pertinent to promoting such change should be the "constants." The topics or units selected should be the variables and often should grow out of the immediate environment and experiences of a class of learners.

Is it grade structure that causes us to be enamored of bits and pieces of learning? Indians in the second grade, explorers in the fourth, and America in the sixth? Is it grade structure that interrupts our flow of curricular thought so that we must think of what is to be covered in the fifth grade? Is it our tendency to think in grade levels that has so delayed the longitudinal look at the program increasingly being advocated in the curricular realm? Is it our tendency to compartmentalize knowledge that has kept us too comfortable with graded lock-step for so long? Which is the cause and which the effect? At any rate, now at long last a view of school organization that squares with pupil realities and a view of the curriculum that aligns with both are coming into prominence. Taken together, they suggest a different kind of elementary school than we have known.

The content of instruction

The teacher's classroom decisions are heavily dependent upon his view of what should be taught and to whom. In the longitudinal curricular view, both the what and the who are seen over a span of years. As a result, whether or not the wet lands are taught in the fifth grade becomes less important than the extent to which each child is deepening his insight into certain effects of environment on patterns of plant, animal, and human life. Whether or not levers are taught in the sixth grade becomes less important than the extent to which each child is developing understanding of principles of force. Whether or not Susan is reading the third book in a given reading series becomes less important than the extent to which her word analysis skills and eye movement are developing at a steady pace. What is taught when becomes less important than what concepts, skills, and values are being learned and how well.

The timing and pacing of learning processes becomes more important than the grade placement of specific learning tasks.

The teacher in the nongraded school is compelled to look deeply into the internal characteristics of the subject matter to be taught. Such a look reveals content differences of considerable import in teaching. Fields such as science and social studies have much in common at the elementary level. There are certain broad principles to be developed: the interdependence of man, the functioning of the human organism, natural forces at work, and so on. There are certain cognitive processes to be refined: collating data, interpreting facts, synthesizing related information, etc. There are certain study skills to be fostered: locating appropriate sources of information, using reference materials, working with others, and so forth. These principles, processes, and skills become threads running along the entire length of the program. What is studied becomes a means to their development. It would be both difficult (in fact, impossible) and unrealistic to define *the* body of content required in these areas for the elementary school. But it is relatively easy to select large problems, topics, or units that permit simultaneous development of these principles, processes, and skills for large groups of students varying widely in both ability and present attainment. Similarly, it is desirable and feasible to use student interests and community-world problems in initiating movement toward further refinement in these areas. The course of studies becomes both a prospectus of the broad, longitudinal principles, processes, and values and a record of the specific topics used by each teacher in developing them. The course of studies is now *not* a listing of topics to be covered grade by grade.

Mathematics, even at the elementary-school level, differs from science and social studies. There are processes and skills to be developed here, too, and these can be exercised through both the solving of social problems and the completion of manipulative exercises. But mathematics has a rigorous internal system that can be learned only by studying the field in its own right, quite apart from social applications. In elementary-school science and social studies, the learner engages primarily in the inductive process of building larger concepts and principles from specifics. In arithmetic, the learner begins with certain concepts and deduces from them. These concepts include number, quantity, and spatial relationships. These must be studied in their own right. The sequence here is determined by the nature of the content itself and advances the learner through an orderly, disciplined process. Large topics, problems, and units do not suffice for this. Nor can large numbers of students of widely differing abilities proceed together through the process.

Music, art, and, to a somewhat lesser degree, physical education are quite comparable but are still different from social studies, science, and mathematics in the elementary-school curriculum. There certainly are specifics to be learned: painters, media, music symbols, games, and stunts. But the purpose now is to develop sensitivity to sound rather than to learn a certain song; to develop painting skills rather than to paint a specific picture; to develop motor coordination rather than to play a particular game. Both the human organism and the field of human expression are viewed longitudinally. At lower elementary-school levels, the pedagogical approach emphasizes the unfolding of the individual. A single stimulus may be used for children of widely varying levels of development but perfomance, likewise, must be expected to be at equally varying levels. After listening to a poem of sun and rain, one child will draw only a yellow circle in the corner of his page. Another of the same age will show the sunlight gleaming through black clouds overhanging lush, growing grass. In time, each child seeks to express a rather precise feeling. He may experience frustration in seeking to bring equally precise skill to the task. Thus, while a given stimulus may motivate many simultaneously, each child requires highly individualized guidance in refining his expressive techniques. Even to be satisfying only to one's self, not to mention to be pleasing to others, creativity in art demands the increasingly rigorous development of insights, skills, and values accompanying the maturation of the human organism.

The language arts differ again from the other fields, although they are closely connected with art and music. To be sure, development of the human organism is important in the learning sequence, but the organic requirements of language usage are developed in all normal children of all cultures by about five and a half years of age. On one hand, more experience is necessary for the refinement of communication. The learner "experiences" something new, he reflects or reasons about his experience, and then he forces his expression through the language structure of his culture. On the other hand, increased understanding of his language structure enhances his interpretation of experience, permitting him to tease nuances of meaning from it that simply are not possible in one whose language insight is coarse and undisciplined. A two-fold pedagogy is required. Learner experiences are used or stimulated with a view to making the learner skillful in communicating them. And language structure itself is studied as a basic discipline. Learners of widely varying abilities can be brought together in the former pedagogy but the discipline itself limits the range of pupils that can productively study together in the latter.

It becomes apparent that a first-rate program of instruction cannot be organized around pupil realities alone. Subject matter realities, too, must be faced. What we know about learners is as useful in determining what we can ignore in teaching them as it is in determining what should be done to help them. Similarly, what we know about the content of instruction helps us to know both when to deemphasize subject-matter considerations and when to follow them rigorously. Placing these two kinds of knowledge side by side provides the flexible framework needed in timing and pacing the learning process.

The timing and pacing of learning

The well-planned curriculum, as we have seen, helps the learner to build desired learning upon desired learning in a continuous sequential fashion. The well-planned curriculum also helps the learner to relate one learning experience to another. Thus, a ten-year-old studying science and social studies might be expected to perceive a variety of relationships between the climate of a given region and the growth of flora native to it. He not only should see such relationships but also should revise his generalizations about them as his own perceptions mature and as new evidence comes to him. Two kinds of timing are involved in such learning. First, contacts with stimuli (books, objects, pictures, etc.) are occurring in such sequence that previous insights into scientific *or* geographic concepts are deepened. Second, the deepening of *both* scientific *and* geographic concepts occurs simultaneously so that a relationship between the two is seen. The well-planned curriculum seeks so to pace the progression of all learning that such deepening of meaning will occur with maximum frequency.

Both graded and nongraded teachers face the problem of helping each child relate learnings sequentially to each other and horizontally to learnings in other curricular areas. But the nongraded teacher has certain notable advantages in seeking so to time and pace the learnings of a diverse class group. He does not have graded content to contend with—that is, content pre-packaged for consumption as though all learners were ready to consume it together. Such pre-packaging assumes that pacing can be determined quite apart from the learners to be paced and that all learners can be put through their paces at about the same rate. This volume rejects such assumptions. The longitudinal view of the curriculum, so compatible with nongraded structure, allows concepts, skills, and values to be developed over the full sweep of the elementary school. Such a view prescribes neither the pacing of pupils along these organizing threads nor specific topics to be dealt with according to a predetermined time table. Consequently, the nongraded teacher is relatively free to select organizing *centers* for instruction (topics, problems, units, etc.) from a wide range of possibilities inherent in these threads. The pupil interest in and readiness for these learning nuclei largely determine the actual selection of what is to be studied. By contrast, the graded teacher, probably equally anxious to provide for learner interest and readiness, is frustrated by a certain inescapable loyalty to the content prescribed for his grade.

Furthermore, the nongraded teacher derives order and system in guiding learners not from a horizontal view of what is appropriate for a grade-level but from the several organizing elements underlying the curriculum and the progression of pupils along them. It is normal to anticipate that a given child will advance along these threads at various rates. Thus, at a given moment, the child's very irregular profile of achievement—perhaps varying several years from learning area to learning area—is anticipated, accepted, and encouraged. The teacher feels not guilt but assurance that he is doing the right thing in permitting a single child to be working at what would be, in a graded system, several grade-levels. The graded teacher faces the same pupil variability (the tables of Chapter 1 are drawn from graded classrooms) but he does not feel the same sense of freedom in dealing with it. For him, order and system are derived from an erroneous but nonetheless generally accepted horizontal view of the curriculum which nourishes the myth that all "normal" children will work at grade-level.

The concept of individualized timing and pacing may appear at first glance to be overwhelming. Actually, it is much less complex and much more meaningful than the concept of individualization that modern theories of curriculum and instruction impose upon the graded school. For decades, the leading texts on elementary education have been advocating instruction geared to individual differences. Teachers, faced with the reality of individual differences, have readily accepted the theory. But they have been frustrated in seeking to apply it. They see a conflict between instruction based on grade-packaged content and the kind of instruction that is suggested by research and theory pertaining to child development, learning, and curriculum. The implications of such research and theory are sufficient to tax the creativity of the best teachers in nongraded schools. But for the graded teacher, forced to face both these implications and the presence of grades and grade standards, the challenge frustrates and often forms an insurmountable block to creativity.

Caught up in such a dilemma, the capable graded teacher effects a compromise. He ignores as best he can the uniform connotations of grade-levels and, for much instruction, groups pupils so that the distance between attainment floors and ceilings in each sub-group is less than in the single large group. This is a partial admission of the inappropriateness of grade standards, because if all children in the fifth grade were really fifth-graders there would be no need to regroup them for achievement. Once this fateful step has been taken, however, the teacher is faced with the whole series of dislocations, justifications, and explanations described in Chapter 4. Textbooks other than those normally assigned to the grade are necessary. Dare one intrude upon the terrain of the next teacher by using textbooks assigned to the higher grade? How does one explain to parents the use of a lower-grade book? Yes, your child is in the fourth grade. No, he doesn't use fourth-grade books; he uses those of his younger sister, Jane, who is in the second grade. How does one explain to children that it's all right to work below grade-level all year but not to be below grade-level at the end of the year? Yes, you've been progressing satisfactorily but we're not promoting you to the next grade. The modern graded teacher has the same information about good instructional practices that is possessed by the modern nongraded teacher. But he cannot practice what he knows about timing and pacing the learning of his pupils, at least not without compromise and hypocrisy.

The nongraded teacher is free, meanwhile, to employ the individualized timing and pacing suggested by modern theories of curriculum and research evidence from the fields of learning and child development. Grouping to reduce the distance between attainment floors and ceilings is for this teacher an appropriate device for modifying the picture of pupil diversity that lies before him. Similarly, grouping based on pupil interest, study habits, and so on may be carried on without reference to the premature and often inappropriate determination of what shall be taught and when, that characterizes the conventional graded school. In effect, the nongraded teacher is free to guide the timing and pacing of learning in accordance with what he knows about the components of the learning act itself—learner, something to be learned, and the process through which learner and the something to be learned become one.

Pupil Grouping and Use of Teachers in Nongraded Classrooms

The nongraded school provides an appropriate structure for continuous pupil progress along the organizing threads of the curriculum. But the individual classroom is the key instructional unit. The principles underlying the nongraded school must be carried over into the nongraded classroom. Since nongrading is an organizational device, it is classroom *organization* that concerns us here. It is important, however, to look also at the evaluation of pupil progress in various kinds of groups to determine the appropriateness of organizational procedures.

This section of the chapter, then, uses some of the preceding curriculum concepts in analyzing the following major alternatives for classroom grouping:

1. Ability grouping whereby class groups are subdivided according to a general criterion of learning capacity such as intelligence quotient.
2. Achievement grouping whereby flexible groups are established on the basis of pupil attainment in one or more skills or curricular areas.
3. Informal grouping on the basis of student interests.
4. Grouping according to the degree of independence, self-propulsion, study skills or other work habits already developed in individual pupils.
5. Various combinations of the above.

Each of these alternatives stems from a basic educational viewpoint in regard to what learning is important and how these learnings can be best accomplished. It follows, then, that each grouping procedure should be accompanied by evaluation procedures appropriate to the goals of such grouping.

Ability grouping

At first glance, ability grouping appears to be compatible with the philosophy of nongrading. The nongraded school is designed to encourage children of varying abilities to proceed at rates appropriate to these abilities. Therefore, it is desirable to establish groups of equal ability within the room or, better still, among several rooms, and let them proceed at different rates. Thus, three third-grade classes might be nongraded and the pupils segregated according to ability. Then, one class would do work usually appropriate for the fourth grade, another class work appropriate for the third grade, and the third class work appropriate for the second grade. If classes were established on a heterogeneous basis, then homogeneous ability groups might be established within each classroom.

But the data presented in Chapter 1 reveal that children do not come in such neat packages. The child with the highest I.Q. is not necessarily the highest achiever. Furthermore, the highest achiever in one area is well down the achievement scale in another. In the fifth-grade class presented in Chapter 1, for example, although children of I.Q. above 120 and below 90 had been removed, the remaining students ranged from 2.7 to 11.2 grades in reading achievement. Several decades of research reveal (1) that student variability is only imperceptibly reduced through ability grouping when a broad range of academic, intellectual, physical, and social traits is considered; (2) that variability in *school achievement* is reduced only about 7 per cent when students of a given grade level are divided into A and B classes and only about 17 per cent when the division is into A, B, and C classes; and (3) that division into A, B, and C classes, accompanied by *separate promotional tracks*, reduces achievement variability about 10 per cent more.[6] Analyses of studies into the effects of ability grouping by Cornell [7] and, more recently, by Petty [8] suggest that curricular differentiation is a more significant factor than ability grouping in encouraging individual progress and academic accomplishment.

Ability grouping is instituted in graded classes, apparently, to create an environment more conducive to individual pupil progress. But the results have been disappointing. The goals sought are attained more readily as a result of *curricular* differentiation. Curricular differentiation is a basic characteristic of nongrading. Grades are pushed out of the picture so that learning activities appropriate to differing abilities, quite irrespective of grade level, may enter in. It follows, then, that grouping on the basis of general ability does not expedite the advantages sought in the nongraded elementary school. Other patterns of grouping must be sought.

Achievement grouping

Research suggests that curricular differentiation is conducive to differentiated pupil progress. It would seem to follow, therefore, that subdividing a class on the basis of general achievement would provide the necessary structure for such differentiation. But, again, the data of Chapter 1 reveal the fallacy in such thinking. The range from curricular area to curricular area for a single child is considerable, usually spreading over several grade levels. This range is particularly great for students at upper and lower levels of the achievement scale, the very children for whom homogeneous grouping is most earnestly pleaded. Children grouped homogeneously on

---

[6] Reported by John I. Goodlad, "Classroom Organization," *Encyclopedia of Educational Research*, Chester W. Harris, ed., 1960 edition; now in press.

[7] Ethel L. Cornell, "Effects of Ability Grouping Determinable from Published Studies," *The Grouping of Pupils*, National Society for the Study of Education, Thirty-fifth Yearbook, Part 1 (Bloomington, Illinois, Public School Publishing Company, 1936), pp. 289-304.

[8] Mary Clare Petty, "Intraclass Grouping in the Elementary School" (unpublished doctoral dissertation, University of Texas, 1952).

a general criterion of achievement remain heterogeneous in the various subcategories of achievement. Grouping on the basis of general attainment, then, is not a precise means for setting the stage for curricular differentiation.

Earlier in this chapter we pointed out that curricular areas differ in significant ways. Some, like arithmetic, are rather rigorous and systematic in their internal organization. A single stimulus will attract and hold the attention of only those children whose background of experience and achievement is such that they can relate to it. Obviously, then, pupils of differing experience and attainment must be subdivided so that groups of considerable homogeneity are established. It is for this reason that grouping of pupils of like attainment is necessary in teaching the fundamentals of arithmetic and the basic reading skills. In most other fields, however, no such rigor exists so far as the elementary levels of education are concerned. A single stimulus will elicit further growth from pupils of varying levels of present attainment. The learning outcome—level of insight or understanding, for example—will vary widely from pupil to pupil. The flexibility in individual progress comes, not from moving a child from group to group according to accomplishment as in arithmetic and reading, but in encouraging and providing opportunity for differing outcomes from a single stimulus situation.

The above analysis, coupled with the earlier discussion of differences in curricular areas, suggests that organizing classroom groups on the basis of present attainment is necessary to differentiated progress in fields like reading and arithmetic. Such grouping is not demanded by fields such as science, health, and social studies. Nongraded and nongraded-type schools such as the Nathaniel Hawthorne School in University City, Missouri, the Cabool Elementary School in Cabool, Missouri, and the Green Bay, Wisconsin, schools have identified 8 to 22 reading levels in the primary unit (normally comprising what would be called grades one to three in a graded structure).[9] Levels can be similarly identified in arithmetic. If the philosophy of the school favors completely heterogeneous classes, then the establishment of reading groups must occur within each classroom. Thus, for part of each day, Miss Thompson's class, with a range from level 5 to level 14 in reading, would be divided into perhaps three groups: levels 5-7 in one group, 8-11 in a second, and 12-14 in a third. A continuous process of evaluation would then provide flexibility in group placement. A child spurting ahead from level 7 would be reassigned to the group

---

[9] See John I. Goodlad, Fred E. Brooks, Irene M. Larson, and Neal Neff, " 'Reading Levels' Replace Grades in the Nongraded Plan," *Elementary School Journal*, 57 (February 1957), pp. 253-56.

comprising levels 8-11. Another child spurting ahead from level 14 would be considered for possible room reassignment, perhaps moving to Miss Smith's class, comprising levels 15-22. It might be decided, however, that other factors favored continuation of the child with Miss Thompson, who would now be forced to extend her reading levels to include level 15. In some nongraded schools, a child comes up for possible reassignment at any time. In others, reassignments of children are considered only at specified intervals ranging from as short as one month to as long as four or five months.

Some nongraded schools, however, regard reading as so central to primary instruction that the child's initial room assignment is determined from his reading level. Thus, if there were 22 reading levels in all and seven primary teachers (grades one to three in the graded school), each of these teachers could be assigned pupils within a narrow reading range of only three to four levels. In this situation, children might be transferred rather frequently from teacher to teacher. To avoid such frequent reassignment, nongraded schools using relatively homogeneous reading groups in establishing classes usually include a larger spread per class, each class overlapping some other class. The room-to-room breakdown might then look somewhat as follows: Miss Brown, levels 1-5; Miss Burrows, 6-11; Miss Henry, 9-14; Miss Silvers, 12-17; Miss Smith, 15-20; Miss Hope, 16-22. Actually, a still larger range would be needed at the upper levels since children tend to grow farther and farther apart as they progress through the school. By initially placing children so that only the lower levels of each grouping are in the class, the volume of class-to-class reassignment is significantly reduced. Even in these classes it is desirable to create reading subgroups during the part of the day devoted to instruction in reading skills. Obviously, such subgroups would be quite homogeneous in regard to reading attainment.

Interest grouping

In all but those curricular areas involving rigorous skills or concepts, grouping according to pupil interests within broadly defined areas is entirely appropriate. In science and social studies, for example, it does not really matter whether or not the class stays close to the *order* of suggested topics. As pointed out earlier, there are certain basic concepts in these fields and the topics of instruction are selected to develop understanding of them. The study of Mexicans is as good as the study of Indians for this purpose—and may be better if the interest is greater in this topic. But there must be a continuing reassurance that prevailing freedom in topic selection actually is resulting in the insights and understandings sought. Almost daily evaluation of an informal sort is essential.

Class discussions provide the sort of interchange among children that reveals the thought levels of individuals. Questions of the "why" rather than the "what" variety force thought processes into the open. Written work should call for analytical behavior rather than mere recall of factual information. Here are a few suggestions for evaluating daily work in content fields such as science and social studies:

1. In a class or large group discussion, first take a mental survey of group participation. Do the responses come from just a few of the more gifted? Do I tend to avoid those who stumble or halt in order to elicit the more polished performance of the better students? Unless opportunity for each child to respond is provided, interest will lag and listlessness will follow. Insights will not be deepened under such conditions.

2. Note the kinds of responses elicited. Are they factual, recall answers? Does the answer demand another question or does it stimulate further discussion and deeper analysis? Two or three really good questions often are sufficient to initiate and carry group discussion that moves from student to student rather than from student to teacher.

3. Check the quality of pupil or teacher summaries. Do they merely summarize facts or do they pull out major generalizations? Even young children can be taught to generalize from specific data but the teacher must set the example.

4. Periodically check the kinds of chalkboard questions stimulating pupil study and research. Questions like "What are the exports of Brazil?" and "What are the chief rivers of India?" are dead-end questions. Once answered, they lead nowhere. But questions like "Why is coffee grown in Brazil?" and "Why are India's rivers so important to the people?" not only call for investigation of many kinds of data but also encourage generalizations that are useful in studying other countries.

5. Use individual and small group study to good advantage. Here are opportunities to find out how individual children are proceeding with important concepts and study skills. Have a child read a portion of a book he is studying, then raise some "why" and "so what" questions with him. You may discover that the concept burden is too heavy and can help him locate a more appropriate volume. At the same time, you are catching an important glimpse of his thought processes.

6. Maintain simple "interest" charts in children's folders. One revealing only reading interests can be most helpful not only in guiding recreational reading but also in identifying catch-hold interest points for other activities. A chart such as Figure 8 will suffice. Each time a child reads a book, a number is placed in

Figure 8

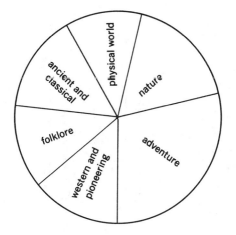

Chart for recording reading interests.

the appropriate "slice of pie" and the title recorded with the number below the chart. At a glance, the teacher is able to determine areas of considerable or limited interest and to plan accordingly.

7. Maintain a single developmental concept chart for the class, as in Figure 9. List the concept areas sought as vertical threads. Identify a given child's approximate present status in a given concept area with a number which you have assigned him. The categories could be further refined into specific concepts, depending on the degree of exactness required.

The data recorded on such charts coupled with the achievement data from the other curricular areas provide needed guidance to the nongraded teacher proceeding without the usual guideline of grade levels. Such data are of inestimable value in determining the most appropriate placement for a given child.

Grouping according to work and study habits

The elementary school is fundamentally concerned with developing learning skills basic to further education. Children leaving the elementary school should be self-propelling to a high degree, able to work independently using a wide range of study resources. Some teachers claim that variations in abilities of this sort, more than any other, compound the task of teaching a heterogeneous class of children. Because of this, one teacher at Englewood, Florida, de-

Modern Theories of Curriculum 95

Figure 9

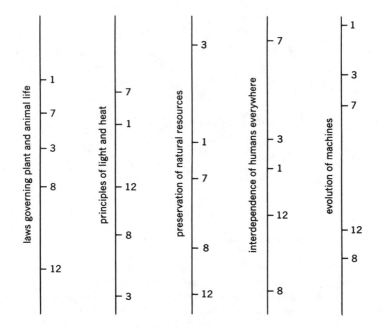

Chart for recording concept development. Numbers on the vertical lines refer to five children being compared.

veloped a technique for grouping based on independence in study. Three groups thus established then became his basic units for many classroom activities. The most advanced group, he knew, was able to proceed with a minimum of teacher guidance. The group lowest in self-propulsion, however, required considerable teacher attention and the most detailed directions in planning its work. The knowledge gained by the teacher in evaluating individuals for these skills has proved invaluable in the guidance of planning, teaching, and pupil placement. A simple chart such as the one for concepts suffices in evaluating each individual periodically.

Pupil grouping and the use of teachers

So far, in discussing grouping, we have stayed within the conventional patterns of the self-contained classroom. But, having broken down vertical grade-levels, we see no reason for not subjecting to critical attention the walls separating classes horizontally.

Several elementary schools scattered across the country are experimenting with plans whereby several classes coordinate their efforts, thus pooling pupils and teaching resources. These new approaches to the use of teachers appear to be of particular relevance to non-graded classrooms.

Let us suppose that there are three classes of students entering their last year of an elementary school. Most of these children have completed five years (irrespective of kindergarten) in the school, a few fast-moving ones only four years, and a few slower ones six years. The range in reading levels represented in the three groups is from 15 to 38, according to the school's classification plan. Under a normal scheme of heterogeneous classes with no attempt at room-to-room grouping for reading achievement, this range would prevail in all three classes. If each class were subgrouped into three for reading, there would be a total of nine groups in the three rooms. The total range in each room would still be from level 15 to 38 and the range in each subgroup would be approximately eight levels (15 to 22 in group A, 23-30 in group B and 31-38 in group C).

Now, let us suppose that the three teachers decide to pool their resources in a team-teaching plan. The three classes are placed side by side and, perhaps, doors are cut from room to room. The three teachers plan their reading program together. The children of all three rooms (a total of perhaps 100) are now regarded as a single group to be divided for reading among three teachers. The teachers divide them into five groups, thus reducing the group-to-group range to four or five levels (15-19 in group A, 20-24 in group B, 25-28 in group C, 29-33 in group D, and 34-38 in group E). Admittedly, the subgroups are somewhat larger than before, but the reduced reading range is the more important consideration in relation to the specific purposes one would want to achieve through such grouping. Since the group-teacher ratio has been reduced from 9 to 3 and is now only 5 to 3, it becomes obvious that only two groups (in contrast to six under the previous arrangement) need be without direct teacher supervision at any moment. More important, however, is the opportunity for flexibility in grouping and the better use of teachers. Such a plan could as readily be extended to arithmetic and, using criteria in addition to or other than achievement, to still other areas of the curriculum.

In Flint, Michigan (where the experiment is with primary-level children), three teachers cooperating in such an arrangement are enthusiastic about the opportunity to pool differing talents. They like the fact that all three are able to observe children's learning and then confer about instructional plans. In Englewood, Florida, teachers are coordinating a new school design with a cooperative teaching plan. Room spaces of from 750 to 2000 square feet are available and are arranged so that there is easy access from room to room. Initial class groupings are quite heterogeneous, but the children of several classes together are regarded as a large "family" in a family "nest" of rooms. Regroupings within the nest occur daily, depending upon the particular activity being planned jointly by all classes comprising the larger family. A very similar plan has been initiated among several upper elementary classes of the Francis M. Price School of Fort Wayne, Indiana. All children have the home base and unified planning inherent in the self-contained classroom along with the specialized opportunities of departmentalization. Time and study will determine whether or not team teaching plans offer the strengths of both departmentalization and the self-contained classroom without the weaknesses of either.[10]

Since the 1957-58 school year, a more elaborate team-teaching project has been under way in the Franklin School of Lexington, Massachusetts. Here, some lessons are taught to large "families" each containing from 75 to 150 children. Some lessons are taught in the traditional setting of the self-contained classroom. Still other lessons are taught to various subgroups divided among teachers in a fashion similar to that described in the preceding paragraph. Sometimes, the subgroups are established on the basis of achievement (for example, in arithmetic or reading) and sometimes on the basis of interests (as in social studies and science). The entire course of studies for each family of children, which may comprise as many as three age-levels, is planned by a team of teachers with a team leader serving as planning chairman. It is hoped that the research orientation of this carefully executed project will provide guidelines for future team-teaching enterprises.[11]

In Conclusion

This chapter has sought to reveal an often-ignored relationship among three aspects of modern elementary education: gross individual differences among those to be educated; a longitudinal concept of curriculum development that prohibits grade-packaging of content; and a nongraded scheme of school organization that en-

---

[10] For further description and analysis of the team teaching innovations at Flint, Englewood, and Ft. Wayne, see John I. Goodlad, "In Pursuit of Visions," *Elementary School Journal*, 59 (October 1958), pp. 1-17.

[11] Some of the issues and the theoretical background for re-examining the teacher-per-class concept are presented in John I. Goodlad, "The Increasing Concern for Effective Teacher Utilization," *The High School in a New Era* (Chicago, University of Chicago Press, 1958), pp. 133-45.

courages continuous pupil progress along the vertical threads of the curriculum. This relationship has then been applied to considerations of classroom organization and evaluation of pupil progress within the nongraded school.

An analysis of bases for grouping pupils has revealed that differences in *both* learners *and* subject matter must be considered in timing and pacing the learning process. The authors endorse a combination of grouping procedures accompanied by a variety of evaluative devices. They do not believe that either departmentalization or general ability grouping has much to commend it. At the same time, they believe that rigorous adherence to the self-contained classroom wherein one teacher and only one works with the class is not justified. There simply is no evidence to tell us how much time one teacher and one group of children must spend together for these pupils to derive the security educators and psychologists recommend (see Chapter 4). Similarly, there is no evidence to show when the contacts can and should be extended to include other teachers and other groups of children. We are convinced, however, that *planned* flexibility in grouping is a key to maximum pupil growth.

Such flexibility should be planned with both pupil welfare and maximum teacher effectiveness in mind. We recommend, first, that each nongraded classroom be organized around achievement groups, interest groups, and work-study skill groups simultaneously. Planned heterogeneity in some curricular areas (e.g., social studies) is as important as planned homogeneity in others (arithmetic and reading skills). We recommend, second, that formal and informal evaluative techniques be devised in such a way that the progress of each child in each area can be readily identified. Visual aids such as charts and graphs are of tremendous help in carrying out this process efficiently. We recommend, third, that grouping possibilities that cut across class lines be considered. Here we would caution against indiscriminate team teaching. The desire of a teacher to exchange his social studies teaching for the arithmetic teaching of another is not a good reason for considering team teaching. The fundamental criterion is whether certain desired learnings can be effected this way with greater consideration for the individual pupil. Rooms cooperating should be viewed together as a larger unit and the children in them as a larger family. Miss Williams, Miss Harris, and Mr. Proctor agree to work together because, together, they can expedite valid educational purposes more readily than by working alone in separate rooms.

When one thinks about the traditional elementary school from the point of view advocated here, a quite different kind of structure emerges. Grade-to-grade and class-to-class barriers dim in significance. Ultimately they are seen as serving no educational purpose at all. Then the viewer is freed to visualize a whole series of exciting innovations that promise better education for boys and girls. The intellectual demand is to see beyond patterns that need not be to the possibilities of patterns that could be.

For Further Reading

Association for Supervision and Curriculum Development. *A Look at Continuity in the School Program.* 1958 Yearbook. Washington, The Association, 1958.

Much of this yearbook is pertinent to the preceding chapter. The reader would find yearbook Chapters 9, "Considering Curriculum Content," and 13, "Promoting Steady Progress Between Grades and Within Grades," particularly helpful.

Jerome S. Bruner. *The Process of Education.* Cambridge, Massachusetts, Harvard University Press, 1961.

A brief but highly regarded statement about what shall be taught and to what purpose. Bruner concludes that children can grasp basic concepts earlier than has been thought possible, through intuitive comprehension.

Goodlad, John I. "Three Dimensions in Organizing the Curriculum for Learning and Teaching." *Frontiers of Elementary Education III,* Vincent J. Glennon, ed., pages 11-22. Syracuse, Syracuse University Press, 1956.

This paper analyzes the considerations that should be taken into account if learners, content and process are to be related effectively. Good timing and pacing of pupil learning depend upon the creative synthesis of all three.

National Society for the Study of Education. *The Integration of Educational Experiences.* Fifty-seventh Yearbook, Part III. Chicago, University of Chicago Press, 1958.

In Chapter 5, Benjamin S. Bloom presents criteria for the selection, development and use of integrative threads in the curriculum. He then applies these criteria to an analysis of the usefulness of major ideas, theories and problems as integrative threads. In Chapter 6, Ralph W. Tyler discusses the general problem of organizing the curriculum vertically and horizontally and then goes on to examine "the way in which experiences of one level can be effectively related to those of another level and the experiences of one area can be effectively related to those in another area."

Thelen, Herbert A. "The Curriculum and the Domains of Knowledge," *Elementary School Journal,* **55** (March 1955), 369-76.

This is a thought-provoking analysis of the role of the major subject-matter disciplines in education. In addition to three domains of more or less objective knowledge—physical, biological, and social—Thelen identifies a fourth which he labels "the subjective world of the individual student."

————, and Jacob W. Getzels. "Symposium: Social Science and Education," *School Review,* **65** (Autumn 1957).

This entire issue is devoted to certain questions of aim, subject matter and method in the curriculum. The several articles, written by specialists in various social science fields, provide excellent examples of some of the demands and limitations placed upon curricular decisions because of the nature of social science subject matter.

Tyler, Ralph W. *Basic Principles of Curriculum and Instruction.* Chicago, University of Chicago Press, 1950.

On pages 54 to 67, Tyler lays out some concepts of curriculum organization. He defines and illustrates the use of organizing elements in providing continuity and sequence in the curriculum.

6. REPORTING PUPIL PROGRESS

IN THE NONGRADED SCHOOL

Introduction

The general problem of reporting pupil progress to parents has probably received as much attention from both educators and citizens as any other educational topic. The Bureau of Elementary Education of the California State Department of Education has reported, in support of this assertion, that "among the many inquiries directed each day to the Bureau . . . the one that surpasses all others in frequency relates to methods of reporting pupil progress to parents."[1] Other state agencies, research bureaus, colleges of education, education libraries, and professors of education also report a heavy volume of requests for information and opinion on the reporting problem. The Education Index annually lists over two hundred writings on matters related to reporting. Therefore, all of the current opinion (of which there is a great deal) and research (of which there is not a great deal of quality) on so extensive and complicated a topic can scarcely be summarized in a single chapter.

It is the belief and conviction of the authors that reporting is neither a greater nor a lesser problem in the nongraded school than in a graded school. Further, we believe that the same general principles that apply to reporting procedures and practices in conventional situations are applicable to nongraded situations. There are, of course, certain minor differences and these we hope to clarify in the discussion that follows. It should be understood by the reader in advance that the chapter aims to discuss reporting in its broadest

---

[1] *California Journal of Elementary Education,* 24 (November 1955), p. 65.

dimensions, with special attention to the effects of nongrading only where appropriate and necessary.

The reporting of pupil progress is essentially an administrative matter, although it is virtually impossible to separate it from its educational effects on the child. Seen at its best, the reporting system is a process of two-way communication between two co-operating sets of adults responsible for the child's well-being, leading to a greater realization on the part of each of the needs, the growth, and the long-range promise of the child. Reporting is seen as an activity in which the child is the focus of friendly, sympathetic, and objective attention, not (as in some unfortunate cases) a badminton bird between two opposing adult forces. The reporting process is seen as the outlet for information summarizing the results of previous programs planned for the child, and as the instrument through which steps are taken toward new and more effective programs for the future.

Idealized as this description may seem, it certainly is an accurate portrayal of the reporting process as presented in current professional writings as well as in statements made by many parents. It reflects not only an important aspect of curriculum planning, but also the "partnership principle" that has developed over recent decades. It characterizes the parent-teacher relationship which is thought to be not only desirable but necessary in a democratic society. It serves as a way of giving substance to that relationship and affords a means for its furtherance and development. Little wonder, then, that so much is being said by parents and teachers about reporting problems, and that there is so much concern about reporting systems that fail to do their job.

Measurement and Evaluation in the Graded and Nongraded School

The vocabulary of home-school communication includes a number of terms that are used somewhat loosely or inconsistently by parents and teachers. "Marks" and "grades" are sometimes used interchangeably, for example, and the processes of measurement and evaluation are sometimes described as if they were reporting activities per se. A word or two about terminology may therefore be helpful as a guide to the discussions of reporting that follow.

Whether they have been carefully and systematically phrased or not, the *objectives* of every school serve as the basis for all educational offerings and for the ways the children's responses to these experiences are viewed. One therefore starts with the objectives, or goals, of a school program when considering how successful or unsuccessful any child's efforts may be. In a graded school, it is customary to think of objectives in terms of the graded structure, each specific objective being more relevant to one grade level than to others. Teachers say that a child normally should have acquired a particular skill or piece of information or attitude by the time he completes a certain grade, or a portion of it. The teacher then plans his program so that the child is exposed to particular opportunities for acquiring such behavior while still a pupil in that grade.

Teachers under any school organization plan need to apply measurement techniques for the purpose of examining the outcomes of instruction, and they usually use symbols or descriptive phrases to express the nature and the value of those outcomes. One by-product of such activities, which go on almost continuously and which are usually expressed in summary terms, is information which can be interpreted to parents and to children by the teachers. Whether this is done by a "marking" system (using "marks" like A, B, C, 93, 85, 77) coded or related to grade norms, or by a marking system related to an individualized longitudinal expectations pattern, or by a descriptive (i.e., nonsymbolic) approach such as written sentences or spoken words, its intention is to satisfy the parent's questions about what is happening to the child in school.

The teacher's expectations for each child's growth in a graded school are frequently expressed or visualized in terms of the calendar that *grade-norms* provide. The placement of material in a grade is based in large measure upon the accumulative experience of test administration, indicating that task x or concept y has been mastered in the past, on the average, by children in the fifth month of the fourth grade. Hence a pupil whose raw score on an achievement test corresponds to a grade-norm of 4.5 is considered to be "on schedule" if the test was administered in January of his fourth-grade year.

As earlier chapters have pointed out, one of the main differences between a graded and a nongraded school is that the learning experiences follow a less rigid time schedule. Objectives are therefore modified principally in terms of timing. Over the total span of the elementary school period a child in a nongraded school has essentially the same aggregate of experiences, involving the same instructional materials and approaches and aimed at the same major goals, but he will have these experiences on a more flexible time-schedule.

When grades as such are eliminated, and the time schedule is modified accordingly, it becomes necessary to discard habits of converting progress data into grade norms. Admittedly this is a difficult step for teachers to take, for in a sense it means the abandonment of a deep-rooted professional vocabulary and of the adoption of very different, and less familiar, ways of looking at growth phenomena.[2]

For when a fourth-grade teacher sees a child's standardized test-score converted into a "grade equivalent" of 5.7, he customarily reacts with confidence that the child is doing quite well, in most situations. This implies that he has confidence in the test, in its applicability to the child's recent school experiences, and in the practicality of comparing his score with those of thousands of other children in all sorts of different situations. This kind of confidence, we fear, is often unwarranted.

What is needed to replace the system of grade norms is a system of more fluid child-development norms, in which each child's reactions represent a separate statistical universe and in which normalcy has primarily an individualized meaning. Helpful as it is to know that a given proportion of all children of approximately the same age are better or poorer at a given task than the child we have in mind, it is far more valuable to know how his performance compares with his own past performance, what appear to be the direction and the rate of his development in mastering tasks in that field, and how well this performance relates to what the teacher has planned for him to do. Out of such knowledge, whether or not it is expressed quantitatively as in a grade-norm, can indeed come valuable clues to the child's future progress.

To the extent that existing norms have some demonstrable relevance to child-development "norms," it may be possible in nongraded situations to salvage many of the present values in standardized tests and other graded materials. This has already happened in some ways in the area of reading, at least insofar as nongraded schools have adopted "reading levels" to replace grade levels. Nearly all of the pilot nongraded schools have taken this step, by adopting a somewhat different *longitudinal view* of the reading skill and adjusting it sequentially (at least) to the needs of each child (see Chapters 4 and 5). Arithmetic, another "subject" in which there is a developmental program, also lends itself quite well to a longitudinal or levels approach in which the general picture of a child's growth can be presented without need for recourse to grade norms. It is evident that the same general reasoning is applicable to spelling, where there is at least some development in skills. In these areas, and possibly in others, the schools need not

---

[2] It means, also, the abandonment of the conventional marking system in all its unpleasant and insidious forms. See the reference to Herbert A. Thelen's viewpoint on this matter at the end of this chapter. Thelan's comments about the confusion over marks and his example of Dr. Watson's report card for Sherlock Holmes should stimulate much profitable discussion.

make very profound changes in their use of textbooks and tests in order to conduct evaluations and reporting programs within the spirit of the nongraded school.

When we approach the broad area of social studies, standards and expectations must be developed in terms of the child's understanding and mastery of content and also in terms of his mastery of skills. There is already available in the literature a very useful and explicit discussion [3] of the evaluation of skills in the social studies. There the techniques and materials used to appraise the learner's behavior are equated with the techniques and materials used for instructional purposes.[4] When considering the degree of proficiency that is desired for a particular individual in a particular skill at a particular time, it is suggested that there should be measurement "in relation to (a) the level of skill previously practiced by the individual in question, (b) the relation of this skill to his other important skill developments, and (c) the degree of adequacy necessary for the performance of his social tasks." [5]

Whenever it is possible for the teacher to describe a child's present skill level in terms of these three dimensions, whether in social studies or in any other curriculum area, then comparisons with the performance of other children assume lesser importance even though they may be of some interest. If the teacher has confidence in the appropriateness of his instructional objectives for each child and the means he selects for achieving them, then he needs only to know how well the child has succeeded at those tasks. The translation of his work-product into a grade norm becomes only of secondary interest at best—more probably it is of tertiary interest, with secondary importance attached to class-wide comparisons. The grade-level referent, in other words, is by no means as important or as useful as many grade-minded teachers would like to believe.

The "partnership principle," implying a mutuality of purpose between teachers and parents, is no less applicable in a graded school than in a nongraded school. It is a valid and important principle for all teachers and parents to appreciate and to exemplify in their communications with each other. The advantage of nongrading is found in the fact that it is not only possible, but probably even easier, for good communication to take place when the deceptive and generally irrelevant grade norms are set aside in favor

---

[3] Virgil E. Herrick and Frank J. Estvan, "Evaluation of Skills in Social Studies," *Skills in Social Studies*, Helen M. Carpenter, ed., Twenty-fourth Yearbook of the National Council for the Social Studies (Washington 6, D.C., The Council, 1953), Ch. 12, pp. 246-261.

[4] *Ibid.*, p. 257.

[5] *Ibid.*

of a more individualized frame of reference. It is more certain that parents and teachers in a nongraded system will approach each effort at communication with the right kinds of expectations for the child, and with less concern for the child's position within an artificial and unrealistic competitive situation. It is more likely that the parent and the teacher will be comfortable together in the discussion of progress measured against the child's own history. It is more likely that the clock and the calendar will be viewed with calm and understanding by the adults as they estimate the rate of the child's learning.

In this section, certain major ideas have emerged:

1. All the learning experiences planned by a teacher in any school are determined by the objectives he has in mind.
2. Traditionally, objectives have been linked with the graded structure, accumulated experience having demonstrated that the average child is able to achieve a given objective by a certain point in that structure.
3. Grade norms are numerical symbols for points in the grade structure, related to the average past achievements of thousands of children.
4. Grade norms lose their usual importance and usefulness when each child is seen as a separate learner with needs and potentialities at variance with those of all other children.
5. A more flexible, individually-oriented, longitudinal growth picture should be constructed for each child, and each manifestation of achievement should be related to this picture rather than to grade norms.
6. In the developmental subject areas (especially reading, arithmetic, and spelling) the longitudinal or levels approach is not especially difficult to substitute for a grade norms approach, since successive stages of process are quite easily identified.
7. In less structured content areas, such as science and social studies, both skills mastery and content mastery can be measured within the three-dimensional framework of (a) what the individual has previously mastered; (b) how the present mastery relates to other skill developments underway; and (c) how adequately the degree of mastery now provides for his needs in that area.
8. Effective home-school cooperation is fostered by the conditions that are associated with nongrading.

Evaluation Through Home-School Cooperation

In the exchange process that is known as home-school communication, information about the child's needs and progress is provided by both parties to the relationship. In the next two sections, each dimension of the process is discussed.

Information the school obtains from the home

Evaluation, and the reporting that evaluation makes possible, is based upon various kinds of evidence. Of the many pertinent facts that exist about a child (his background, his history, his relationships with others, his behavior in and out of school, and so forth), some can be discovered with relative ease by the teacher and some are more likely to be known by the parent. Implicit in the partnership principle is the fact that the home willingly supplies relevant information and evidence to the school, not only the information required by law but other evidence as well. Obviously this kind of partnership takes time to develop, and grows only within an atmosphere of mutual trust, mutual respect, and mutual concern.

There are routine procedures for the collection of certain data. At the time of a child's school registration, for example, the family contributes a certain amount of information as a matter of course and in accordance with well-established custom. This includes details of family organization and membership, vital statistics of the child, usually a brief health history, and sometimes an inventory of the child's needs as requested on a form provided by the school. If the child has been in school before, it is usually the family that provides information about previous school experiences and copies of report forms or transfer slips. All such data serve as the nucleus of the child's permanent school record folder.

When a parent is willing to discuss his perception of the child's needs in complete detail at the outset, it is obviously possible for the school to save much valuable time in getting to know the child and in planning a program with the help of the parents. How much additional information a parent will volunteer or provide at initial registration time depends upon many things, one of which is the skill of the school representative who handles the registration procedure. Preferably this should be a professional person, not a secretary. Another factor is the parent's confidence in school people. If his experiences in the past and in other schools have been satisfying and rewarding, and if the teachers and administrators have been highly professional and competent in their dealings with him, the parent is more likely to assume the competence of teachers in the present school situation. When dealing with the parents of a transfer student, therefore, a school man is likely to become very conscious of his dependence upon the general competence of his brethren in the profession!

Parents usually see their children with less objectivity than teachers, but with far greater knowledge of the child's history and with a more comprehensive view of the child's habits and reactions. They see him in his daily relations with family members, his pets, friends and neighbors of greatly varying ages, doctors, dentists, ministers, and all sorts of strangers. They observe the choices he makes in use of free time, spending his allowance, selecting companions, recreational reading, and countless other activities. They hear him talk about his school experiences, his teachers and classmates, his successes and failures, and his perceptions of the values of his education. They gauge his interest in school, his feelings toward the people in the school, and his relative enjoyment of life both in and out of school. Some of these things, of course, the parents may not see or comprehend very well; but clues to such aspects of the child's development could be extremely useful to the teachers seeking to know their pupil better than they do. It is indeed regrettable that schools have had relatively little success in tapping this invaluable source of help from parents.

One of the reasons for this failure is that school people have not created the conditions that would lead to a freer exchange of information; another is that they have not known what questions to ask of parents. Again, we are reminded that too few schools have given adequate attention to the refinement of their objectives in terms of the specific behavioral outcomes sought. When objectives are vaguely or abstractly phrased (examples: "good health"; "tolerance for others"), teachers may not understand them as well as when objectives are expressed more precisely: "to understand how periodic dental care can influence the condition of one's teeth and mouth"; "to know the roles of basic foods in body-building"; "to cultivate habits of eating proper foods in balance with each other"; "to have a genuine interest in many types of people"; "to appreciate man's unique obligations to domestic animals." Some of these examples would have even more precise subcategories in the teacher's mind. By understanding one's own goals for children, and the behaviors that are related to the goals, it is possible to see where a parent's descriptions of behavior might be useful. And along with this understanding, the teacher should develop a real skill in the detective work of questioning.

Consider, for example, the sharpness that is missing in questions like "Does he eat well at home?" or "Is Jimmy tolerant of others?" or "Does Jimmy enjoy school?" While these are not necessarily poor questions, and they may serve quite well as warm-up questions, it is clear that more probing will probably be needed before the discussion gets around to some of the specific behaviors from which the teacher gets clues to the real needs of the child and the real effects of his instruction.

For the teacher needs to know, at the appropriate moment, whether Jimmy's behavior at the dentist's office or at the dinner table has any relationship to the health curriculum, whether the way he treats the Hennesseys' dog or chooses the children for his birthday party is influenced by some of the social studies lessons, whether the attitudes he reveals to his parents about the science fair or his recent flop as a committee chairman are similar to his apparent reactions in the school. These and other clues can be of inestimable value to a teacher. Many parents are sufficiently observant, articulate, and interested to provide such details with little prompting. The difference between getting or not getting these details from other kinds of parents is, as often as not, to be found in the command a teacher has of the details in his work.

It should not be overlooked that teachers also have a number of ways to obtain information about the child's home life and behavior directly from the child. An example would be a written exercise in which the child is asked, "Tell us a story about what happened to you this morning at breakfast time."

Other principles involved in the process of obtaining information from the home will emerge as we discuss the reverse process and the various ways in which parents and teachers are brought together in the interest of the child.

Information the home receives from the school

Every public school has the obligation to provide parents with three kinds of information about the individual child:

1. A complete and accurate picture of the child's own potentiality and the extent to which his progress in school measures up to that potential.
2. An approximate description of the relative standing of the child within his own class and his own school.
3. An approximate description of the way the child's potentiality and progress compare with other children of his age throughout the United States.

By far the most important of these three is the first. Unfortunately, it is also the most difficult. Much of the time, educators beg the first question by answering the second and third, assuming that these answers also cover the first. This practice is especially characteristic of school systems where the validity and usefulness of grade norms and of uniform expectancy standards are not questioned. It therefore deserves a close look.

Almost always when teachers attempt to compare a child's performance with the national population, this is done through standardized test data and similar indices of the "normal" as it has been defined at each age (grade) level. In a nation of some 50,000-plus school districts, each legally entitled to operate a distinctly unique educational program and with many cherishing the idea of the self-contained autonomous classroom, it is rather amazing that there should be such widespread dependency upon standardized tests. Even when we acknowledge that most school districts are not very different from the others in the broad, general structure of their curricula, it should be obvious that local emphases and variations in approach make it nearly impossible to make valid comparisons between any two school systems (or even any two classrooms) on the basis of a given standardized test. Nonetheless, we assume that such comparisons are reasonable and proceed accordingly. Therefore some children sit at their desks every now and then to be tested and respond to questions, a large proportion of which may as well be printed in classical Arabic for all their relevance to what goes on the rest of the year for them. It is no secret that some other children spend a good part of the year specifically preparing for the tests, which in the teacher's mind may be the best available description of his course of study.

Whether or not this is too strong a charge, the fact remains that it is doubtful that teachers learn very much, except in a very broad sense, about the progress of a child when they depend upon standardized tests for the evidence. They *do* see in a rough way how his overall progress pattern compares with other American children, but this is more useful over a period of years than it is at any one moment. This being the case, the disclosure to parents of exact scores or grade equivalents is a rather foolish, if not fraudulent, practice.

Data showing the relative standing of a child within his class are always of great interest to parents and are sometimes a useful index to the future position of the child within the school and even within the community. On the other hand, class rankings are at best subjective and are likely to change as conditions change. Teachers well know how parents can misunderstand and misuse information or impressions they receive of a child's class ranking. Frequently, too, classes have an uneven or unusual distribution of talent within them, so that a child who ranks at approximately the middle of one class on an arithmetic-computation exercise might actually rank somewhat above or below the middle in terms of the entire community population or some more average group with which he might be compared. The school staff should therefore be extremely careful not to create wrong impressions in the minds of parents with regard to the relative rank of a child within a class, or for that matter regarding the school's own interest in the establishment of such rankings. One way of avoiding such trouble is to discuss the child's relative position in a number of different categories: e.g., he is among the best spellers, but nearer the middle in arithmetic reasoning, and for the moment he is lagging behind the majority in developing a fluent writing style. This is better than saying "He tends to be an average student in the group," with no further elaboration.

Since the relative standing of the child in his class or within the national population is not a very desirable or accurate basis on which to describe his progress, we return to the position that an individualized picture is what must be given to the parent. How can this picture be given to parents? It would seem that this is a relatively simple task in some areas, if teachers will but take the time and the trouble to gather appropriate evidence.

In the area of handwriting, for example, it would be relatively easy for the school to provide parents with tangible evidence of the child's growth. Why not keep a permanent folder of handwriting samples, dated every few months throughout the child's elementary school career? Whether looseleaf or bound in some way, such a folder could be extremely useful to each succeeding teacher, and to the parent, in observing what happens to the child's ability to form letters and symbols over the years. In the folder could be kept a "handwriting measuring scale," either one that is commercially available or one locally prepared (the latter would be better, if the commercial scale uses graded norms). Here, too, could be kept a summary of the specific suggestions given the child (and the parents) at various times regarding needed handwriting improvements. Over the years, the folder might have a very positive effect upon the child's handwriting and upon the parents' understanding of the progress made. Eventually it could become a cherished family souvenir of the child's school experience, as well as a useful source of research data.

It can be seen that the foregoing idea has applicability to many other areas of the school curriculum. Selected and typical samples of the child's efforts in creative writing, in graphic art, in arithmetic computation and problem solving, and in other areas could serve not only as the basis for periodic review of his progress but also, in the aggregate, as a panoramic view of the child's total development. Too much of what a child does is lost forever in the school's and the family's records, partly because there exists no systematic means of retaining behavioral evidence.

Nor does evidence have to be restricted to what may appear on paper. The tape recorder and other forms of sound recording now make it possible to retain samples of a child's speech patterns, musical skills, and other sound-producing behavior. This is a relatively unexplored possibility partly because of the cost but chiefly because of its novelty. Considering that a two-hour tape can be purchased for only a few dollars, and that such a tape begun at the kindergarten level could record a decade or more of "sound behavior," it would seem that the cost factor is scarcely a real barrier.

These are only examples, but they show what might be done to arrange more effective longitudinal reporting. We now return to a consideration of how the data of pupil growth get into the record, some of the problems that arise as we communicate the data to parents, and some of the factors that influence the adequacy with which the teacher performs the reporting role.

The Reporting Process

How the process begins

The process of understanding and evaluating the child begins in the school's very first contacts with the family, in some cases even before the child begins nursery school, kindergarten, or the first primary year, as the case may be. To the teachers in the pre-school and in the primary there falls a special responsibility for building up the child's cumulative record folder and for acquiring vast amounts of information about the child as a learner and as a human being. To them, too, falls the special responsibility for interpreting these data to the eager, interested parent. Often the kindergarten teacher is the first adult in the child's experience who is able to view him objectively, and hence the parent's early conferences with the kindergarten teacher may afford the first real opportunity to acquire information about the child as others see him. Inevitably, this means that some parents will seek to confirm their belief that the child is unusually bright and has a distinguished future. For other parents, it may mean that deep insecurity about the child's normalcy or about his prospects of even marginal success will eventually reach the surface of discussion. The hopes, fears, and perceptions of many types of parents about all sorts of children will enter into the teachers' contacts with them; and to handle the many delicate problems that arise the teacher needs operating guidelines to follow.

We hold as a general rule for teachers to follow in the early years, that *it is wisest and safest to proceed slowly in arriving at judgments about a child's academic-social-physical-emotional potential, and to be cautious in sharing these judgments with parents.* For convenience in future reference, let us call this Rule A. It is based upon the belief that children arrive at school with such varying backgrounds and histories, and such differing motivations and means of expressing themselves, that it is almost impossible to be sure of their strengths and weaknesses after a mere year or two of association. The child who is initially glib, happy, and quick to respond to stimuli may be a future drudge who has come out of a highly verbal, school-oriented, nourishing home environment similar to that the teacher values. The youngster who answers a surprising number of the intelligence-test questions may have a copy of the test in his dresser at home. The child who sulks in the corner most of the day may simply be resentful that the school is interfering with some other valued experience, and after a year or two of emotional growth may become the star of the class. However bizarre these illustrations may seem at first glance, they are not particularly extraordinary, and they serve merely to confirm, as Buttercup sings so mysteriously in *Pinafore,* that "things are seldom what they seem."

The avoidance of judgmental statements in the early years, as commanded by Rule A, is by no means a technique for avoiding the reporting function. It is, rather, a prudent posture from which excellent reporting can be done. It seems not only safe, but sufficient, in the kindergarten and primary years to provide parents mostly with objective, descriptive statements regarding the child's work, progress, and problems. "Jimmy is now reading with fewer pauses for word recognition than several months back; he uses his 'free' time mostly in the library corner; he is sometimes chosen by the others for team captain or group leader; he is learning to write the more difficult letters (such as n, r, d, e) in less time; he reads music more accurately than most children, and always greets Miss Treble with a smile." These are more accurate and more useful than "Jimmy is doing well in reading; he loves to read storybooks; he is popular; his handwriting is getting better; and he seems to be gifted in music."

Over a period of time, all of the evidence presented in chiefly *descriptive* form will begin to take shape in the parents' and the teachers' minds as larger pictures of the child's strengths and weaknesses, of his uneven pace of development, and of his probable position in the academic hierarchy. As these pictures emerge, it becomes more defensible to sum them up in judgmental statements of apparent validity. While a diagram could scarcely present this concept with any claim to quantitative accuracy, perhaps the following picture, Figure 10, will serve to convey the general idea.

Reporting later progress

Having pointed out in Rule A that teachers should be extremely chary of labeling the general potential of children in the

114

Figure 10

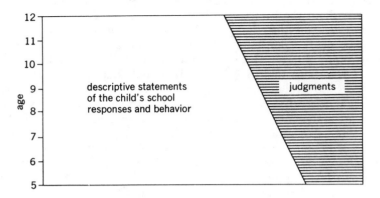

Content of reports to parents.

early years, we now propose a second rule which at first glance may appear to contradict the other. Rule B tells us: *Unless the school has discharged its obligation for complete and realistic reporting to the parent by the time the child is approximately 9 to 11 years of age, there is the very real possibility of trouble ahead.* "Complete and realistic" is intended in the foregoing sentence to be in harmony with Figure 10, implying that the relative minimization of judgmental statements need not detract from either the fullness or the clarity of the picture that is drawn for the parent.

Rule B recognizes that there is possible harm to the child and to the home-school relationship if the parents persist in believing that he has more or less potential than is indicated by the school. This is a point well understood by most teachers, especially in the case where parents expect too much. Whenever a child's potentiality is seen by teachers as essentially normal or average, the realization of this information may not be pleasant to the parents concerned, particularly if the parents have high ambitions for the child and are themselves academically oriented. In such cases, it may take several years before the school staff is able to convince the parent that average academic success is the best that may be expected, and it may take longer than that before pressures for impossible performance disappear. Children whose potential is below average sometimes face even sterner difficulties, and the teachers' reporting and communication problem may be equally serious.

One of the relatively common experiences of teachers and administrators is to be confronted, both publicly and privately, with the charge that the school has withheld the truth (to wit, the bad news that a child is doing poorly) from the parent. Usually, the charge includes the lament, "and now it's too late for us to do something about it." Rule B is intended to prevent this charge from being made in the future.

Let us consider the possible explanations why this charge might be made against the school. The child is in the sixth grade, and is doing poorly. The parent protests that this is the first time he has even been told that the child's potential is low. In this case, four possible explanations come to mind: (1) there has been a sudden shift in the child's pattern that both the home and school failed to anticipate; (2) the parent is misrepresenting the facts, itself a possible indication of the school's failure to communicate; (3) he is telling the truth, which may be an indication of either cowardice or ignorance on the part of the kindergarten or primary staff; or (4) he is holding stubbornly to an unwholesome illusion or dream about the child that the school has thus far been unsuccessful in destroying. None of these is a satisfactory explanation as far as the school is concerned, but the one the school ought to be most fearful of is number (3). Rule B tells teachers to be neither cowardly nor careless, and above all that they must be thorough.

Incidentally, it would be possible to describe the reverse of the foregoing problem while illustrating the same principles. A parent might claim to have discovered, late in the elementary grades, that his child has more ability than he has been using and developing. Rule B tells us that this also should never happen.

Other dimensions of the reporting process

In the beginning of this chapter we acknowledged that reporting is essentially an administrative matter, and it was implied that other aspects of instructional service to the child are more central to the major work of the teacher. Curriculum planning, actual teaching, and the process of evaluation are major functions as contrasted with reporting. We have described the great importance of good school-home communication and in the foregoing section have indicated how sensitive, even explosive, the question of reporting can be in the lives of both parents and teachers. We pause now to consider certain other dimensions of the reporting problem.

First, the need for reporting serves as a stimulant to better curriculum planning. It helps to keep the teacher on his toes, alert to many aspects of a child's development that might otherwise be overlooked. It helps him to remember the family circumstances that bear so importantly on the child's school achievement. It provides a special incentive to focus his mind upon the over-all needs of the child, and to set aside special times when his progress story is summarized. In brief, it compels the teacher to reveal to others how well he knows each child and how well he goes about planning the child's school experiences; and by exposing his competency to the public it serves as an incentive to do his best. It is therefore probable that the teacher learns more about his pupils because the reporting system demands that he acquire this knowledge, than he would if he were under no particular obligation to reveal such knowledge. This knowledge then becomes a part of the professional record and an additional basis for teaching decisions. The result must be better teaching. *The reporting that teachers do to themselves is at least as important as the reporting teachers do to parents,* and the latter is frequently a stimulant to the former.

Another value of the reporting process is that it serves to provide parents with valuable information about broader matters than their own children's growth. Much of what is done in the name of reporting pupil progress is actually concerned with public relations or even parent education. Parents frequently have no adequate factual basis for understanding the progress of the child as the school sees it, and preliminary to discussion of the specific youngster's work is the need for understanding the school's aims and practices. Sometimes a relatively extraneous matter, such as the school bus schedule or the absence of a lunchroom or a vague misgiving about the school's policies on Valentine exchanges, is more prominent in a parent's mind at conference time than the germane facts about Junior's schoolwork. The efforts of teachers to untangle these problems, or to bring about better parent understanding of the broad aims of the school, should not be charged off to the reporting function even though they become enmeshed with it.

The way a report card or report form is designed and phrased is in itself a vehicle for parent education, as are the handbooks, bulletins, study groups, speeches, and other devices used to explain what the schools are trying to do. Similarly, face-to-face contacts between parents and teachers can in many ways be an effective means of parent education.

Alternative methods of reporting

A group of teachers preparing to launch a nongraded primary unit in Vestal, New York, sent questionnaires to 43 school systems which are using or have used a nongraded plan. Twenty-seven responses were received and summarized.[6] Regarding the types of reports to parents in use in these communities, conferences were

---

[6] Maurie Hillson, "The Analysis of the Questionnaire on the Ungraded Primary," a report to the Clayton Avenue Study Group on Individual Differences (New York, Vestal Central School, New York, 1958), 16 pp. Dittographed.

named by 18 systems, letters to parents by three, a report card using numerical or letter grades by six. Eight of the communities reported the use of various combinations of the foregoing. Similar studies of reporting procedures in graded schools over the country likewise show that there is a great deal of variation in practice. It is therefore desirable to review the various alternative approaches in use.

While there are many different approaches to the reporting process, they have a great deal in common with each other and in the final analysis they are differentiated primarily by (a) whether they present much or little information, (b) whether they are presented unilaterally on paper, or through two-way face-to-face contact, and (c) whether they are done skillfully and accurately. As a general rule, a unilateral paper approach employing symbols (e.g., 93, 85, 77, 69; A, B, C, D, F; S-I-U; 1-2-3-4) tends to present little information by its very structure; whereas a face-to-face conference inevitably involves the exchange of hundreds if not thousands of words. Therefore it becomes evident at the outset that the traditional comparison of "report cards vs. parent conferences" is an unfair (or at least limited) one and does not provide an adequate basis for judging the merits of various procedures. These means should be examined in terms of the underlying problems and principles involved in their use, and the limitations or advantages thereby revealed.

The report card based upon a comparative marking system was at one time the predominant mechanism for reporting pupil progress, although supplementary reports in the form of teachers' comments, notes, letters, personal interviews and conferences, and other exchanges of information have always been used to a certain extent. There is little need to document at this point the gradual disillusionment of parents and teachers with the comparative marking system itself, and the corollary movement toward more useful and realistic means of conveying progress information to parents. The classic statement on the competitive marking system by Snygg and Combs [7] remains useful as a commentary on the devastating effect the system can have on personality development. A more recent study by Otto and others [8] indicates that children are motivated by many more things than the marking or reporting system used, that a compara-

[7] Donald Snygg and Arthur W. Combs, *Individual Behavior* (New York, Harper and Brothers, 1949), pp. 223-5.

[8] Henry J. Otto, Melvin A. Bowden, M. Vere Devault, Joseph J. Kotrlik, and James A. Turman, *Four Methods of Reporting to Parents*, Bureau of Laboratory Schools Publication No. 7 (Austin, The University of Texas, 1957), pp. x + 247. See especially pages 222-35 for discussion of children's motivations and competitive reporting systems.

tive marking system is an inadequate and unsatisfactory device for motivating children, and that the removal of such a system by no means eliminates the element of competition in children's school lives.

Many authors remind us that not only the marking system, but the validity of the marks themselves, is open to question. Otto points out "the complicating fact that teachers' marks are influenced by many factors other than achievement, such as pupil behavior and cleanliness." [9] Indeed, the extent to which extraneous or irrelevant factors enter into teachers' marking decisions may be exceedingly great. Battle [10] carried on a study involving 24 matched pairs of high school students and six teachers of four major subjects. The students sorted 90 coded items on values (religious, economic, political, aesthetic, social, hedonistic, physical, ethical, and theoretical), placing them in the relative order in which they were cherished by themselves. The teachers sorted the same cards in terms of the "pattern of cherishment" they would consider ideal for the pupils. The study confirmed with reasonable confidence the hypothesis that when pupils of similar aptitude, age, and sex are related to particular teachers, the value patterns of those who receive good marks in a particular subject tend to have higher correlation with value patterns considered ideal by the teachers who determine the marks than do the patterns of pupils who receive low marks in the subject.[11] A similar result was obtained when the pupils were related to a group of teachers, and when pupils were related to teachers and to other pupils simultaneously. Reflecting on these results, Battle comments, "it seems reasonable to conclude that in determining school marks the teacher expresses bias in favor of the pupil who tends to have a pattern of values similar to the teacher's ideal.[12]

Such studies as these tend to destroy whatever basis may remain in teachers' minds for adhering to the prevalent grading and reporting system. They show that it is both unwise and unprofitable for schools to emphasize competitive and comparative marks as a stimulant to pupil production and to use these marks as the chief basis for reports to parents. There is also plenty of evidence to suggest that parents agree with this view and are generally receptive to plans based on sounder and broader principles.

The comparative marking system is based upon grade-level-

---

[9] *Ibid.*, p. 217.

[10] Haron James Battle, *Application of Inverted Analysis in Study of the Relation Between Values and Achievement of High School Pupils* (unpublished doctoral dissertation, Department of Education, The University of Chicago, 1954), pp. vii + 113.

[11] *Ibid.*, p. 58.

[12] *Ibid.*, p. 66.

expectancy standards and upon the child's rank in his class in terms of those standards. It would of course be possible to report this information by means of a written statement, or in a face-to-face conference, and presumably such a report could have far greater meaning than an A-B-C-D-F report card because of the greater elaboration which would be entailed. Such a report, however, would still suffer from the limitations and inadequacy of the principles upon which it was based. There is no necessary correlation between the use of a conference approach and the abandonment of grade-level-expectancy standards. Therefore when teachers speak of plans based on "sounder and broader principles," they must be careful not to imply that the principles are inherent in the mechanism of reporting. While the principles may find expression through the mechanism, or through several mechanisms, they remain separate.

A mechanism somewhat related to the A-B-C-D-F report, and its nearly obsolete sister the percentage (93;85;77;69) system, is the symbolic report in which the child's performance is measured against his own presumed ability. A symbol "S" (for satisfactory) may be used to indicate that the child is doing as well as can reasonably be expected, a U (unsatisfactory) or an N (needs to improve) or some similar symbol when he is not. Sometimes there is included an O (outstanding) or an H (honors) or some other exalted symbol when the teacher wishes to offer special praise or commendation. The symbol I is used to indicate "improving"; and this plan is frequently called the S-I-U reporting plan in the literature. Along with the A-B-C-D-F report, the S-I-U was one of four methods examined by Otto and others [13] in a study confirming the general professional opinion that the S-I-U plan is basically sound and popular, but leaves parents inadequately informed on the *relative* standing of their child among his agemates. Again, it may be noted that a face-to-face or detailed written report based upon the philosophical and psychological premises of the S-I-U report card could be far more informative than the other but still fail to provide the additional dimension of comparative information.

A system somewhat similar to the foregoing is one in which the numbers 1 (rapid progress), 2 (satisfactory progress), 3 (acceptable progress), and 4 (little or no progress) are used to denote the kind of growth a child is making in the various curriculum areas and categories of school behavior described on a card. Some school systems use this type of report in combination with relatively detailed statements written by the teacher.

It would be difficult to recount all the variations of the "rating sheet" device that can be found in fairly common use. Based upon

---

[13] Otto *et al., op. cit.,* see pp. 35-7, 209, 212-13.

either a comparative scale or a scale applicable only to the child's own capabilities, such devices range from those asking questions (answered "yes" or "no") to those describing the child's position on various continua of behavior or achievement (e.g., consistently pays attention; usually pays attention; tends not to pay attention; never pays attention). It should be noted that although such checklists are sometimes used as a school-to-home reporting device alone, it is perhaps more common for them to be used as one basis for a face-to-face discussion.

The narrative report from teacher to parent, whether as a separate technique or in association with a symbolic or checklist report, is a widely supported means of communicating pupil progress. Sometimes the school system prescribes a certain amount of structure for such letters, as for example, a printed form on which there are large spaces for comments in specified categories. At the other extreme, the teacher may simply write a letter following his own impulses entirely. Customarily, of course, a carbon copy of the letter is retained in the child's file. The chief characteristic of the narrative approach is that it is extremely flexible and allows the teacher to provide a great deal of useful information within the context he chooses to construct for the parent. Among its limitations are that some teachers are less fluent (and even less literate) than others; that letters are very costly of teacher time and effort (especially when clerical services are limited); that teachers are frequently reluctant to say negative things on paper; and that teachers may omit references to things that would ordinarily be included if a checklist were on hand as a reminder.

The personal note or letter, as opposed to the official narrative report, undoubtedly plays an important part in the reporting system but usually represents an extra rather than a regular service. Letters occur at such irregular and unpredictable times that it is customary to think of them more as public-relations than as reporting devices.

The "group letter" (a letter, mimeographed or dittoed, sent to all parents) is a practical device used by some teachers for communicating with parents. One school, described by Hardy,[14] uses group letters for a variety of purposes, including the raising of questions to help prepare for parent-teacher conferences; describing plans that are underway for a new unit in one of the classrooms, and inviting suggestions and comments; suggesting activities that might be carried on in the home as a supplement to classroom lessons; introducing a teacher's general plans for the year, or describing some of the specific goals the teacher has in mind; dis-

---

[14] Charlotte Hardy, "Communicating with Parents by Letter," *The National Elementary Principal*, 37 (September 1957), pp. 233-38.

cussing the social structure and the social learnings of the group; or summing up the progress that has been made over the term or year. It is noted that sometimes a group letter may be designed to help a particular parent or small group of parents with a problem by commenting upon it without identifying the affected parents directly.[15] While it is apparent that the group letter also falls into the category of public relations as readily as the category of reporting, it can serve as an excellent source of information about the children's school experiences as seen by the teacher, and also gives the parents an additional insight into the professional and personal character of the teacher. It seems reasonable to assert that for this reason, if no other, the group letter may well be a means of hastening the development of mutual understanding between the home and the school.

There are several different devices in the category of face-to-face reporting procedures. The most common of these is the parent-teacher conference conducted in the school building, routinely by advance appointment, with the teacher giving general direction to the conversation. Conferences conducted in the home are another means of face-to-face reporting.

The home visit is a relatively little-used device, however, despite the many obvious advantages of such visits. Notably, it serves as a means of enabling teachers to obtain a fuller and more accurate picture of the child's home environment and the family's make-up which in turn may make it easier to understand the child and his needs. It also offers a certain convenience to the parent, since many find it difficult to leave the home for conferences, and others feel less comfortable in the school building than in the security of their own home. But there are also some hazards in home visits, one of which is that a minority of parents regard them as an invasion of privacy or at least an intrusion. Sometimes, too, teachers encounter awkward or embarrassing situations during home visits.[16] On the whole, however, it would seem that much could be gained by a general increase in the use of this method of meeting and talking with parents.

Racine, Wisconsin, uses home visitations in grades 1-6 during the third and fourth weeks of school in the fall. In the teachers' handbook on reporting pupil progress, there is a three-page mimeographed section affording information on purposes, time and scheduling, procedures, and methods of recording home visits. It

---

[15] *Ibid.*, p. 237.

[16] An amusing story of a teacher who was offered a bottle of beer and wondered whether or not to accept it is told by Harl R. Douglass in "Why Visit the Homes?" *The National Elementary Principal*, 37 (September 1957), pp. 242-3.

emphasizes that "we are not prying into home affairs which do not concern us, but . . . we are anxious to understand the backgrounds of our children and to establish with parents warm and friendly relations which will help us to do the best job with the children. Most parents will welcome an opportunity to talk to teachers on this basis." [17]

That parents *do* feel this way is well supported by the relatively few studies that have been made about parent reactions to reporting systems. It seems to be especially true in communities where the nongraded organization pattern has been in operation. In Austin's study,[18] involving 915 parents in a community where the parent-teacher conference is the principal vehicle for reporting progress, 31 per cent of the families indicated the belief that home visits should be given increased emphasis. While this raises many questions, not the least of which is the administrative problem of time, it represents a recommendation worth more serious consideration.

The parent-teacher conference conducted in the school, it is safe to say, *is the approach most universally advocated in the current literature on reporting, and* beyond that *is probably the most fruitful and effective single means available.* This is not to advocate its exclusive use but rather to indicate its relative superiority. Many of its advantages have already been described or implied previously. Among them are the freedom of both parties to ask questions and to offer more adequate explanations. Illustrations and examples can be reviewed in detail; misunderstandings can be clarified at the time they arise; the comparative-competitive elements of the report can be reduced to their proper perspective, in effect submerged in the broader and more important data under discussion; and the parent and the teacher can get to know each other as colleagues, possibly even as friends.

On the negative side are the obvious administrative problems, answers to some of which appear later in the chapter. There is the difficulty that some parents, especially the fathers and the working mothers, either cannot or will not take the time for conferences. Some of the same limitations noted for the narrative report are involved, including occasional lack of verbal (and even social) skill on the part of teachers. One of the most serious drawbacks of conferences, however, has been that teachers sometimes do not know their pupils as well as they ought, and such shortcomings are more

---

[17] Racine Public Schools, Division of Instructional Services, "Reporting Pupil Progress: Teachers Handbook, Second and Third Grades" (Racine, Wisconsin, undated), p. 3.

[18] Kent C. Austin, *The Ungraded Primary Unit in Public Elementary Schools of the United States* (unpublished doctoral thesis, University of Colorado, 1957).

likely to be evident to parents as they meet and talk with teachers than if they merely sit at home and puzzle over the symbols on a piece of paper.

Another difficulty with face-to-face discussions is that they lead teachers and parents more rapidly into consideration of intimate details than do the less personal and less complete forms of communication. Sometimes there is the danger that a parent will allow himself to volunteer more information than he intended to upon arrival, and then regret his impulsiveness. Sometimes the teacher will precipitate discussion of intimate matters by his questioning procedure. There is a fairly serious hazard involved, possibly resulting in alienation of the parent, when a conference leads into questions of the child's emotional problems and, sometimes inevitably, of the family's home life. It may be that too many teachers nowadays venture into the role of the highly trained therapist or analyst without an adequate awareness of the harm they may do by getting beyond their depth. Nearly all such instances probably stem from the best intentions on the teacher's part, and a strong desire to be of maximum help on the problems of the child and the family. The increasing tendency of school people to approach these problems has apparently cost much goodwill and even the confidence of school patrons.

A recent commentator on this problem pointed out that "more and more, at least in 'sophisticated' school circles, we hear the comment that parent-teacher conferences nowadays too often take on the aspect of psychiatric counseling sessions. Parents have complained that they come away from a school interview with very little idea of how Jackie or Julie is getting along with reading or social studies. But they have an ample supply of adjectives describing the child's behavior and a definite feeling of having themselves been 'sized up' and evaluated in analytical terms." [19] To the extent that this feeling may be widespread, there is much room for reappraisal not only of teachers' conference techniques and behavior, but of the very purposes of the conferences as seen by the teachers.

That teachers will vary considerably in their approach, in their insight, in their ability to communicate, and in discretion is of course self-evident. Maves reports a study,[20] based on an analysis of sixty tape-recorded conferences, indicating that both teachers and parents could be separated into "high-level" and "low-level" performers in conference situations. Some of the factors associated with high

---

[19] Dorothy Barclay, "When Teachers Grade Home Life," *The New York Times Magazine,* November 24, 1957, p. 69.

[20] Harold J. Maves, "Contrasting Levels of Performance in Parent-Teacher Conferences," *Elementary School Journal, 58* (January 1958), pp. 219-24.

performance were the establishment of rapport, use of specific illustrative incidents and of samples of the children's work, evidence of planning for the child's future development, and use of commendation of children. One of the negative factors was "direct, inept questioning which fails to elicit responses from the parents and leaves the teacher in the dominant role." [21]

With the realization that there are weaknesses or hazards involved in almost any reporting system in use, we may properly ask what would be the best procedure, or combination of procedures, to follow? In the final chapter of their study, Otto [22] and his colleagues offer one plausible answer. "The salient feature of an adequate reporting plan," they say, "should be the individual parent-teacher conference. The general consensus is that there should be at least two regularly scheduled conferences each year, these to be supplemented with other conferences as needed for individual cases." [23] They go on to recommend intervening written reports (checklists or notes) two to four times a year, and state that, since the conference is certain to provide the necessary comparative information, these written reports "can and should be different from the conventional report card using the symbols of a comparative marking system." [24] Such an answer, expanded to include the occasional use of home visits, may well represent the expression of an ideal for which all school systems might strive.

Presumably the school will take parents' preferences and needs into account in any effort to establish a reporting program approximating the ideal just described. Before they can expect to achieve this goal, however, the schools must expend much time, energy, and money on the in-service training of the teachers and in the provision of an administrative environment conducive to top-quality reporting.

In-service training in reporting techniques

Reporting is one of the most complex and important functions of the teacher, and it deserves prominent attention both in the pre-service training a prospective teacher receives in the college, and in the program of professional study that is conducted by the employing school system. In every school there should be frequent attention paid, not only to informing the teachers of prevailing philosophy and practice in reporting, but to the broad, professional

---

[21] *Ibid.*, p. 224.

[22] Otto *et al.*, *op. cit.*, pp. 201-36.

[23] *Ibid.*, p. 213.

[24] *Ibid.*, p. 214.

issues involved. School-home communication is one topic that should always have some current meaning for a local school staff.

Teachers rarely cease to need help in the techniques of reporting, especially if they are regularly engaged in any form of written or face-to-face reporting. Many systems, aware of the teachers' need for help in planning and conducting parent-teacher conferences, for example, have devoted a great deal of time, energy, and material within the in-service program to this problem. The subject of conferences and reporting is often included in teachers' workshops and meetings. Handbooks and bulletins, containing recommendations on conference and reporting techniques, are frequently issued to teachers.

Sometimes sociodrama (or at least, role-playing in "mock conferences" or other demonstrations of actual practice) is employed as a means of imparting conference skills and ideas to teachers, especially those new to the system. In Park Forest, for example, it is customary for several veterans to stage a series of make-believe conferences during the preschool workshop for newly employed teachers. The parent roles are varied, ranging from cooperative and friendly parents to those whose attitudes or difficulties pose a complicated problem for a teacher conducting a conference with them. Interestingly, the veteran teachers who engage in the role-playing have frequently reported that they acquired new sympathy for the parents' viewpoint as a result of their "performance." In other communities, tape-recorded conferences are heard and discussed in teachers' workshops.

There are, of course, a number of other ways that the mechanics of conducting a conference can be demonstrated to teachers unfamiliar with the approach. Fortunately, teacher-training institutions themselves are doing a more thorough job on the conference method, and are arranging for student teachers to have some experience with face-to-face progress reporting, so that many new teachers are now better prepared to conduct conferences.

Written guides for parent-teacher conferences vary tremendously in their nature and quality from school system to school system. Among the best guides we have seen is that furnished teachers in the elementary schools of River Forest, Illinois. Among its features are an outline of the values of the conference for the child; emphasis upon the confidential nature of the conference method, and hence upon the school's obligation to be as forthright and informative as possible; emphasis upon the virtues of the teacher being a good listener in conferences; ideas for writing up the conference report; advice to avoid reporting information in the personal-social area about which the parents can probably do nothing, or which would be so threatening that communication would be very difficult; advice to use descriptive rather than judgmental statements in problem areas; and a section with sample comments dealing with various typical personal-social problems of children.

One of the most elaborate and useful manuals prepared for the guidance of classroom teachers in reporting pupil progress is the "Report Card Manual" issued in Van Dyke, Michigan. Looseleaf and joined with paper fasteners, this manual includes mimeographed pages of instructions and suggestions, along with samples of forms used and guides to other sources of help. Excellently organized and skillfully reflecting the school system's basic aims in its reporting program, the manual features seven pages of "sample comments" which suggest positive, analytical, and encouraging ways that teachers can phrase their remarks about children's habits, progress in subject matter, special abilities, and school attendance.

Another community with a strong history of in-service development activities, where teachers are given excellent support in reporting pupil progress through handbooks on the topic, is Racine, Wisconsin. Racine's reporting system includes home visits in grades 1-6 during the third and fourth weeks of school; report cards in grades K-6 twice during the year and again at the close of the year; and parent-teacher conferences in grades K-6 during the middle of the school year. Handbooks on "Reporting Pupil Progress" are issued to teachers, and these include a pocket for sample forms as well as separate mimeographed sections on each of the three types of reporting that are used.

It has been noted that where face-to-face contacts are the primary means of reporting, the need teachers have for reinforcement in technique is especially great. The more experience a school system and its personnel have with the conference technique, and the stronger its over-all relationships with parents have been over the years, the more likely it is to have worked out a solid and efficient system such as that of River Forest.

Previous descriptions [25] of that system in the literature have emphasized the importance of parent support, of continuous study and adaptation at the staff level, and of keeping the welfare of the child as the central purpose of any reporting system. Teachers operating within such a climate tend to develop many sources of strength and help for dealing with difficult problems. Examples are two brief

[25] Wallace E. Sugden, "Continuous Study Is Necessary," *Childhood Education, 24* (February 1948), pp. 277-79.

Wallace E. Sugden, "Co-operative Planning for Developing an Achievement Record," *Elementary School Journal, 47* (June 1947), pp. 571-74.

Robert H. Anderson and Edward R. Steadman, "Pupils' Reactions to a Reporting System," *Elementary School Journal, 51* (November 1950), pp. 136-42.

dittographed bulletins produced in River Forest by a committee on mental health, one on "How I Try to Help Children Who Are Overly Aggressive in their Behavior" and another on "How I Try to Help the Shy Child." While not directly intended to influence teacher behavior in parent conferences, these bulletins are in effect a useful tool to the teacher as she prepares to confer with the parents of children who fall in the aforementioned categories.

The local system need not depend upon in-service guides developed locally to help its staff acquire skill and insight in reporting techniques. A number of very helpful publications [26] are available on the topic, and can serve as the basis for in-service study and discussion. The administrator should see that they are available and devise means for calling pertinent ideas and suggestions to the attention of the staff.

Enabling Teachers to Evaluate, Record, and Report

If teachers are expected to carry out extensive programs of evaluating pupil progress, recording and analyzing evidence of change, and reporting in full detail to parents and the school officials, then means must be found for helping them to fit such tasks into their crowded work schedules. One teacher in River Forest has estimated that the conference procedure requires, on the average: 45 minutes for writing up the conference material; 30 minutes for a preliminary conference with the child; minimum of 30 minutes for the conference with the parent; and 15 minutes for writing in comments after the conference. Multiplied by the number of pupils involved, at least twice a year, this results in a sizable number of hours. If parents want complete reporting, as assuredly they do, then public officials and school administrators must insure that teachers have the time, the training, and the resources to do the job. In some communities, where enlightened leadership has persuaded the community to keep pace with the school's service needs, this will not prove to be a difficult task. In places where the community is still trying to run a comprehensive, up-to-date program

---

[26] See, for example:

Grace Langdon and Irving W. Stout, *Teacher-Parent Interviews* (New York, Prentice-Hall, Inc., 1954), pp. xii + 356.

Association for Supervision and Curriculum Development, *Reporting Is Communicating: An Approach to Evaluation and Marking* (Washington, D.C., the Association, 1956), pp. vi + 57.

Katherine E. D'Evelyn, "Good Techniques for Conferencing," *Childhood Education, 32* (November 1955), pp. 119-21.

Nora Weckler, "Problems in Organizing Parent-Teacher Conferences," *California Journal of Elementary Education, 24* (November 1955), pp. 117-26.

within the general budgetary and staffing framework of the early 1900's, however, it may take a massive effort.

This effort will involve the provision of several separate but related services. One of them is the availability to the teacher of adequate leadership and consultant services. In the authors' opinion an adequate staffing policy would provide a full-time principal (or equivalent assistant) for every 12-14 teachers; a guidance specialist for every 600 children; qualified consultants or co-workers in such areas as remedial reading and special education; and a central research and supervisory staff capable of resolving complicated questions of procedure and strategy. Also needed is adequate secretarial service for the school: a full-time secretary for the principal, plus an additional half-time person for every five teachers above a minimum figure, let us say, of eight. Indeed, these may be conservative figures in view of all the current interest in teacher aides, clerical aides, instructional secretaries, and other forms of nonprofessional support.

The use of paid nonprofessional assistants in elementary schools has received a great deal of attention in recent years. Stemming in part from the shortage of teachers and in part from recognition of the fact that present-day teachers necessarily engage in many routine clerical and administrative tasks that might be done by assistants with less training, a number of efforts have been made to include such assistants in the school personnel structure. Probably the best known of these efforts has been the Cooperative Study for the Better Utilization of Teacher Competencies, in Bay City, Michigan. The 1955 report [27] of this study includes a great deal of detail stemming from job analysis and time studies of teaching, and also descriptions of the numerous duties carried out by the teacher aides. Another publication in which there is extremely useful discussion of the professional tasks of the teacher, and of the nature and distribution of the elementary teacher's work, is the 1954-55 report of the Yale-Fairfield Study of Elementary Teaching.[28] These and similar studies promise to shed much light on the broad range of duties for which teachers are now commonly held responsible, and the extent to which it is feasible and desirable to delegate or share them with other adults.

[27] *A Cooperative Study for the Better Utilization of Teacher Competencies.* Second Printed Report, 1955 (Mount Pleasant, Michigan, Central Michigan College, 1955), 32 pp.

[28] *Yale-Fairfield Study of Elementary Teaching. Report for 1954-55,* Clyde M. Hill, ed. (New Haven, Connecticut, February 1956), pp. xiv + 321. Also available in an abridged edition prepared by Burton P. Fowler (New York, The Fund for the Advancement of Education, 1956), 141 pp. A more recent report of the Yale-Fairfield Study, entitled *Teacher Assistants,* was published in July 1958.

In Bay City and in Flint, Michigan,[29] aides are used in situations where an unusually large number of students are in the charge of a teacher or group of teachers. A teacher receives assistance from an aide, for instance, when she works with a class approximately twice the "normal" group in size (50-60 children); or a team of two teachers plus a teacher aide may deal with 96-100 children in three adjoining classrooms. The "Norwalk Plan," introduced in four elementary schools of Norwalk, Connecticut in September of 1958, is another team plan in which a nonprofessional teacher aide assists two teachers (one known as team leader, the other as cooperating teacher) in their work with 75 to 85 pupils.

Somewhat different approaches are in use in other places where secretarial aides are provided. One of these is Davidson County, Tennessee, where an experiment is being conducted in the use of instructional secretaries.[30] Each secretary serves approximately seven teachers, each working with class groups average in size. In the Franklin School in Lexington, Massachusetts, a project in team-teaching includes the provision of 80 hours' weekly secretarial service to a staff of eighteen teachers, working with about 480 children. A number of other schools with average class sizes have reinforced their school-secretarial staff in recent years in an effort to relieve teachers of certain bookkeeping, materials-preparation, and record-keeping tasks; and in some cases they have added part-time or full-time secretaries whose chief duties are to type conference reports and other progress records for the teachers.

Not only secretarial assistance per se, but various means of reducing the difficulty of routine tasks will be needed. While it may be straying afield from the specific mission of this volume to suggest that many "duties" (such as collecting for charity drives, selling milk and meal tickets, serving as unpaid bank tellers) of today's teacher ought to be eliminated, it is undoubtedly pertinent to suggest that the paperwork and clerical tasks associated with reporting could be simplified. For one thing, reporting forms could be redesigned and printed in such a way that they are easier to complete. Some districts (an example is Corona, California) have their progress reports printed in multiple copies with inexpensive, single-use carbon paper inserted, with copies arranged so that the same basic form can be supplemented in subsequent periods. Where a carbon copy of a report remains in the school's hands, laborious

---

[29] See "The Teacher Aide Experiments in the Flint Public Schools" (Flint, Michigan, April 1958). 16 pp. Multilithed.

[30] See George Peabody College for Teachers, The First General Planning Conference, August 13-15, 1957. Peabody-Public School Cooperative Program, p. 52. See Appendix C, "An Experiment in the Use of Instructional Secretaries," pp. 14-20.

transposition of marks and comments onto another permanent record can be eliminated.

It would also seem reasonable that, in a day when virtually every college graduate has some competence on the typewriter, a typewriter should be available to each teacher. At one time when postwar government-surplus equipment became available to schools at virtually no cost, Park Forest was able to provide almost every teacher with a typewriter. The administrators noticed with interest that this led not only to an increase in the quantity of information included in written progress reports, but to some heightening of teacher morale during the busy reporting periods.

Similarly, teachers can make good use of other labor-saving equipment. Adding machines with tapes make it easier to calculate and to verify attendance and other statistics that go into reports. Tape recorders and dictating machines make it easier for teachers to get some of their progress summaries, letters or reports to parents, and recollections of children's work and behavior into the record. Only a very few school systems have attempted to make such equipment available to teachers, whereas in industry and in other professions these aids are in very common use.

Space is another necessary feature of a good progress-reporting system, especially where face-to-face conferences are involved. Private or semi-private work areas where teachers can retire to concentrate upon their paperwork are quite frequently provided in modern schools. Suitable and comfortable space in which private conferences with parents can be conducted, however, is more rarely available. Some of the Park Forest schools are provided with small, attractive "conference rooms" for the express purpose of enabling teachers and parents to talk together in comfort and privacy. These are located in the administrative suite, so that the school secretary may serve as a receptionist and so that the office waiting room is also at hand. Other schools provide an attractive lounge, sometimes known as the "parents room," where conferences may be held. The larger the school, the more likely it is that two or more such spaces are needed, so that more than one conference can be scheduled at one time.

Another, even greater, need is time for conferences. Here the prevailing practice is either to designate certain after-school time, to dismiss school for all or part of a day during conference weeks, or to provide substitute teachers for those who are holding conferences within the regular school day.

In Shorewood, Wisconsin, for example, the Board of Education has authorized 2:30 P.M. dismissals on a total of eighteen days a year, in regularly scheduled blocks of time, so that conferences may be held between 2:30 and 4:30 P.M.[31] Since conferences are usually a half-hour in length, this arrangement makes possible a fairly large number of conferences in a year's time. The plan is typical of many that are found in elementary schools using the conference system. It involves a "compromise" on the source of time, taken partly out of the normal teaching schedule and partly out of the teacher's own time. Dismissing school early certain afternoons is generally more popular with parents than procedures which call off school for an entire afternoon or even an entire day for conference purposes. It is also less likely to run afoul of the attendance laws in many states, where a "day" must be a certain length (usually four hours) for state-aid and other legal purposes.

Included among the many arrangements and forms of help that a teacher needs in order to do a good job of reporting the child's progress is the provision of an adequate, historical record of the child from the time of his first association with the school.

The child's permanent school record

The cumulative record folder ought to include every fact and statistic related to the child's history and background, in which the school has an interest. Since it also serves certain legal, administrative, and documentary purposes outside the classroom teacher's immediate concerns, it will inevitably become a fairly bulky folder unless some means can be found for simplifying central records. If a school system makes a consistent effort to gather this evidence together, it is probable that the folders will become quite bulky after a while. It may even reach a point where teachers are discouraged from handling and reading the great mass of available material. It is therefore appropriate to have a periodic housecleaning of the folders, with an eye to removing all but the most relevant and useful contents. Materials of lesser usefulness may be either set aside in a central storage area, or destroyed altogether. Folders should not be allowed to become so full of paper that they become a storage problem for the teacher. Some schools keep two cumulative folders for each child, one complete folder kept in the principal's office and one streamlined folder in which are kept materials most likely to be needed by the teacher in her day-to-day work with the child. While this requires additional secretarial work, it can be minimized by the use of extra carbon copies as often as necessary.

Many cumulative folders have places for photographs, and it is helpful to add a picture approximately every two years. The names

---

[31] Louis Romano, "Finding Out What Parents Want to Know," *Elementary School Journal, 58* (November 1957), p. 89.

of all family members, with birthdates of siblings, should be occasionally rechecked by means of a follow-up records questionnaire. This inquiry should include questions about others living in the household, such as grandparents or maiden aunts. Several lines are needed for recording changes in address, telephone, parents' employment and office address, name of physician to be called in case of emergency, and other data subject to change or amplification. The child's birthdate, and the serial or code number of the official document from which the birthdate was taken, should be recorded ineradicably, since sometimes schools are called upon to confirm birth records when the original documents are lost by fire or other disaster.

Sometimes health information and the health record are kept separately by the school nurse. The cumulative folder, however, should include at least the most important health data such as history of surgery, known disabilities or health weaknesses, and special instructions regarding the child's participation in physical activities.

The school history of the child is recorded somewhat differently in a nongraded school. In fact, it may be helpful if a locally prepared, printed folder is used instead of forms commercially available because the latter are geared to grade norms and usually employ the phrase "grade level." The recommended headings for the columns recording school history would be: (1) school year; (2) days enrolled; (3) days attended; (4) days absent; (5) teacher's name and/or room number; (6) classification; and (7) other information. Those categories are sufficiently flexible so that almost any nomenclature (such as "primary" or "fourth grade") can be used. If a child transfers to another room during the year, two lines can be bracketed together or furnished separately as need be. The "other information" column can be used to record end-of-year "promotions" or assignments, or comments about general progress, or almost any other data needed.

The academic progress of the child may need little other than summary documentation on the cumulative folder itself, especially if carbon copies of report forms and conference reports are kept in the folder. One school insures that such forms will not be lost by furnishing a special pocket for them in the folder. Another uses a metal fastener, and attaches two-hole-punched copies of the reports to the folder by that means.

Intelligence test results and other evidence of intellectual potential should be recorded with special care. Some school systems provide a generous space for additional "comment," adjoining the place where ability test scores are recorded, so that teachers' estimates of the child's probable strengths and weaknesses can be included. It would seem wise to expand upon this practice, not only because such information would be useful but because the very process of preparing such estimates could become a means of each teacher's discovering more about her children. All too often, ability tests are simply administered and recorded in a perfunctory manner, so that whatever diagnostic and interpretive value they may have is lost.

It would seem that a red "caution" slip should be stapled to the I.Q. column of a child's folder, until at least two (preferably three or four) separate tests are included in the record. Too many schools base their performance expectations upon a single test, usually one administered in the preprimary period of the child's life, and all too frequently presenting an inadequate or inaccurate picture of the child's real potential. Simple arithmetic errors might cause a teacher to record a 93 I.Q. for a child genius, or a 147 I.Q. for John Q. Average. Furthermore, some children approach their first intelligence test with temporary attitudinal advantages or disadvantages, such as the child whose overanxious parent warns him to "do a good job on that test or else!"

The recording of achievement test information in a nongraded school represents a serious policy problem. So long as the tests are translated into grade equivalents or norms, one of the evils we are trying to eliminate persists in an important way. This calls for an imaginative and creative approach at the local level. Perhaps the record folder can be designed so that it provides columns for the actual scores, then columns for locally-derived symbols to interpret the scores longitudinally, and then columns for grade norms with asterisks denoting "for unofficial reference only." The grade norms problem is a somewhat less serious one if the data are presented graphically, as for example in the profile charts accompanying certain standardized tests. When parents and teachers deal with *visual* pictures of growth rather than the abstract pictures that grade norms such as 6.3 or 4.7 represent, it is easier to view a child's progress in the way it ought to be viewed in a nongraded school.

Somewhere in the folder there should be a record of the child's special interests, accomplishments, and progress-related experiences. Most schools ignore these things in the official record, or at best record a comment or two about hobbies and music lessons. There should be room for an annual "nonacademic" inventory, where the teacher can describe the child's over-all progress. Much of this information, of course, might be furnished by the parents.

It is also important to keep the record up to date insofar as family changes and important family events are concerned. Sample entries might be: sister Kathy stricken with polio, June 1, 1958; paternal grandfather, very close to Jimmy, died in March, 1959; twin daughters born to older sister, living in adjoining flat, August,

1958; father traveled to Australia on company business for six months during 1958-59 school year.

How the child *feels* about his school experiences, and the parents' perceptions of the child's school progress, should be recorded wherever possible. A good two-way progress-reporting system, which affords parents the opportunity to volunteer and to discuss such information with the teachers, is the most likely means of obtaining these data.

Information about the social and emotional development of the child may be somewhat more difficult to organize systematically, but it is highly important to assign some space in the cumulative folder to this category of progress information. Whether this is best done by providing blank spaces for teachers' summary comments, by attempting to devise statements to which a symbolic response can be made, or by providing pockets specifically intended as a file for documents about social-emotional growth will depend upon the sophistication and the wishes of the teachers. Probably copies of progress reports, conference records, and anecdotal reports will be the major source of such information.

It might be helpful if the principal or teacher in a nongraded school would prepare, at the end of each year, a very brief mimeographed statement describing the history of the child's class, or age group, since it first entered the primary unit. Such a statement could be very useful if ever the child's folder is transferred to a graded school, or if a high school guidance counselor (or equivalent person) ever encounters the child's "nongraded" record without an appropriate background for understanding it. Park Forest, for example, formerly included a fairly complete description of its ungraded primary school plan in each folder of a pupil transferred to another community. Follow-up correspondence indicated that the welfare of the children was well served by this device, and many of the communities involved seemed to appreciate the information that was given.

The Progress-Information Needs of the Child

Up to this point the chapter has dealt primarily with the needs and the interests of parents and teachers insofar as the child's growth is concerned. In view of all this concern about reporting practices, and especially since so much is being said about "keeping the focus on the child," it is extremely curious that so little of the literature deals with the reactions and feelings of children in relation to the reports their parents receive. One of the few available discussions of this topic comes from California where the Committee on Reporting to Parents of the Cooperative Council on In-Service Education focused its attention upon the problem in a many-sided approach.[32] The committee asserted that many children want their parents and teachers to know one another, that some children want to take part in parent-teacher conferences, that some children are anxious about the conferences, that children want their parents to appreciate their efforts and to understand them better, and that parents vary widely in their attitudes toward marks and conferences. That children and their parents need more help in understanding marks on report cards, and that children should be more actively involved in conferences between teachers and parents were among the conclusions of this study.

An earlier article [33] describes the reactions of eighth-grade children, whose prior experience had been entirely with the parent-teacher conference type of reporting, to a system in which for the first time they encountered letter marks (A, B, C, D, F) used in conjunction with other evidence. Their reactions appear to support the idea quite clearly that children value the conference system in the lower grade levels, and also that children frequently feel their parents are dissatisfied with them as a result of their school marks.

Both of these reports clearly lead to the notion that much valuable information on the reporting problem could be obtained by more extensive and careful research into children's reactions and attitudes. Such research is especially needed where reporting practices are linked to a nongraded school operation, and it is to be fervently hoped that doctoral studies and other research will be made in this all-important area.

It is well known that children sometimes have anxieties about their "report cards" and the ways their parents will react to them. When reporting is done primarily by a conference method, the child may have another kind of anxiety, namely the lack of knowledge about what the parent and teacher discuss. One teacher has reported [34] that he alleviated this concern by arranging pupil-teacher conferences in advance of the parent-teacher conferences. Not only did this afford the teacher an additional opportunity to understand the child and his needs, but as one child put it, "I feel better now that I know what you're going to say to my parents." [35]

There is reason to believe that many children have such feel-

---

[32] Sybil Richardson, "How Do Children Feel About Reports to Parents?" *California Journal of Elementary Education*, 24 (November 1955), pp. 98-111.

[33] Robert H. Anderson, and Edward R. Steadman, *op. cit.*

[34] Joseph Moray, "Pupil-Teacher Conferences," *Elementary School Journal*, 58 (March 1958), pp. 335-6.

[35] *Ibid.*, p. 336.

ings, and that teachers should try to meet these needs through conferences and other devices.

> Teachers should be encouraged to provide many opportunities for children to talk about the school activities which are difficult for them and to evaluate their own progress and needs. Marks and reports deeply affect children's security and self-respect and their attitudes and motivations for learning. Teachers should feel justified, therefore, in spending adequate time in group activities and in individual conferences with children to make sure that the children are developing clear understandings of marks and reports that are made to their parents.[36]

Some teachers include the child in part or all of the conference held with a parent. The so-called "three-way conference" [37] presumably meets the need of the child to acquire an understanding of the matters his teacher and parents are concerned about, and allows the child to contribute his own ideas and problems. Sometimes the child is invited to sit in on the entire conference; sometimes he is present for the first part of the conference and then the adults engage in more private discussion guided by the child's reactions and responses. Undoubtedly there is room for more three-way discussions in reporting programs, and techniques will be developed for capitalizing upon the child's ideas in conference situations.

Closing the Gap

This volume is written during a period of great national concern for the adequacy of public education and the effectiveness of the schools in developing the innate potentialities of children. Quite possibly this concern would be even greater if parents and teachers were more fully aware of the extent to which ineffective reporting practices are detrimental to the welfare of children. Since so much of what is done in the name of reporting prevents or inhibits children from developing their innate capacities, it is surprising there has not been a greater outcry against such ineffective practice.

A major thesis of this volume is that the traditional graded organization is one of the most inhibiting forces in children's lives. In practice, it is at the level of reporting progress that the full impact of the graded system usually makes itself felt. It is probably impossible to change reporting practices without in some way influ-

---

[36] Richardson, *op. cit.*, p. 111. See also R. Murray Thomas, "Talking with Students," *Judging Student Progress* (New York, Longmans, Green and Co., 1954), pp. 350-57.

[37] L. T. Camp, "Three-way Conferences Assist Lay Participation," *Educational Leadership,* 15 (April 1958), pp. 418-21.

encing the graded structure, just as it is definitely impossible to ungrade a school without overhauling, modifying, or adapting the reporting system accordingly. In the final analysis, it is through the reporting system that the child acquires from the school organization many of the basic facts on which he judges his own worth.

In the long run, reporting serves no purpose more important than enabling the child to understand himself better and to be better understood, so that he may develop his potentialities to the maximum. Our purpose in the schools is to help people discover and develop the talents that reside within them.

That few men ever achieve the greatest possible development of their innate physical, spiritual, and intellectual capacities is certainly one of the great tragedies of the universe, in this as in all earlier centuries. It seems quite reasonable to claim that most children grow into less healthy, less moral, less thoughtful, and less informed men than might have been predicted for them in their cradles. Certainly there are many forces at work to prevent man's achievement of perfection, and the schools are often relatively feeble in offsetting them. But the gap between what the schools *are* doing to offset them, and what the schools *might* do, remains great enough to tease out some speculation about changes in educational systems and man's eventual destiny.

One highly useful and graphic description of the gap between man's potential and his actual achievement is presented by Dr. Joseph W. Still. Figures 11 and 12, devised by Still, are drawn upon the basis of his observations and general knowledge of human physical and intellectual behavior.

The upper lines in each chart indicate the physical and psychological potentials of normal people, with peak periods shown for various typical activities. The lower lines indicate how the majority of people fail to measure up to the indicated potential.

Reflecting upon the reasons why so many people fail to achieve their physical and mental potentials, Still states, "It seems pretty clear that it is not because of poor heredity but because they fail to discover that they are able, if they choose, to make more of their lives." [38] The schools contribute significantly to the views people hold of their own talents. The schools do this in part through their systems for evaluating and reporting children's progress in various aspects of development. It remains to be asked whether the failures of discovery to which Still refers can be traced at least in part to those systems.

Throughout this chapter we have tried to emphasize that the

---

[38] Joseph W. Still, "Man's Potential and His Performance," *The New York Times Magazine* (November 24, 1957), p. 37.

Figure 11

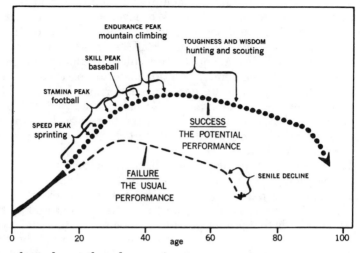

The physical growth and ages of man.

Figure 12

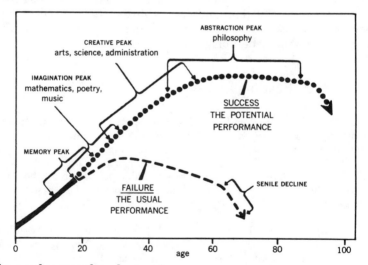

The psychic growth and ages of man.

Chart redrawn after Joseph W. Still. Reproduced with the permission of the author, who indicates that the figures are intended as artistic rather than scientific curves.

reporting process and the evaluation procedures out of which it grows can be deceiving and damaging when the reporting base is the grade-level-expectancy pattern. We have described alternative means of measuring and describing growth, and have noted a number of principles to guide the school staff in reporting to parents. We have indicated that adequate curriculum planning, adequate means of measuring outcomes, and adequate means of describing the child's growth pattern are necessary under any form of school organization, graded or nongraded. We have acknowledged, however, that school systems engaged in thorough and zealous studies of these matters will undoubtedly work harder than teachers content with existing procedures.

The reporting of pupil progress in a nongraded school is inherently no more complex than in a graded school, and can lead children and their parents to have a far better understanding of themselves. The discovery of one's own potential, unconfused by the dubious standards that grades provide, can be an exciting and wonderful experience for a child, and such experience is more likely to be found in a school where teachers are unfettered in their teaching and evaluation decisions by grade-mindedness. It is more likely to take place when parents and teachers collaborate, with a realistic frame of reference to guide them, in treating the child as an individual. It is more likely to take place in a school where teachers spend a great deal of time and energy in the study of curriculum objectives and learning outcomes. And this, we contend, is what *every* teacher should be doing.

For Further Reading

Of the references already cited in the foregoing chapter, the reader will probably find *Four Methods of Reporting to Parents,* by Otto and others, to be of particular value for further reading. Also of great importance are the volume by Langdon and Stout, *Teacher-Parent Interviews,* and *Reporting Is Communicating,* the pamphlet published by the Association for Supervision and Curriculum Development. Other suggested readings are:

Herrick, Virgil E., John I. Goodlad, Frank J. Estvan, and Paul W. Eberman. *The Elementary School.* Englewood Cliffs, New Jersey, Prentice-Hall, Inc., 1956. Chapter 15, "Policies and Practices in Marking, Reporting, and Promoting," presents some guiding principles and a very useful discussion of current practice.

Rothney, John W. M. *Evaluating and Reporting Pupil Progress.* What Research Says to the Teacher, No. 7. Washington, D.C., Department of Classroom Teachers and American Educational Research Association of the National Education Association, 1955. 33 pages.

A summary of research on the evaluation and reporting of pupil progress is made, including sections on the assessment of school achievement and of personal-social development. A bibliography on research references as well as general references is provided.

Seidman, Jerome M. (ed.). *Readings in Educational Psychology.* Boston, Houghton Mifflin Company, 1955.

Chapter 13, pages 311-35, presents six selected readings on "Reporting Development and Achievement." The authors include Ruth Strang, David H. Russell, Dorothy Rogers, Beatrice Ford Parker, and Katherine D'Evelyn, all of whom have been prominent among students of the reporting problem.

Thelen, Herbert A. "The Triumph of 'Achievement' over Inquiry in Education," *Elementary School Journal,* **60** (January 1960), 190-97.

This important statement exposes the conflict between methods of testing children and ways of measuring what children have learned. It furnishes examples of the conflict between education and achievement as school goals, and it poses alternative uses of evaluation to guide teaching.

Thomas, R. Murray. *Ways of Teaching in Elementary Schools,* New York, Longmans, Green & Co., 1955. Chapter 20, pages 531-42, presents a brief but useful discussion of evaluation and reporting of pupil progress. The chapter includes a sample report form as used in the Omaha Public schools.

Thomas's *Judging Student Progress,* also published by Longmans, Green & Co., 1954, is excellent for its thorough discussion of evaluation procedures. Chapter 13, "Marking and Reporting Student Progress," is of particular interest.

Several of the periodical magazines in education have devoted entire issues to the topic of reporting. Of these, there are two that appear to be of special value: the November 1955 issue of *California Journal of Elementary Education,* and the September 1957 issue of *The National Elementary Principal.* These are commended to the reader's attention.

7. TOWARD REALISTIC STANDARDS AND SOUND MENTAL HEALTH

Introduction

The increasing concern with which the American people have viewed the problem of mental health over recent decades is scarcely in need of further documentation. That a great proportion of Americans suffer from mental disease or illness and that most if not all disorders have their origins in unfortunate (and usually preventable) experiences of childhood have been substantiated well beyond reasonable doubt. For the educator and the parents with whom he is allied, these are sobering thoughts and a challenge to the combined resources of the school and the home. This chapter describes those relationships between the mental health problem and public school administrative practices which may provide important clues for future progress.

Not only the educational services to children, but the administrative and psychological environment within which they are rendered, influence the children's perceptions of the school and of their relationship to it. It follows that these perceptions will vary from child to child, as for example from children who are well suited to satisfying the school's demands to those who are not. Since these perceptions are inevitably related to the mental health of the child, it may be well to attempt a description of how nongraded and graded schools affect children before proceeding to a consideration of mental health as a general school problem.

In order to depict in more personal terms the ways in which organizational arrangements influence children in their development, let us take a few hypothetical children [1] through the primary

---

[1] Robert H. Anderson, "The Ungraded Primary School as a Contribution to Improved School Practices," *Frontiers of Elementary Education*, Vincent Glennon, ed. (Syracuse, Syracuse University Press, 1955), Vol. 2, Ch. 4.

grades by way of the graded and the nongraded patterns. First, we shall consider the cases of two cousins, whom we shall call Jane and Judy. We shall postulate that they are exactly the same age, that they have virtually equal academic potentiality, and that they live in two different cities. In the autumn of the school year which follows their sixth birthdays, Judy is placed in a nongraded primary class, while her cousin Jane, many miles away, is assigned to a typical first-grade class.

When the entire family gathers at Christmas time at Grandmother's house and the reunited cousins begin to compare notes on their school experiences, the girls discover that they are both using the same preprimer and are doing just about the same things in their classrooms. Their mothers, while drying dishes together afterwards, confide in Grandma that other children in their home neighborhoods seem to be farther along in their reading than Jane and Judy. Jane's mother is worried that Jane might not "pass" in June. Judy's mother does not express her concern in the same way, but says that she hopes Judy will perk up during her primary schooling.

In June, assuming both girls make the same limited progress, the children's letters to Grandmother might be full of school news.

From Jane: Either "I failed first grade and I am very unhappy" or "I passed, but teacher says that I must do much better next year."

From Judy: "I am still in Primary."

Needless to say, the failing of Jane could bring this example to an unhappy end. Jane's bitter experience with failure, her possible distaste for future schooling and the repetition of preprimer work, and her family's disappointment could add up to a most unfortunate situation. Whatever Judy's ultimate success, a line between Jane and Judy would appear to have been somewhat sharply drawn at this point. At least for the next year or two, family reunions with an apparently more successful Judy might not be a happy prospect for Jane.

So that we may continue our illustration, let us give Jane the benefit of the doubt and arrange for her to be promoted to the second grade. When she arrives at school in September, the chances are that her second-grade teacher will hope and expect that she has already mastered the first-grade work, and will press her for a higher quality of academic production than is within her power. The label "second grade" on the door and in the teacher's mind might be a constant hazard for Jane, and along toward spring, minus a miracle or an unusual spurt on her part, the specter of failure again might be weaving in and out of the child's life.

While this has been going on some miles away, Judy would have returned in September to a room labeled "Primary—Miss Asyouare," and resumed her reading and other classwork approximately where she had left it in June. Her teacher, let us hope, has no "second-grade" fixation in her mind, and she views Judy's progress without special concern for her comparative academic achievement as of June. She does try, of course, to get maximum effort out of Judy and her classmates, but not out of any particular anxiety to cover the so-called "second-grade work" within the time allotted. (See Figure 13.)

By June of the second year, it is quite possible that Judy will be a notch or so ahead of Jane because of the presumably more favorable administrative and psychological environment within which Judy works. Even if we do not give this advantage to Judy, however, the fact remains that Miss Second Grade has scarcely any choice at the end of the year but to fail Jane under the policies of many graded school systems. Even if she does not withhold promotion, the child's future in the hands of Miss Third Grade is less

Figure 13

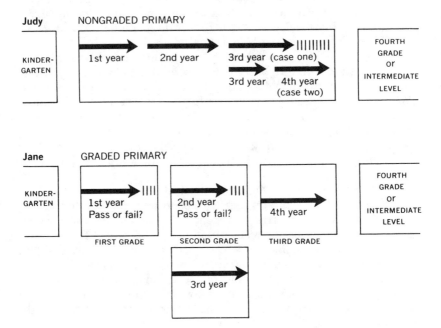

Two slow learners in the graded and nongraded school. Each arrow represents a year's academic progress.

144

promising than it was in her present classroom the September before; and somewhere along the way Jane is threatened with trouble unless her teachers and parents handle the situation with far more skill and good luck than one normally has reason to expect. For a child like Jane, the whole graded arrangement has therefore raised periodic barriers and obstacles which are indeed difficult to overcome.

Judy, on the other hand, moves into her third year of primary training still relatively free of the pressures and troubles which beset Jane. She starts out in September where she ended in June, in a room labeled "primary," the same as before, and moves along as rapidly as it is possible for her to go. At this point among others the ungraded arrangement makes its beneficent effects felt.

Let us re-examine the third (and fourth) year story for Judy, as depicted in Figure 13. The two possible alternatives are shown as case one and case two:

Case one. Because of the alleged psychological advantage to Judy in the ungraded situation, we will assume that the accumulative benefits of a continuous and uninterrupted program begin to accelerate Judy's school progress.[2] This means that Judy might in the third year record more than a year's gains, to a point where by June her teacher could feel justified in promoting her to a fourth grade. How fortunate that the axe of failure was not there to fall on Judy's head the two previous Junes!

Case two. Assume that the child does not make unexpected or unusual gains, and her school progress (and general development) in the third year is less than the staff agrees is necessary to meet minimum standards for fourth-grade admission. She then returns to primary school for a fourth year of work. Perhaps as far as Grandma and the other relatives are concerned, this puts Judy in the same boat with Jane. But does it? Consider where Jane is starting her fourth year, compared with Judy. Consider also where the two children are likely to be by the following June. Consider the kind of nonpromotion pressure which Jane endured, contrasted with the relatively failure-free system by which Judy was classified each June!

In order to visualize the impact of graded and nongraded structure upon children who are gifted or superior academically, it

---

[2] This is not an unrealistic assumption. Several communities using flexible promotion practices have reported that children who started slowly, and were originally thought to be slow learners, seemed to "catch fire" after a year or two and make unexpectedly rapid progress thereafter.

may be helpful to consider the Jane-Judy illustration in approximately its reverse operation. Let us find one more set of cousins, call them Jack and Jill, and arrange for them to arrive at Grandmother's house for a family reunion on Memorial Day. What would this family conversation be like? Jack, who attends a graded school, might be somewhat envious of Jill because she is already at work on the more exciting stories in the second reader. Jack's teacher is a bit fearful of entering Miss Second Grade's domain ahead of schedule and is obliged to be content with other "enrichments," as his teacher calls them.

By the middle of the second year, both children would undoubtedly be ahead of the normal schedule (i.e., the schedule followed by the majority of their classmates). Both, because of their giftedness, would probably be the subject of much faculty discussion at their respective schools, the burning question in each case

Figure 14

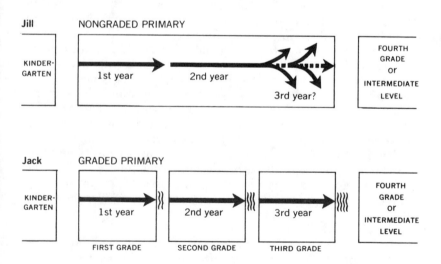

Two gifted learners in the graded and nongraded school. Each arrow represents a year's academic progress.

being the child's official classification in the years immediately ahead. (See Figure 14.)

Now let us assume for a moment that neither child is sufficiently mature in *all* respects to merit consideration for acceleration, i.e., gaining a year's time. For Jack, the psychological and administrative barrier which probably exists between grade levels in his school could quite possibly mean less opportunity. Many educators are convinced that grade-mindedness in teachers has been one of the reasons for the profession's failure to do what should be done for gifted children. While it may be apparent on the surface that Jack, who needs to remain with his agemates, should receive a richer program and the stimulation of more challenging assignments, the ability and the willingness of grade-conscious teachers to provide such experiences without trespassing upon the "territory" of their upper-grade colleagues is often limited.

In Jill's case, the nongraded organization pattern lends itself very well to her needs during the initial period in which she is hitting her stride as well as later on, when a richer program at a slower pace is the staff's prescription. The same lack of concern with grade barriers which enables Jill to penetrate second-grade materials during her first year would tend to operate in her teachers' minds as they plan for her third-year program. For Jill, it seems to the authors that it would be psychologically and administratively easier for the teacher and staff to "fatten" her program and adjust to the range of her interests and abilities as they develop. (Again, see Figure 14.)

Continuing with the illustration of Jack and Jill, the intellectually gifted cousins, let us change the conditions of our analysis by agreeing that both youngsters are sufficiently mature in all respects to merit acceleration. In other words, we will suppose that all the available evidence in both cases indicates that it would make good sense if the children were to find themselves in the fourth grade after only two years of primary schooling. This implies that the children are not only doing superior work for their age, but they also are unusually mature in other respects (physiologically, emotionally, socially, etc.) and increasingly interested in the things which appeal to the children who entered the primary program a year earlier than they.

How does the "gain" of a year's time take place? In Jill's case, there is essentially no problem since she moves along without grade barriers to cross. By the end of the second year she will have arrived at the fourth-grade threshold with the complete primary program behind her: no gaps, no material skipped, no hurdles uncrossed. If she happens to have changed teachers and class groups along the way, it was done by means of a simple transfer from one primary room to another, not by a change in *grade* levels. (See Figure 15.)

Figure 15

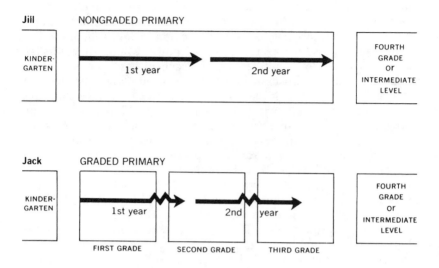

The acceleration of two gifted learners in the graded and nongraded school. Each arrow represents a year's academic progress.

Jack, on the other hand, encounters two important obstacles in moving toward a fourth-grade assignment in less than the typical three-year time span. One of these obstacles, which appears twice along the way, is the difficulty of crossing over a grade barrier during the school year. Nearly all graded schools have come to accept the inevitability of some children falling behind the regular schedule, and work at a lower level is frequently possible within a graded classroom for the benefit of the Janes and the Judys previously described. Few, however, feel comfortable in dealing with children whose work should be at a *higher* level than the present grade. There is much talk about "enrichment," and often a successful enrichment curriculum is found to be in operation for the benefit of the Jacks and Jills. Less often is *advanced* work that is vertically more difficult, rather than horizontally difficult, made available to the able child. As a result, a boy like Jack may find it virtually impossible to move ahead into regular second-grade work while he is still in the first grade, or into regular third-grade work while he is still in the second grade, except by means of very special arrangements worked out by the school staff *after* their decision to accelerate the child.

The second obstacle Jack encounters, one closely related to the first, is the problem of his administrative classification. Whereas Jill simply moved ahead without particular incident or fanfare, the existence of grade labels in a graded school tends automatically to dramatize the uniqueness of Jack's double-promotion, or skip-promotion, or grade-jumping, or whatever the maneuver is officially called. This means that Jack becomes a kind of rarity in the school: the jackpot winner, the star pupil, the grade jumper, the boy who beat the system. While most of this recognition will probably please Jack, it might also tend to embarrass and possibly even hamper him as he strives either to live up to these titles or regain a normal place among his classmates. An unnecessary and distracting self-consciousness could become quite a liability to Jack as he seeks to make the academic and social adjustments involved. The academic adjustments alone would be difficult enough, since in many situations he must work independently to acquire the skills and information stemming from lessons and experiences he will not have shared with his new classmates.

Inasmuch as grade norms and the notion of "average" are very closely related to each other, it might seem at first glance that the nongrading of classes has less emotional and intellectual impact upon the average child than upon the Janes, Judys, Jacks, and Jills we have described. This is a view worth exploring.

Let us take a third set of "identical" cousins, John and James. John, as it happens, lives in a city where he attends a nongraded primary class which began in September following his sixth birthday. James, who like John would be considered a normal, average youngster on the basis of academic aptitude tests, has been assigned to a first-grade class. At Christmas time, over the turkey during a family reunion at Grandmother's house, the boys find that they are both using practically the same books, are learning to write by the same method, and are both just about ready to start the primer in their reading groups.

The following September, James prints a letter to Grandmother saying, "I am now in second grade, and we are reading in our new second readers." John also prints a letter, saying "I am in Primary. Our group has nice new readers." Twelve months later, both boys again write to Grandma (perhaps in crude cursive strokes) proudly evidencing further progress. Again John says, "I am still in Primary," whereas this time James has a "third-grade" label to use. Finally, in June of the third year, Grandmother receives two fairly legible letters in which both boys announce, "I have been promoted to the fourth grade." (See Figure 16.)

On the surface, the school experiences and progress of these two children are nearly identical. Being "normal" and "average," both children in the illustration reached the fourth grade in the length of time which a century of experience has led educators to define as typical for children of their age. However, there is reason to doubt that these definitions have valid meaning for a significant proportion of children, as is so generally assumed.

All discussions of "normal" and "average" children are somewhat theoretical because both terms refer to concepts rather than actualities. John and James are the fictional representatives of their normal age range, a term which itself needs amplification. In one sense it means all healthy children of 90-110 I.Q., born into rela-

Figure 16

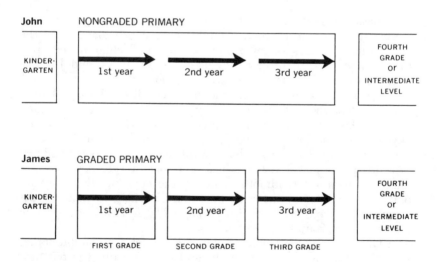

Two "average" learners in the graded and nongraded school. Each arrow represents a year's academic progress.

tively typical American families during the same month (let us say March, so that the boys are age 6½ in September of their first primary year). In another sense, much less realistic and yet a key element in the graded-school rationale, it means all children of 90-110 I.Q., born during a given 12 months time span (let us say November through the following October 31), who enter first-year-primary work as a group.

We need only re-examine Figure 16 in the light of this discussion to realize how unrepresentative the figure is of the growth patterns of even "normal" or "average" children. Were we to assume that John's I.Q. is 107 by contrast with an I.Q. of 96 for James, for example, the arrows showing James's progress might well have been pictured slightly to the left in each case. Were we to assume, on the other hand, that James was born seven or eight months earlier than John, the arrows showing his progress might be pictured slightly to the right. Countless other conditions might be enumerated that would alter in some degree the picture of relative "normalcy" in progress given in Figure 16. We might, for example, show one of the children getting off to a slow or a fast start, or having plateau periods and spurts along the way, or having family troubles or other obstacles to normal school progress. We might further alter the picture by postulating emotional or other differences that might lead the boys to react in varying ways to the motivational and other uses the teachers may have made of the end-of-year promotion system in their dealings with the children. In this latter area, in particular, seems to lie a powerful argument against the notion that "average" is a useful concept and that all children can be handled and classified in the same general way.

Children's Motivations

Implicit in the operational philosophy of the schools attended by Jane, Jack, and James is the idea that the children will be stimulated to work more earnestly because of the promotion-or-failure mechanism within the graded system. Each grade purportedly represents a set of standards, and the requirement that those standards be met is presumed to have a desirable motivating effect upon each child's behavior. This notion is now seriously challenged on a number of fronts.

Motivation is a very complex problem and cannot be considered apart from numerous other factors that influence the behavior of children and adults. It is extremely difficult to generalize about the ways children are motivated or the ways they are likely to react to classroom situations because so many variables must be taken into account. The administrative climate within each school system, and from school to school within the larger community, is one of the variables. In gross terms, many schools and school systems have the graded system in common; in actuality, gradedness may have slightly different meaning as an atmospheric factor in any single school compared with the rest. Another variable of an administrative sort is that of physical environment, with some schools architecturally attractive and well equipped while others are dingy and poorly provided.

In Chapters 5 and 6, grouping practices and reporting practices have been revealed as variables within the total environment that may have a crucial bearing upon the child's perception of his school experiences. Literally hundreds of other variables can be described: probably the most important of these deal with the personalities of the people (children, parents, teachers, supervisors, etc.) involved.

There is fairly general agreement that differing social structures and social climates within schools and classrooms have a strong influence upon the ways children get along with each other and their teachers, react to learning situations, and go about solving their personal and academic problems. Classroom social structure and social climate are significantly influenced by the teacher's personality and by her teaching "style" or approach. Classroom atmosphere is similarly influenced by the social configuration of the school neighborhood, by the nature of each child's family background, and by the various factors that go into the child's individual personality as a school client.

From many experiments and studies in the past quarter-century or so have come a number of different theories of learning, with several variations within each major theory.[3] Learning theorists disagree on a number of important points, one of the most important having to do with the question of how children are best motivated to learn. Motivation, of course, is only one of the conditions upon which learning is dependent. Ryans [4] lists a number of qualitative conditions that are necessary for learning in every situation: the learner must be capable of multiple response, of variability in re-

[3] For one discussion of these theories see Ernest R. Hilgard, *Theories of Learning* (New York, Appleton-Century-Crofts, Inc., 1948), pp. 7-17. Reprinted in W. A. Fullagar, H. G. Lewis, and C. F. Cumbee, *Readings for Educational Psychology* (New York, Thomas Y. Crowell Company, 1956), pp. 1-10.

[4] David G. Ryans, "Motivation in Learning," *The Psychology of Learning*, Forty-first Yearbook of the National Society for the Study of Education, Part II (Bloomington, Illinois, Public School Publishing Co., 1942), Ch. 7, pp. 289-331. See pp. 289-90.

sponse behavior, of profiting by or through experience; the response pattern to be learned must be structurally and functionally possible for the learner; there must be internal and external energy changes in the environment, the intensity of these changes exceeding the threshold of the behavior to be learned; there must be a first occurrence of the response pattern as a result of trial and error, problem solving, and other factors. He also lists quantitative conditions for learning, which will vary in degree and upon which the rate and the permanence of the learning are dependent: the condition of the organism (age, "capacity," fatigue, etc.); repetition; and motivation. The latter includes the preparatory set of the individual (drive, concomitant behavior, related experience) and incentive appropriate to the set, the attainment of which results in reinforcement.[5]

Reinforcement operates to build up or to strengthen the tendencies of individuals to behave in certain ways. Punishment and related mechanisms of control are used to reduce or eliminate tendencies to behave in ways opposite to those that are reinforced and rewarded, or both. Skinner, defining education as "the establishing of behavior which will be of advantage to the individual and to others at some future time," [6] notes that the educational agency arranges reinforcements for the purpose of conditioning the learner. Good grades, promotions, keys, medals, diplomas, prizes, and other reinforcers are all associated with the generalized reinforcer of approval. Certain privileges, job opportunities, and other avenues to economic and social advancement may depend upon scholastic achievement and therefore serve as reinforcers. However, it is noted that the economic consequences and the honorific reinforcements of education become weaker and less important as more and more people are educated and social security increases: fewer special advantages are now contingent upon education, and fewer students seek to amass wealth or escape the threat of poverty.[7] As a result, it is claimed, teachers turn to such alternative methods of control as making the teaching more interesting, supplying more and better aids to learning, and creating more "favorable circumstances for the execution of the behavior to be controlled." [8] In such situations the "spurious reinforcements" of educational control (grades, prizes, promotions, and so forth) are replaced as much as possible by the "natural" or "functional" reinforcements that are embodied in the intrinsic value of the behavior learned. Every effort is made to en-

---

[5] *Ibid.*, p. 290.

[6] B. F. Skinner, *Science and Human Behavior* (New York, The Macmillan Company, 1953), p. 402.

[7] *Ibid.*, p. 406.

[8] *Ibid.*

courage the learner to recognize these values and to appreciate their probable future usefulness.

Symonds, in a discussion [9] of pupils' motivations for learning, lends further support to the idea that many of the traditional reinforcements of educational control are indeed spurious. Here it is indicated that the winning of acceptance and approval are deeper motives for learning than teachers have realized. It is claimed that "striving for external tokens of approval in the form of tangible rewards, prizes, badges, and marks is subordinate to striving for direct recognition and approval from a parent, a teacher, or a peer." [10] Again, "behind mastery is the need for proving oneself and winning the approval of others in almost every normal case." [11]

The teachers' ways of viewing and recognizing each child's achievement and progress are critical to the child's morale and wellbeing, especially if Symonds is correct in his belief that children strive to succeed to a very great extent because of a need for recognition and approval. Pearson goes so far as to claim that "the child who toward the end of the term becomes worried lest he not be promoted to the next grade is not worried about this but is worried lest his teacher and his parents will not reward him with love if he is not promoted." [12]

Under the graded system, teachers tend to give pupils the rewards and approvals they seek only when they produce work that is thought to be at least "average" for that grade. Those who are incapable by nature, or those potentially capable but who are temporarily behind schedule, are regularly denied the approval they want because the symbolic evidence of such approval is withheld. Even the child of average achievement, though not denied the approval symbol known as "promotion," may feel that the teacher's approval is only partial if the mark is a "C" or a "B" (less than the teacher awards to other approved children), or the praise is in terms like "adequate" and "satisfactory" rather than "very good!" or an occasional "this pleases me very much!" Thus many children who are doing their best possible work often receive real or imagined rebuke (or its equivalent) under a graded system. This in turn may lead to bewilderment, disappointment, frustration, and even anger in the hearts of such children.

For the child who is, by virtue of superior ability or back-

---

[9] Percival M. Symonds, "What Education Has to Learn from Psychology," *Teachers College Record*, 56 (February 1955), pp. 277-85.

[10] *Op. cit.*, p. 285.

[11] *Op. cit.*, p. 284.

[12] Gerald H. J. Pearson, "A Survey of Learning Difficulties in Children," in *The Psychoanalytic Study of the Child*, Vol. 7 (New York, International Universities Press, Inc., 1952), p. 329.

ground, able rather easily to satisfy the minimum standards of the grade level, the system is little better as a stimulant to good mental health. When his schooling is governed by grade-minded teachers, such a child is often prevented from developing as rapidly as possible and as richly as he might. Here the problem may not be difficulty in obtaining symbols of success (and therefore the teachers' and the parents' love), but rather the deluding simplicity of the process. Success in terms of standards easily satisfied is a far different prize than success in the face of genuine challenge. In a discussion of the need for esteem, Maslow makes this observation:

> We have been learning more and more of the dangers of basing self-esteem on the opinions of others rather than on real capacity, competence, and adequacy to the task. The most stable and therefore most healthy self-esteem is based on *deserved* respect from others rather than on external fame or celebrity and unwarranted adulation.[13]

In the graded school the bright child may deprive himself, or be deprived, of the true fruits of honest labor by accepting, even welcoming, the ceiling that grade levels may impose on him. Not only could this lead to indolent or nonproductive work habits, with eventual conflict and disappointment when rewards no longer come as easily, but it could also warp his perception of maturity and progress and even stunt his capacity to reach greater heights.

Whatever the level of their potential ability, children as a whole must have a very different interpretation of school standards than do adults. In fact, there is a disappointing lack of information in the psychological and educational literature on the ways children perceive such things as grade organization, marking systems, teachers' efforts to motivate learning, and such related matters. What actually happens in a child's mind when his teacher reproves him by saying, "That's not the way fourth-graders behave," or "Now you are acting like a second-grader"? What does a child think and feel when a teacher says, "We don't study that until fifth grade"? What, beyond its meaning in terms of teacher approval, does a child understand in the sentence, "You are reading x months (or years) above (or below) the normal standard for children in this grade"?

We can only speculate upon such matters, but there is good reason to believe that grade norms and standards are only an abstraction to the elementary-age child. It is doubtful that children below high-school age can translate the numerical and letter symbols of the graded system into terms or actions they can really understand. It seems unlikely that many children can make a realistic or

---

[13] A. H. Maslow, *Motivation and Personality* (New York, Harper and Brothers, 1954), p. 91.

accurate connection between the quantity and the quality of their own performance, as they see it, and the notions of grade standards and of adequacy that are held by adults. Possibly children know that third grade is "higher" than first grade in somewhat the same sense that three pennies are greater than one. The terms "easier" (for a grade below) and "harder" (for a grade above) appear to have fairly useful meaning for children, but this may have more emotional than intellectual impact upon them. It may well be questioned whether children have any basis, other than a kind of blind faith in the adults' statements, for whatever notion they have of the grade scale and their relative position on it. To the extent that any of these speculations may have a basis in fact, many teachers in graded schools are in hopelessly poor communication with their pupils.

It also seems likely that the graded system has certain negative implications for child growth and development in the broader sense. "How does a fourth-grader behave?" and similar questions have certain connotations for each child which may stereotype how fast he is allowed to grow up, or required to grow up, and this may be out of balance with his true developmental tendencies. For the gifted child, or for the child who has been given an early start in the home toward self-reliance and independence, the stereotype may serve to repress and suppress growth if enforced too literally by the teacher. For the less able child and the child with less emotional strength, the stereotype may produce situations of severe stress and frustration.

The stereotypes of grade expectancies and of grade-mindedness also influence children's attitudes toward each other. A system that ranks pupils in terms of each other's success will engender more unwholesome rivalry than a system where the success of others is not necessarily related to one's own success. When variations in growth and progress are seen as a natural thing, not as deviations from a desired norm, they can be more easily accepted by children. The child's ability to earn the approval of other children, not only that of adults, is measurably increased in the environment where grade-mindedness is absent. Threats of ouster from the group, or deprivation of success symbols, or similar negatives are less present in this situation, and the child is more likely to work comfortably and securely at a pace that makes sense for him. He is more likely to take a positive interest in the progress of those whose pace exceeds or falls behind his. Individual differences, because they are accepted at face value, become a source of group strength instead of factors that upset the graded apple-cart. Comments in support of these assertions are quite numerous in the literature collected by the authors during the questionnaire study reported in earlier chapters.

Children's Anxieties

To overlook or to underestimate the anxieties of children as a major factor in their ability to learn would also be a serious mistake. The psychoanalytic literature has in recent years included several valuable discussions of the problem of anxiety, and at least one [14] of these has translated the insights of psychotherapy into guideposts for teaching. Stavsky notes that psychotherapy and teaching both embody an interpersonal relationship between an adult and a child, and also that the teacher's techniques, though not those of the therapist, "are intrinsically anxiety-reducing or anxiety-controlling techniques." [15] Among the examples of these techniques that Stavsky describes are knowing how to motivate for learning; showing sincere interest in children; showing respect for individualism; using patience; avoiding ridicule; using sensible praise; avoiding partiality; and possessing the capacity to forget past unpleasant relationships with the child.[16] Such techniques, it is contended, "are actually approaches which reduce or control anxiety, and . . . result in a teacher-pupil relationship that is relatively free of anxiety and in the establishment of a comparatively secure road for the development of the learning process." [17] While Stavsky makes no specific mention of promotion practices and grade-level-expectancy standards, it is quite obvious that the anxiety-reducing techniques he advocates would be somewhat easier to apply in the nongraded school environment.

"Failure" as an Educational Concept

In the public mind, and even quite uniformly within the profession, there persists a notion that fear of failure is a desirable motivating force for children in school. Sometimes the critics of so-called progressive school practices believe that their proponents are attempting to shield children from all failure, and they see this as unrealistic in view of "the way things are in the hard-knocks, outside world." A few words on this general problem may therefore be in order.

Most men learn as much, if not more, from their failures as from their successes. Eagerness to avoid failure and to profit from

---

[14] William H. Stavsky, "Using the Insights of Psychotherapy in Teaching," *Elementary School Journal,* 58 (October 1957), pp. 28-35.

[15] *Op. cit.,* p. 30.

[16] *Ibid.*

[17] *Ibid.*

mistakes is as characteristic of the culturally approved personality as is the philosophic view that man is imperfect and bound to err at least to some extent. Life is in many ways a procession of trial-and-error experiences in which failure serves a useful purpose for the individual in his search for ideas and skills and self-understanding. Trial-and-error is in fact an essential part of learning, and the educational institution must provide many ways for the individual to seek both widely and creatively for new behavior. In providing such psychological freedom, it must also provide psychological safety: to wit, error and failure must be tolerated without undue penalty. The individual needs experience with failure as well as with success, and profits from the opportunity to encounter failure at little more than the price he would pay for success. Out of such encounters can come the insights into how similar failures can be avoided, a keener awareness of both self and situations in which the self is seeking success, and techniques for accepting or coping with failure when it is again encountered.

When the individual enjoys both the freedom to make mistakes and protection against penalty for failure, his questing activities are certain to be more numerous and more bold, and hence his chances for enjoying frequent success are enhanced. On the other hand, the penalizing of failure tends to reduce the freedom of trial-and-error and restricts questing for answers. Thus any deliberate use of failure and the fear of failure as presumed "incentives" to learning arises out of ignorant or willful disregard of known truths.

There is another dimension to the obsolete theory that the fear of failure may stimulate learning. Failure that results when an individual attempts something within his capacity or power is a very different thing from failure that results from attempting the impossible. When we fail at something we might under different circumstances achieve, the failure may serve as a healthy stimulant to greater effort and the alteration of circumstances. This explains many, if not most of man's greatest achievements, including the attainment by Roger Bannister (and, subsequently, a number of others) of the "four minute mile" in the world of sports. We have learned that for some men, under perfectly controlled circumstances of training, diet, and other preparations, it is possible to perform such seemingly impossible feats. And yet we do not expect most track athletes to be able to run a mile in four minutes upon demand; nor do we believe that in the predictable future any man will be able to run a mile in, let us say, three minutes and a half. Here physiologists and others would probably agree that man's capacity for sustained stress, for intake and use of oxygen, and related factors impose a predictable outer limit closer to 225 or 230 seconds than to 210. Therefore no "miler" is ever sent out under serious instructions from his coach to run the distance in 3:30.

Yet we often make similar demands of children in school, or at least schools have frequently done so in the past. To insist that a certain child should have completed, with total success, the first-grade reader by June of his first primary year may be essentially as unreasonable as to insist that he run a four-minute mile. To confront certain children with a never-ending series of demands, few if any of which are within their capacity to accomplish, is as senseless as it is useless. What physiologists and psychologists and others would probably agree is beyond the predictable outer limit for a given individual should never be expected of that individual. And yet grade-mindedness and the graded system have, many times, caused teachers to expect of children what they could not do.

Nor is that the extent of these crimes against children. To expect more than is reasonable is one thing. But to react to the resulting failure situation as if the child, and not the system, were wrong is another. That thousands of school systems have made efforts of various kinds to adjust the system to the child is highly gratifying; that so many others have not, however, and that less than a hundred have thus far tried to effect a complete adjustment is in many ways discouraging. Certainly grade-mindedness continues to be a powerful force; and the fear of failure is still seen by many teachers as a useful weapon.

Making Success Possible

There is another dimension to the problem of what may reasonably be expected of the child. We might describe as the antithesis of failure the striving of children for success. In the foregoing paragraphs we have argued against unreasonable expectations, or the commitment of children to situations in which failure is the likely, even inevitable, outcome. Conversely, this is to argue for the situation in which success is possible, even likely. It is to recommend that tasks be planned which are within the capacity of the child, that expectations be so geared to existing abilities that the child's needs for success will be satisfied.

Nor is this to argue for an extreme position in which life becomes unnaturally easy for the child, in which trial-and-success completely replaces trial-and-error, or in which an inflated and unrealistic sense of power develops in the child. Obviously it would be no service to the youngster to shield him from all failure, or to dull his desire to reach the stars beyond his fingertips. Mental health is, among other things, a state of balance between security and aspiration. Security and success belong together. Here we suggest that the desire to exceed one's grasp is more likely to spring from a foundation of security and success than from a foundation of failure.

Aspiration, or goal-striving behavior within a range of difficulty, has been the topic of a growing number of research studies. A review [18] of some of these studies indicates among many other things that the person who has experienced success will tend to have a more realistic attitude toward both success and failure than the person who has experienced failure. This seems to suggest that the opportunity to enjoy success on a fairly consistent basis is a necessary prelude to understanding one's own limitations as well as one's strengths and potentialities. It argues for the maintenance of an environment in which the pace of activities will generally be well adjusted to a given child's talents, and in which subtle or direct pressure to "keep up" (or "stay back") with the fictional average of the group is absent. In the nongraded school, each child's daily efforts are regarded to be successful or unsuccessful only in relation to the child's own pattern of growth. When success comes too seldom, new conditions can be rather easily created in which successes can be enjoyed more often. The relative position of other children is noticed less, and the teachers' approval and pleasure can be expressed in the presence of the successful individual and his colleagues with complete honesty. In a graded school, any given "success" is almost inevitably measured, at least to some extent, against the fictional yardstick of grade-level-expectancy; therefore, the teacher finds it difficult to maintain the child's feeling of persistent success and on dramatic occasions (report-card time, promotion time, testing time) must deny or even withdraw some of the success symbols.

Admittedly the situation is not altogether black-and-white, especially since children do not always hold the same notions of success and failure that are held by their teachers (who themselves seldom agree in the interpretation of specific academic behavior). Research seems to indicate that

> the feeling of success and failure does not depend on an absolute level of achievement. What for one person means success means failure for another person and even for the same person the same achievement will lead sometimes to the feeling of failure and sometimes to the feeling of success.[19]

---

[18] Kurt Lewin, Tamara Dembo, Leon Festinger, and Pauline Snedden Sears, "Level of Aspiration," *Personality and the Behavior Disorders*, J. McV. Hunt, ed. (New York, Ronald Press Co., 1944), Vol. I, Ch. 10, pp. 333-78.

[19] *Ibid.*, p. 374.

Even when used with appropriate flexibility and moderation, grade standards are a rather poor basis for interpreting academic behavior if their meaning is inconstant from person to person or within the same person from moment to moment.

One of the traditional arguments in support of the graded structure is that it gives to children a competitive experience similar to that which characterizes adult life. This argument presumes that adults strive to satisfy certain generally accepted standards and that in the process there are inevitably those who "make the grade" and those who do not. While this description may be somewhat over-simplified, it is accurate enough to reflect a fairly general viewpoint among the adult population.

We may well ask whether adults are regularly exposed to the fear of failure and the unilateral expectancy standards that they indirectly advocate for their children. In actuality, the "school of hard knocks," as adults sometimes describe their working environment, is a more tolerable place for most of them than is generally acknowledged. Men and women select occupations, build friendships, and establish life patterns on the basis of their successes and satisfactions. One might indeed claim that each person not only finds his own level, but by and large derives pleasure from his activities at that level. Furthermore, the extreme diversity of adult pursuits affords nearly everyone the opportunity for relative success, and except in such gross terms as economic position and social prestige it is impossible to comment with assurance on the relative happiness or even the worth of different men.

If we are to face these facts, then the public elementary school may be one of the few places where a person can find himself involuntarily engaged in an unfair competition. The future barber, or banker, or biologist finds himself in virtually inescapable association with all other kinds of children; later in life, he will compete (and associate) primarily with other barbers, or bankers, or biologists. While we are quick to appreciate the many values accruing to children, and eventually to society, from the democratization and socialization the school promotes by bringing children together, it seems reasonable to ask that in so doing each individual not be deprived of his fair chance for success. If this means that the future barber does not master certain operations in mathematics until several years after the nascent banker or the biologist has done so, let it not be lamented as a decline in standards but appreciated as a sensible solution to a difficult problem. And let each child *enjoy* the victory of a task completed!

Nonpromotion and Personality

Chapter 2 showed the negative effects of nonpromotion, a concomitant of the graded system. That chapter serves as suitable substantiation for the statement by a group of Helen Heffernan's students, that "nonpromotion is devastating to the personality of children. It deadens initiative, paralyzes the will to achieve, destroys the sense of security and acceptance in the family circle, and promotes truancy and delinquency." [20] Along these same lines, Wrightstone summarizes the research on this topic by stating:

> Nonpromotion affects the personality of the pupil unfavorably. Clinical studies of children who have failed show that there is a loss of self-confidence. Self-respect is undermined. The feeling of security, so necessary to mental health, is usually weakened and feelings of inferiority are increased.[21]

In this present chapter, in which attention is focused particularly upon mental health, we are relating the influences upon personality of the entire promotion and grading system, not only the subcategory of nonpromotion.

Nonpromotion alone is not the problem. Its elimination, as for example through the adoption of a policy of continuous promotion, leaves the school with most of the troubles it had before. Automatic or continuous promotion for everyone is scarcely the perfect answer to the problem. It is a solution that "begs the question, and fails to solve the educational problem underlying nonpromotion, . . . it gets rid of the symptom without remedying the cause." [22] The cause, as we describe it in this volume, is grade-mindedness itself. The graded system, from which grade-mindedness stems, is based upon notions of motivation, of human development, and of human organization that are almost entirely outdated.

The nongraded plan, on the other hand, is free of the restrictions and the inconsistencies we have deplored. It is a solution that takes realities into account and places no false labels upon a child's status or progress. It leads teachers to deal with each child's needs

---

[20] "What Research Says About Nonpromotions," *California Journal of Elementary Education*, 21 (August 1952), p. 44.

[21] J. W. Wrightstone, *Class Organization for Instruction*, What Research Says to the Teacher, No. 13 (Washington, D.C., National Education Association, May 1957), p. 5.

[22] Willard A. Elsbree and Harold J. McNally, *Elementary School Administration and Supervision* (New York, American Book Company, 1951), p. 150.

quite apart from the needs of the others. It imposes no penalty upon teachers when their pupils penetrate advanced ground or remain on a lower level, so long as each child is making as much satisfactory progress as could reasonably be expected. It requires a broader view of the school enterprise and probably a greater amount of individual lesson planning, but for most teachers these would be a very modest price to pay for the benefits received.

For the child, school changes from a game of pass-or-fail to the more serious and uplifting business of making the most of oneself. The false satisfaction enjoyed by the above-average child in a graded situation is replaced by the sober responsibility of maximizing one's talents for learning. For the less able child, a state of nearly continuous frustration is replaced by an atmosphere in which there is frequent success and therefore a more genuine incentive to further learning. Even for the typical child, school life takes on a more wholesome perspective and the inducements to learning are more genuine.

Within such an atmosphere, it is contended, a healthy and cooperative group spirit will more likely develop. Individual mental health is more certain to be fostered.

Building Stronger Adults

If some of these contentions are valid, then it seems possible that through elimination of the grade barriers schools will be better able to develop strong mental health as well as academic growth in their students. In an atmosphere where a child's earnest efforts have a fairer chance of being appreciated, it would seem that success would breed success and children would become self-sufficient and wholly secure more rapidly and more frequently than in the graded setting.

Self-sufficient adults, realistically mindful of their limitations but positively oriented to capitalize upon their strengths, are certainly needed in our society at the present time. The graded system makes it harder to produce them, or requires a kind of hypocritical waiver of the rules in order to do so. It tends to narrow the minds and the operational freedom of teachers, and in effect make them conformists. The attendant effects upon the minds and the emotions of the children may be equally bad.

In the so-called "Rockefeller Report" published in 1958 there is reference to "the social ceilings on individual performance" that appear to exist in modern society as obstacles to the full development of individual talent.[23] The effects of these ceilings are seen as a danger to the creative spirit of men:

> Some of our more discerning critics are uneasy about the current aspirations and values of Americans. They sense a lack of purpose in Americans: they see evidence that security, conformity, and comfort are idols of the day; and they fear that our young people have lost youth's immemorial fondness for adventure, far horizons, and the challenge of the unpredictable.[24]

Whether or not "conformity" in a negative sense has been gaining ground in the United States because of the schools, it seems to be commonly assumed by many of the writers on this subject (notably Whyte in *The Organization Man*) that there is at least a relationship.[25] The forces that may be causing Americans to lose their individual identity, it is arguable, are certainly not unlike the forces that have prevented the teaching profession from completely shedding the graded school structure and all of its implications about the sameness of children and the likeness of their responses. Faceless children, all turning the same page at the same moment, all climbing the same steps at the same time, all seeking the same goals . . . these would be a caricature, possibly extreme but undoubtedly to the point, of the average, grade-norm personalities so much teaching appears to countenance.

The Teacher's Mental Health

In recent years there have been a number of studies which suggest that emotional instability and various psychotic or neurotic behavior patterns are found with alarming frequency among public school teachers. The existence of this problem is generally associated with such factors as the prevalence of unmarried women in the profession, the relative lack of opportunity and economic security for men teachers and those for women with dependents, the relatively low social status enjoyed among the professions by teachers,

---

[23] From *The Pursuit of Excellence; Education and the Future of America*. © 1958, by Rockefeller Brothers Fund. Special Studies Project Report V. Reprinted by permission of Doubleday & Co., Inc., Garden City, New York. See especially pp. 13-15.

[24] *Ibid.*, p. 45.

[25] For an interesting discussion of the research on school "adjustment" of children, see Wesley Allinsmith and George W. Goethals, "Cultural Factors in Mental Health: An Anthropological Perspective," *Review of Educational Research, 26* (December 1956), pp. 429-50. See especially pp. 441-47.

the extraordinary demands that are made of the schools in today's rapidly changing world, the ambivalent attitude of taxpayers toward teachers, and certain common practices of personnel administration found in the schools.

Jersild [26] has described some of the problems that teachers face in their personal and professional lives, noting that the search for meaning is one of the teacher's two chief concerns, the other being anxiety. He refers to such related problems as loneliness and hostility, suggesting here and there that teachers (like other groups of people) have all too few and too limited means of mutual understanding and communication. Some practices and features of the school are seen as indirect channels for venting hostility, as for example "the rigidities that appear in course requirements . . . or . . . 'the great areas of meaninglessness' so often found in school situations." [27] While Jersild argues effectively for individual self-discovery and for an emphasis upon personal significance in connection with everything teachers seek to learn and to teach, his volume is rather sobering in that it confirms the enormity of the problem of building adequate mental health in members of the teaching profession.

The mental health of teachers is an expanding field of research, and hopefully there may be great progress in understanding the needs of both in-service and preservice teachers. A number of promising clues to truly effective personnel administration, one example being the teaching-team concept, are already under exploration. At the same time, it is a rather curious and depressing fact that only a very few writers in the fields of mental health and public school administration have recognized the extent to which the graded school pattern, and in particular the grade-mindedness which it has bred, may have contributed to personality disorder and emotional conflict among American teachers.

This sweeping generalization cannot easily be discussed in the whole, not even when broken down into the single problem of mental illness of teachers, because there are admittedly so many other causes or antecedents of mental illness than the accused grade-mindedness. Our purpose is to describe grade-mindedness as *one* potential cause of such illness. In the graded structure there have existed, almost without challenge, conditions that ought certainly to be eliminated as a part of the crusade for better mental health, for teachers as well as for children.

To us it seems that the teacher who operates within either a

---

26 Arthur T. Jersild, *When Teachers Face Themselves* (New York, Bureau of Publications, Teachers College, Columbia University, 1955).

27 *Ibid.*, pp. 115-16.

deliberately grade-oriented framework, or one where grade labels are still in use but frequently ignored, has less opportunity to enjoy peace of mind than one whose working environment has been non-graded. It would be difficult to prove or to disprove this contention, and even harder to assign any quantitative value to the advantage allegedly enjoyed by the nongraded teacher; yet certain aspects of this advantage would be difficult to deny.

We believe that a certain amount of confusion exists within the profession now that grade labels have generally lost what was once universally accepted as their meaning. Just as a high school diploma now has several shades of meaning in the eyes of college registrars, employing officials, and critics of the schools, so does the phrase "promoted to the *x*th grade." We believe that the breakdown in professional acceptance of grade standards, symbolized chiefly by the frequency of so-called social promotions and the widespread practice of continuous promotion, has placed many teachers in the position where certain of their decisions cannot be explained with logic. Intellectual honesty becomes rather difficult for the teacher, not only in dealing with parents and children but in facing himself, when abandoned beliefs have to be mustered in defense of such decisions. It is no less difficult for the teacher when certain decisions that are in the best interests of children have to be explained as if they were extra-legal, or somehow improper. So long as the language and the philosophy of one system remain partially intact while another language and a conflicting philosophy are equally prevalent, it seems inevitable that guilt feelings and a sense of embarrassment will occasionally disturb even the most skillful of teachers.

The confusions and irritations of this situation must also have a debilitating effect upon staff relationships. Where grade labels and traditional promotion practices have more "validity" in one teacher's eyes than in another's, proper performance becomes a matter of dispute, and relationships between teachers become strained.

As has been indicated earlier, teachers as a whole are known to be a relatively conservative group both in their personal lives and in their professional attitudes. Nonetheless, it seems unlikely that there are many schools in America today where an overwhelming majority of the teachers hold with conviction a nineteenth-century belief in grade-level-expectancy standards and associated promotion practices. If such beliefs were to be seen as the far-right end of a philosophical continuum and the beliefs expressed in this volume were seen as the far-left position, it may be that the distribution of all American elementary teachers would resemble a rather tall and quite symmetrical bell curve with the extreme positions quite thinly populated. It may even be, hopefully, that the median position would be slightly left of the center.

Related to this supposition is a belief that nearly all school systems have the entire range of viewpoints represented on their staffs. Although school systems frequently attract personnel because of their reputation for one or another kind of philosophical emphasis, teachers frequently base their job-seeking on factors (geographic location, personal and family connections, and the like) other than philosophy. Thus it seems quite certain that every staff, including some of those where a nongraded pattern is already in operation, faces to at least some extent the problem of conflicts in philosophy and confusion in practice.

To summarize the meaning of this chapter and of others that have preceded it, it is our belief that the well-being of teachers and children alike is jeopardized by the continued use of grade labels. In the few "right wing" communities where their use is as straightforward and unequivocal now as a half-century ago, the frustrations for the majority of teachers may be few, but the impact upon children's personalities must be literally devastating. In the few communities at the opposite end of the continuum, the teachers may have many problems but they are spared at least the embarrassment of professional double-jointedness; the children, presumably, have significant advantages in their search for healthy ego satisfaction and in the development of their potential.

For the vast majority caught in the middle, life appears to be full of many contradictions and frustrations. These communities, in most of which the meaning of grade labels has been modified to suit present-day understandings of children's needs, do a disservice to their teachers by retaining the administrative machinery and the nomenclature of the system they have silently renounced. The teacher who operates on an essentially nongraded basis (which is good) comes up inevitably, and even frequently, against situations in which he is forced either to behave on a graded basis or to pretend that he is so behaving (both of which are bad). And if this appears to be an overstatement or an exaggeration of his plight, then one need only ask, "How strong must the forces of grade-mindedness be, if they prevent us from behaving overtly the way we want to behave, and often do behave, but which behavior we sometimes have to avoid at the expense of our self-respect?"

For self-respect is one of the cornerstones of a healthy personality, and a healthy personality is one of the indispensable requirements of a teacher. To entrust the young to anyone less than healthy, self-assured, and confident in the professional role he assumes is to invite serious trouble. We are reminded of Paul Witty's statement, that "studies have revealed that the frequency of personality disorder is very high among children in the classes of unstable teachers." [28]

For Further Reading

Allinsmith, Wesley, and George W. Goethals. *The Role of Schools in Mental Health*. Monograph Series No. 7, Joint Commission on Mental Illness and Health. New York, Basic Books, Inc., 1962.

Of several relevant chapters in this volume, Chapter 3, "Dealing with Mental Illness in Schools," is of particular interest. The authors acknowledge the important contribution that a nongraded arrangement can make toward the reduction or elimination of mental illness in children.

Association for Supervision and Curriculum Development. *Fostering Mental Health in Our Schools*. 1950 Yearbook. Washington, The Association, 1950.

This volume contains three major sections, one of which discusses the child's motivations and another of which describes factors determining behavior and development.

Bruner, J. S., J. J. Goodnow, and G. A. Austin. *A Study of Thinking*. New York, John Wiley and Sons, Inc., 1956.

An analysis of strategies in the utilization of information for thinking and problem solving. This volume is of value in explaining the cognitive processes and their relationship to human activity. The individual is seen as a dynamic person and *a priori* motivated.

Fullagar, W. A., H. G. Lewis, and C. F. Cumbee. *Readings for Educational Psychology*. New York, Thomas Y. Crowell Co., 1956.

In addition to the Hilgard reference cited in the foregoing chapter, the reader will be interested in the five selections, pages 225-79, on emotional and social development. In Part III there is a selection by Otto and Melby on "An Attempt to Evaluate the Threat of Failure as a Factor in Achievement." Also of interest is Ruth Nedelsky's selection on the teacher's role in the peer group, pages 436-46.

---

[28] Paul Witty, *Mental Health in Modern Education*, National Society for the Study of Education, Fifty-fourth Yearbook, Part II (Chicago, University of Chicago Press, 1955), p. 1.

Maslow, A. H. *Motivation and Personality*. New York, Harper and Brothers, 1954.

In this volume Maslow presents a systematic psychology in which an essentially optimistic view of man's potentiality prevails over what the author sees as negative, constricting aspects of many current psychological theories. The reader would find Chapters 5, "A Theory of Human Motivation," and 12, "Self-actualizing People: A Study of Psychological Health," of particular interest. Chapter 17, "Normality, Health, and Values," offers a view of normality which suggests the need for redefining family training and educational processes along more positive lines.

National Society for the Study of Education. *Mental Health in Modern Education*. Fifty-fourth Yearbook, Part II. Chicago, University of Chicago Press, 1955.

All of this yearbook is relevant to the discussion of the foregoing chapter. Of particular relevance would be Chapter 3 on motivation and learning, Chapters 7 through 9 on mental health practices, and Chapter 13 on the mental health of the teacher.

Nebraska Symposium on Motivation, 1955. Marshall R. Jones, ed. Lincoln, University of Nebraska Press, 1955. One of a series in Current Theory and Research in Motivation. Includes papers by Abraham Maslow, David McClelland, James Olds, Helen Peak, Julian Rotter, and Paul T. Young. McClelland's paper on the social consequences of the achievement motive, pages 41-62, may be of special interest.

8. THE ESTABLISHMENT
OF THE NONGRADED SCHOOL

Introduction

Reference has been made in earlier chapters to the surveys conducted by the authors in a number of communities known to have had early experience with nongraded school programs. In one of these studies, respondents were asked to describe their plans in operation and also to answer a series of questions about their experiences with nongrading. Specifically, they were asked:

1. Since what year has the plan been in operation?
2. Which "grades" have been replaced by a nongraded plan?
3. What contributed most to the successful development of the program?
4. What were the most difficult blocks or problems to overcome?
5. What advice would you give to other school systems contemplating the introduction of a nongraded plan?

It was found that the majority of these programs were about seven years old, although a few reported that they had started between ten and twenty years earlier, and few were only two years old. With few exceptions, the plans were limited to the "primary grades" (1, 2, and 3).

Tables 7, 8, and 9 summarize the information gathered from questions 3, 4, and 5, respectively.

Table 7 is an attempt to summarize the factors which, in the judgment of thirty-four school administrators or supervisors who completed the questionnaire, contributed most to the successful development of nongraded programs. The item mentioned most frequently is a strong interest and desire on the part of the teaching staff. Next in frequency were careful study by the staff of other plans in existence, and effective use of P.T.A. and other public-relations channels. The response categories as presented in the table overlap each other considerably, but it is possible to state with confidence that the majority of explanations for the success of nongraded programs falls in either of two major categories: (1) that teachers engaged in serious and continued study of the plans before and after they were adopted, and (2) that parents' understanding of the

Table 7

Factors contributing to the successful development of nongraded programs (as reported by thirty-four communities)

factor	frequency of mention
Strong interest and desire on the part of teachers	13
Careful study by the staff of other plans in existence; local research	12
Effective use of P.T.A. and other public-relations channels	10
Staff concern about pupil retentions and related pupil adjustment problems	8
Parent conferences; parent meetings	8
Special interest and leadership shown by a teacher, principal, superintendent, or supervisor	8
Continuous parent-education emphasis	7
Successful efforts to explain and promote the plan to parents	6
Very careful planning, step by step	5
Help given by other school districts and college personnel	5
Success of the program in a pilot school, leading to more general adoption	4
A friendly press and other publicity measures	4
Cooperation and harmony among the teachers	4
Moving slowly	3
Initiative shown by parents themselves in promoting the idea	3
Approval and support by the Board of Education	2
Permanency of staff personnel	2
The prospect of success for children and teachers	2
Conservative admissions policy in first year; care in determining which children to admit to nongraded groups	2
Help from central guidance and testing personnel	1

plans was so crucially important that various devices for enabling parents to study and to learn about the plans were employed.

In Table 8 are reported those blocks or problems that were encountered by the responding school systems. It is of interest to note that the preponderance of these problems involves limited flexibility

---

Table 8

Problems or difficulties that had to be overcome (as reported by thirty-four communities)

problems or difficulties	frequency of mention
Grade-level-expectation habits of teachers	10
Reluctance of traditionalists among teachers to try something different	9
General problems of providing understanding to parents	7
Problems of retraining or orienting new staff members to the plan	6
Problems of designing an appropriate report card or reporting procedure	5
Grade-level-expectation habits of parents	5
Dealing with the parents whose children need more time in primary	4
Continuous influx of new pupils and parents unfamiliar with the plan	3
Fears and doubts of teachers	3
Students moving away who have been under the plan ("loss of investment")	3
Problems of grouping and classifying children	2
Insufficient materials for various achievement levels	2
Leaders too impatient, not really thoroughly informed	2
Problems of being a "pilot school" among traditional schools	2
Insufficient number of other schools in school district using the plan	2
Teachers violating the operating rules in one way or another	2
Reticence or inability of staff to explain the plan's basic values to parents	1
Creating an adequate nomenclature for the new system	1
Persuading Board of Education to approve the new plan	1
State-mandated reports requiring grade designation	1

Table 9

Recommendations to school districts contemplating the introduction of nongraded plans (as reported by thirty-four communities)

recommendations	frequency of mention
Take time to get full parental understanding and consent	13
Get the cooperation of *all* teachers and staff members; common philosophy and knowledge	10
Move slowly, evaluate every move	9
Work closely with your P.T.A., and keep them informed on progress	8
Introduce the plan in one grade at a time, over a period of years	6
Have a sound program of testing and evaluation	5
Help teachers toward a complete understanding of child development	5
Study other nongraded plans in operation; adapt as necessary	4
Don't do it simply to be doing something *new;* it takes desire and hard work	3
Above all, understand what you are doing and why	3
Report carefully to parents on pupil progress	3
Use the conference method of reporting pupil progress	2
Emphasize the plan in teacher recruitment	2
Get Board of Education support in the early stages	2
Work with teachers first, then parents	2
Give plenty of consideration to unbiased teacher judgment	1
Make sure that leaders are the best informed of all	1
Protect teachers from large class size	1
Prepare and assist faculty (e.g., help from aides)	1
Never use the word "experiment"	1
Don't be discouraged by disappointments or setbacks	1
Have a strong program for the entrance of children	1
Be sure secondary teachers are well informed	1
Work toward system-wide plan (one school isn't enough)	1
Have a good publicity program in newspapers, etc.	1
Have a plan for explaining system to parents new to the district	1

or enthusiasm on the part of *teachers,* rather than parents. It should be noted here that some of the communities that reported the discontinuation of nongraded plans, in another part of the study not related to Table 8, mentioned the lack of teacher cooperation and failure of teachers to give adequate explanation of the plans to parents as major causes for lack of success. If lack of parental support and understanding can be attributed at least in part to the lack of the teachers' enthusiasm and understanding, then this information along with Table 8 affords convincing evidence that the teaching staff is the key to success in any venture of this kind.

This is substantiated in many ways by the information in Table 9, which summarizes "the most significant advice" that the communities operating nongraded plans would give to others contemplating the introduction of such plans. Here the underlying theme is that an adequately informed staff is the key to obtaining parental consent and to the discovery of appropriate machinery for implementing the philosophy which the staff comes to share.

Another recurring suggestion is that a nongraded plan cannot, or should not, be rushed into being. Only a relatively few communities—the postwar suburbs, for example—have the advantage of starting with an entirely new staff establishing its own precedents. Most communities have long-existing policies and traditions and a substantial proportion of the teachers are veterans with well-established ideas about school organization patterns, and time must be allowed for teachers and citizens to discover how harmoniously the nongraded approach may fit the really basic wants and needs of the community and contribute toward the realization of long-sought goals. Without allowing sufficient time for such discoveries, the questionnaire respondents advise, much long-run support can be lost.

Preparing the Way

American public education is essentially a conservative enterprise. Teachers are a relatively conservative group within the population, and the citizenry seems to react more nervously to changes in school practices than to many other kinds of social change. Any effort at major reorganization or improvement in the schools, such as the initiation of a nongraded plan within a single school or a group of schools, must therefore be done with great care. It is a complex task, calling for the mobilization of many forces and the skillful application of many psychological or social principles.

The suggestions in Table 9, offered by thirty-four school systems presently operating nongraded programs, provide useful clues about how to prepare the way for nongraded classes in other communities. Additional clues may be found in the literature on the sociology of school systems and on the processes of effecting changes in institutional operations. Certain basic principles emerge from the suggestions and clues found in these sources. One of them is that institutional changes may be initiated at almost any point in the personnel hierarchy. Another is that full acceptance of the arguments for change by the status leaders in the hierarchy (especially the superintendent) is highly desirable, if not indispensable. Yet another seems to be that the initiating group should consolidate its position by insuring that it fully understands the new idea and by laying careful plans for its promotion, before any widespread exposition of information and plans.

Initiation of the idea may actually come from any level within the staff hierarchy, or even from the community outside the school. It is probable that in many school systems there is no one who knows much about nongrading. The first person who happens to read or hear about nongrading may be a teacher, a principal, a supervisor, the superintendent, a parent, or an interested citizen. Many communities have commented on the special interest or initiative shown by various kinds of persons, as shown in Table 7.

A professional person or a lay citizen may first become injected with the spirit and the workings of the nongraded school in a variety of ways. In a population as mobile as that of the United States today, it is increasingly likely that a given community may open its doors to a family whose former residence was in one of the places where a nongraded school was, or is, in operation. The professional literature and other sources of professional communication are paying more attention to nongrading and related matters. Teachers themselves are more mobile than formerly, and in more frequent touch with college and university people whose interests converge on the problem of school organization.

The exact extent to which professors of education are familiar with, and enthusiastic about, the nongraded plan is not known. The probability is that there is much interest, and that considerable attention is now being given to questions of reorganization in both undergraduate and graduate courses in education. In addition, a number of professors have many opportunities to discuss these questions as they engage in consultative work. Some college instructors, stimulated by their class and field experiences in this area, have begun to concentrate specifically on the nongraded-school movement as a college course topic. Some courses dealing entirely with nongraded school organization are already known to be in existence, and indications are that other institutions will offer such courses as interest in the topic grows. Most of the newer textbooks in elementary education devote some space to nongrading, and probably this will lead to more discussion in a variety of courses.[1]

Whatever the source of original interest and information, and no matter who in the organization first espouses the cause of nongrading, it is quite clear that the first major step is to infuse the superintendent and his administrative-supervisory staff with the necessary understanding and enthusiasm.

By and large, the history of nongraded plans in this century is a story of the zealous dedication of individual leaders to an idea. Almost without exception, the relatively few communities that have adopted a nongraded system have done so because key people within the schools have labored mightily and persistently to impress upon their colleagues and their patrons that the elimination of grade classifications is not only theoretically desirable but actually feasible. Rarely have nongraded programs been launched without the highly enthusiastic support of the superintendent of schools and his principal staff officers. Nongraded programs have scarcely ever succeeded in buildings supervised by principals with less than great confidence in the wisdom and the workability of the idea. Solid and unanimous support of nongraded programs at the administrative level, in other words, appears to be an indispensable, vital factor in their success.

How the superintendent and his staff will become so inspired depends not only upon their own professional perceptions and philosophy, but also upon the nature of their contacts with the university people, with their own employees, and with people in the community, as well. This is illustrated by the experience of several administrators who have been associated with nongraded schools. In one New York community, for example, the superintendent and a building principal were initially "sold" on the nongraded plan by a persistent parent who had previously lived (and served as a P.T.A. president) in an Illinois community using

---

[1] Possibly the first institution in the United States to offer a professional course dealing exclusively with the nongraded school is the Central Washington College of Education, Ellensburg, Washington. Education 470: The Ungraded Elementary School, was first offered in the summer of 1957. The instructor was Miss Jettye Fern Grant, Supervisor of General Elementary and Kindergarten Instruction in the public schools of Berkeley, California.

Another pioneer in teaching about nongraded schools was the State University of New York, State Teachers College at Cortland. Dr. Maurie Hillson, who has since become Associate Professor of Education at Bucknell University in Lewisburg, Pennsylvania, was the instructor who designed and offered the course.

an ungraded-primary system. In an Iowa town, the initial impetus for an administrative study of the nongraded idea came from a teacher who shared with his colleagues a paper he wrote on the topic as part of a summer course at the state university. One California superintendent acquired his first enthusiasm for the plan as the result of a casual conversation at an Atlantic City convention with the enthusiastic principal of a partially nongraded school. The superintendent who introduced the ungraded primary in Park Forest, Illinois, first learned of the plan when his godchild became one of the first beneficiaries of the pioneer program in Milwaukee, Wisconsin. It is therefore possible to light the spark of initial interest and enthusiasm in a variety of ways.

After the administrators have acquired a thorough understanding of the nongraded arrangement and have developed a desire to investigate its merits, the second step is to acquaint the rest of the professional staff with it. Here the alternative courses of action are almost limitless, in the same sense that in-service education may be of many, many types. Each school will doubtless examine how its recent professional program was established for clues to appropriate procedures for bringing staff energy to bear upon a study of nongraded plans.

Whether to begin with an information campaign aimed at the entire staff or with one involving only the teachers most immediately concerned will be one of the first questions to settle. Obviously this will depend upon the size of the school system, its internal workings and politics, the recent (and long-range) history of the in-service program, and similar factors. Large school systems have tended to launch nongraded programs (and other improvements) on a school-by-school basis, using as pilot schools those that for various reasons are most "ready" for the new program. Milwaukee's plan, now extended to nearly all of its schools, began modestly in a single school and required many years before receiving city-wide acceptance. Some systems have originated staff study groups comprising only those teachers (usually of the primary grades) who would be participating in the program directly, whereas others have included upper-grade and high-school teachers in all phases of the deliberations and planning. No blanket rule can be laid down, but it would seem that best results can usually be obtained by beginning with informal, intimate discussion groups involving the teachers directly affected and then gradually expanding the circle of participation after the nucleus group has ironed out most of its preliminary questions and problems. In a small school system this might mean initial discussions involving only the first-grade teachers, or primary-grade teachers, for example, followed by meetings including all elementary teachers, and eventually a series of predecision meetings involving the secondary-school staff. In a larger system, it might mean a similar sequence of meetings on a school-by-school basis.

One of the advantages of restricted discussions during the exploratory stages is that it makes allowance for the traditional grade-mindedness and subject-mindedness of typical upper-grade and secondary-school teachers. While these are the teachers who stand to gain the most from serious examination of the nongraded proposal, they are also the least likely to understand and support the idea when it is first introduced. The elementary teachers are less likely to be overpowered by instinctive resistance from their tradition-bound colleagues if given time to weigh the arguments and muster supporting evidence. Eventually, of course, everyone on the staff should become involved in the planning and thinking, and the high-school teachers are likely to benefit in countless ways as the "contagious health" of a successfully nongraded program becomes apparent.

For reasons that will be evident in the pages immediately following, the administrators may find less staff resistance to the idea of nongrading than they had anticipated. The teachers in nearly all elementary schools and school systems in America have been engaged over the past ten or more years in studies of problems to which nongrading is at least part of the solution. While there are differences of relative readiness, with some schools requiring more time and study than others before nongrading could be successfully introduced, there are probably not very many schools in the United States which have not been moving (consciously or otherwise) in the direction of a nongraded program. Witness the almost universal interest in report card reform, in the question of promotion vs. nonpromotion, in provision for individual differences, in providing for the needs of typical children, and in the adaptation of the curriculum to the needs of the child. Serious study of any one of these problems must lead inevitably to the question, "What about this century-old system of dividing children into grades?"

Most of the temporary solutions which have been worked out for these problems make a mockery of the graded system. Certainly 100 per cent promotion and the variations of it represent little more than an effort to "get around the law." Similarly, the newer progress-reporting systems are designed in large measure to free the participants from the strait jacket of grade-expectancy standards. Almost any effort to modify the school program to fit the special needs of each child destroys or limits the usefulness of a grade calendar and the standardized pacing of learning events.

If these assertions are valid, then the efforts of the administration (or other proponents of change) to focus staff attention upon a promising solution ought to be well received. Planting the new idea is not actually a very difficult problem in those schools where the teachers have been continuously concerned with problems of promoting, of reporting, and of individualizing instruction. And where teachers have *not* been concerned with these problems, it is probably too early in the development of that staff to begin serious consideration of nongrading.

There are a number of ways of presenting the topic to the staff. One way may be to interest the teachers through reports by the principal on the discussions of nongrading which take place in administrative staff meetings. Another may be to interest the local planning council or similar group whose concern may be the determination of agenda for the local in-service program. Some staffs are close-knit and informal and may respond to ideas thrown into regular meetings or even the informal gatherings of teachers within the working day. These and many other ways may be used to excite enough interest that the staff will agree to take steps to increase its understanding of the nongraded arrangement and how it works.

Once a professional staff has agreed to investigate the merits of a nongraded program, the attack may proceed on several fronts and in a variety of ways. A thorough acquaintance with the growing literature of nongraded plans is one of the first prizes to seek, and can be facilitated by the assemblage of a central library on the subject. A number of the school systems which operate nongraded programs, besieged from all sides by requests for help and information, have mimeographed or printed brochures and pamphlets that may be obtained free or for a small charge. Articles and other materials such as those included in the chapter bibliographies of this volume can be made available. A collection of sample progress-report forms, reports on local promotion statistics and standardized test results, photographs and other pictorial materials which illustrate the local situation, and similar materials would be useful additions to the library and study center. As a general rule, the most desirable arrangement is one that puts copies of the most pertinent materials permanently into the hands of all concerned; while this involves a certain cost in purchasing and reproducing the materials, it represents a long-run economy.

Sometimes it is possible for members of the staff to visit schools where the nongraded plan is in operation. Actually the value of such visits is more likely to be psychological than informational, since the apparent "normalcy" of affairs in the nongraded schools is more readily visible than are the subtle mechanics of operation which differentiate it from a graded school. Visitors to a nongraded school may or may not notice the absence of grade labels on the doors and in the speech of their hosts, but they are sure to notice that the principal and his teachers have not been lynched by their townspeople, are apparently healthy and happy, and are evidently surviving what may in prospect have seemed a slightly hazardous undertaking. If they are astute observers, they may also detect dozens of things (e.g., the range of textbooks and instructional materials in use, the kinds of motivational devices employed, the absence of appeals to conformity) which reflect the more enlightened approach to education that the newer philosophy embraces.

Reading about the experience of others and seeing other plans in operation are useful concomitants of local staff discussion, but they are less important than the give-and-take which enters into such discussion. Here is where the special and unique factors in the local situation need to be fitted into the universal framework. Here is where Doubting Thomasina needs to be convinced, where the peculiar strengths and weaknesses of each teacher will need to be taken into account, where specific strategy will be worked out, and where the presence or absence of appropriate leadership will make itself felt.

How long and how deep this local discussion should be is the job of the plan's proponents to determine. Conceivably there are schools so happily staffed and so ready for this sort of progress that only a meeting or two is needed to weld them into action and get the policy campaign underway. Most schools would probably need an average of six months to a year of thorough staff study before they could be ready for this next phase. Some would need several years of preparation, especially where leadership is less effective or less inspired. Only a few schools would need a longer time to make ready: these would be the ones which have been less concerned with individual differences, report card reform, and similar problems, and in which the initial break-through has yet to take place.

Intelligent acceptance by the professional staff of the basic philosophy of a nongraded plan must be secured before any action is taken that goes beyond the discussion stage. This requires not only skill in gauging the true feelings of the teachers, but a great deal of patience. Additional time spent in helping teachers to increase their knowledge about, and their enthusiasm for, the nongraded plan may be a good investment against the plan's failure. Repeatedly in the authors' correspondence with administrators of school systems that have attempted a nongraded plan has appeared the admonition, "Be sure your entire staff is well informed and in favor of the idea!"

Introducing the Plan to the Parents

Let us say that the staff has reached the point where it has an excellent working knowledge of the nongraded philosophy and its mechanics, and has further resolved to work toward the establishment of a nongraded program in the present primary and/or intermediate grades. The next step, then, is the development of a plan for presenting the proposal to the community.

Ideally, the in-service professional program for the staff ought to be geared in some way to the school system's parent-education and public-relations programs. In many schools, representatives of the P.T.A. and other groups participate regularly in the in-service program, especially as it relates to curriculum development. In many schools there are regular study groups and other devices for bringing parents and teachers together to discuss educational and child-rearing problems. In such schools as these, it is quite likely that some of the more interested and well-informed parents will have participated in the original studies which led to the decision by the teachers to establish nongraded classes. These parents will become the shock troops, the couriers, the spokesmen, and the allies of the teachers in their drive for support. Expanding the size of this group, through public meetings and other devices, will be an appropriate step to take.

Obviously the Board of Education represents the most important single group to be convinced of the merits of the proposed plan. Boards of Education, of course, vary a great deal in their quality and their make-up, and some will be closer to the ongoing professional activities of their employees than others. A definite plan for approaching this group and involving it in the phases of the study will be needed before a decision has been taken. Ideally, the superintendent and his staff will keep the Board well informed on the nature and the progress of all of the staff's in-service activities. This implies that the Board members would become aware of the staff's interest in nongraded programs in advance of the time that policy recommendations might be expected to come before them for approval. The superintendent, estimating the progress of the project and the readiness of his Board to review it, might encourage individual board members to join in certain of the study activities and field visits, to acquire a background for the decision that must eventually be made. Thorough and complete records should be kept of all study activities so that it will be as easy as possible for Board members to acquaint themselves with the history and the status of the project.

Convincing parents and Boards of Education of the merits of

a nongraded school program is actually a less difficult task than it may appear to be at first glance. Laymen generally view educational problems with a more objective, open mind than many teachers realize, and logical solutions to school problems are often more readily accepted by the nonprofessional than by the habit-ridden professional whose mind-set may obscure the facts involved. Witness, for example, the fact that parents have been more sympathetic than teachers to report-card reform, to such allegedly controversial curriculum innovations as "sex education," to adequate library services in schools, to more aesthetic experiences within the curriculum, and so on. The history of the nongraded school seems to bear out this assertion: whereas few schools have reported failures due to parent resistance, a number have reported that programs could not be launched or had declined after they were begun, because of stout resistance from grade-minded teachers. In addition to emphasizing the importance of having all teachers really convinced of the idea's worth, this situation seems to confirm the notion that parents in most communities are remarkably inclined to support (or at least, tolerate) the efforts of teachers to break away from the graded system.

Some parents can be expected to support the change with particular zeal and enthusiasm. These will include parents whose own experience as children was less than satisfactory because of the existence of tightly defined grade classifications. For example, there are among parents (and teachers) working with today's generation of school children fairly large numbers who in their own childhood "skipped a grade." Apparently very little formal research has been done on these people, except for the unusually gifted. The authors, at least informally, have discovered through widespread questioning and interviews that a large proportion of such persons express mild to severe regret over their "skipping" experiences. While professional men in particular express appreciation for the time which was gained in launching their careers, many confess that the literal "skipping" of virtually a whole year's groundwork, in addition to the social and related problems which they encountered simultaneously, caused many difficulties which took years to iron out. It seems quite probable that any thorough research into the feelings and attitudes of these double-promotion cases from the last generation would show these people to be generally antagonistic to the system. Quite probably, many would join the general trend against double-promotion which is observable in the United States in the past decade or two. They would almost certainly turn out to be the most enthusiastic supporters of the nongraded school plan, which permits none of the "skipping" mentioned above, but which encourages rapid progress under more desirable circumstances.

Therefore, the support of many parents seems to be assured if the staff can show how the nongraded school solves some of the problems which parents themselves have experienced. As in all school-public relations, the enthusiasm and support of the professional staff is the real key to preparing the way with parents for a nongraded school. It is difficult to imagine a community of parents, represented by their Board of Education, denying a staff the opportunity to attempt a nongraded program if the staff very clearly believes it to be desirable and knows how to go about it.

Reaching the Whole Community

Once a staff has received authorization from the policy-making Board of Education to launch a partial or complete nongraded program, its next step is to prepare the general public for the events which will follow. A broad-scale campaign of publicity and information must be planned. Here everything depends upon the solidarity and enthusiasm of the total staff, since questions will be asked not only of the zealous leaders and the teachers directly affected, but of everyone else involved. All members of the staff should be in a position to answer these questions, and of course their answers should reflect their confidence in the wisdom of the new arrangement. Faint praise or direct criticism from members of the staff at any level could easily undermine the efforts of the others.

Not to be overlooked in the earliest stages of the information campaign is the power of the local press. The adoption of a nongraded system is a newsworthy and important step for a community to take, and the local editors are certain to show a great deal of interest in it. Given only half the facts, or little impression of the staff's enthusiasm for the plan, the editor could do real damage to the project with the wrong sort of news reporting. The staff would do well to invite the newspaper people to its meetings, provide them with large quantities of basic data, furnish charts and other visual material to illustrate the characteristics of the plan, and otherwise provide them with the ingredients of accurate, interesting, and complimentary news stories. Probably this sort of close cooperation with the press will need to continue for a number of years, until no further possibility of misunderstanding or erroneous reporting remains.[2]

---

[2] Newspaper staffs have turnover, too. One new photographer created a minor headache for a nongraded school staff by his printed caption, "Second Graders Visit Dairy Farm." In this case, both the teacher who was present at the picture taking and the editor failed to inform the newcomer of the school's organization plan.

Information about the new program needs to be passed along not only to the parents directly involved, but to various public and nonpublic agencies dealing with children. Doctors and dentists often query children about their school status, and with a little coaching can be persuaded to use some other phrase than "what grade are you in, Johnny?" Church school leaders, who often base their Sunday-school grade placements upon the public school's decisions, can ordinarily be persuaded to adopt a nongraded scheme of classification if shown the reasons for it. Scout groups, youth clubs, the public library, public health agencies (e.g., the groups dispensing the Salk polio vaccine by age- or grade-levels)—these are examples of the organizations whose awareness of the absence of grade labels can be helpful to the success of the public school program. Precautions taken with such groups, reducing the public tendency to talk and think in terms of grades, are of course only relatively useful; but at least they increase the public's appreciation of the school's earnest desire to accomplish its new goal.

Getting the word to parents who will be immediately and directly affected is a more obvious, and in many ways a simpler task. The importance of a strong P.T.A. (or equivalent) is demonstrated here again, since schools or school systems with good home-school communication and rapport have a real advantage in getting information to their patrons. If there is a parent-sponsored home-school newsletter, or similar periodic bulletin to parents, this can be used as a channel for communication. Meetings of homeroom groups, or study groups, or the general membership can turn attention to the proposed plan. Person-to-person telephone campaigns, either to announce meeting plans or to pass along actual details of the nongraded system, can be carried on. Small groups of parents can be invited to school on a staggered schedule for discussions involving key staff members. Individual parent-teacher or parent-principal conferences can be scheduled. The past habits and working patterns of the school and parent groups would of course influence the type of approach to be used.

The Board of Education and school administration may elect to produce one or more bulletins, newsletters, or pamphlets describing the nongraded program and plans for instituting it locally. The Board may also wish to sponsor official meetings and discussion groups. It will almost certainly request that maximum individual parent-teacher contacts be used as a means for informing parents of the new program. Among other things, it will wish to clarify the questions most frequently raised: Is the educational program undergoing a basic change? What about the reports of pupil progress to be received by parents? What if we move to a community which still follows the graded plan? Is my child about to become a guinea pig in some "progressive" experiment? and so on.

To insure adequate long-range publicity and goodwill, some school systems have regular programs of communication with parents of preschool children. One school maintains an up-to-date list of preschool siblings and sends an annual "newsletter" (addressed to the child, but of great interest to parents) to the home until the child is eligible for enrollment. It is easy to see how this excellent device could be put to good use as a means of alerting the preschool child and his parents to the revised "rules of the game" under which he will operate in the future.

Many schools also maintain good relations with nursery schools serving their neighborhoods. Nursery-school teachers can be of great help in preparing both children and parents for the nongraded program lying ahead; at least, they can employ the proper vocabulary and avoid the idea of "passing" to the kindergarten. Usually nursery schools sponsor periodic parent meetings or discussion groups, and the public-school principal or his representative would almost certainly be welcome to speak to the parents about the nongraded program at one of these meetings.

Preparing the Way with the Children

There are essentially two ways to start a nongraded program. One is to institute it in the first year only, when the children enter the lowest "grade level" involved, and expand it to a more advanced group each year. The other is to decree the abolition of existing grade levels over the entire span (e.g., grades 1-3, or 4-6, or 1-6) as of a given moment, trusting that children will gradually forget the grade labels that they once were assigned. The first plan, recommended by many (see Table 9), has the advantage of allowing the gradual indoctrination of each successive group of children and their parents into a pattern which becomes more easily accepted as the years go by. It has the disadvantage of requiring a three-year period or more before all grade labels are dropped. It also is awkward in some ways for the surviving graded class just ahead of the first nongraded class. Despite these limitations, the gradual approach has been used much more widely than the swift-stroke approach.

When the gradual approach is used, the children who will need the most attention and guidance will be the spearhead group, the first class to be without a grade label. This work usually begins in the kindergarten, where the teacher, the principal, and others explain to children that beginning next year with their class they will be called "Primary" (or whatever term has been selected) children rather than "first-graders." A continuous campaign is conducted to edit the grade labels from their speech and to substitute the appropriate designatory language. The kindergarten teacher avoids the concept of "passing in June," and other promotion-related phraseology. While these may seem like minor considerations, the fact is that they set the stage for the more important precautions and procedures which follow the next year.

The close relationship of kindergarten services to the general success of a nongraded program deserves further examination at this point. It seems to the authors to be more than a coincidence that practically all of the communities known to be operating nongraded programs operate kindergarten programs as well, and have done so for many years. It may be argued that the educational climate in those communities where kindergartens exist, and especially in those where top-level administrative people give frequent public expression to the values of such services, is far more likely to lead to the inauguration of a nongraded program than the climate in communities where kindergarten has not been regarded as important. In fact, it would seem reasonable to argue that the leaders in communities without kindergartens who seek to develop a nongraded program might regard as their first job the creation of sentiment in favor of kindergarten services within the staff and the parent group.

Among the obvious reasons for this would be that the school would be enabled through kindergarten services to make a far more accurate appraisal of each child's needs and potentiality, prior to assignment to the graded (or nongraded) years. Another is that kindergartens in operation tend to be more "nongraded" and flexible than any other level, and that the child's mental health is more likely to develop along desired lines in such a climate than in one where the weight of the graded system is omnipresent. This is not to claim that all kindergartens are well run along lines conducive to positive emotional growth of children, since many are not; [3] but kindergarten teachers are generally more free to meet the real needs of children than are most grade teachers, and the effect of this may be very positive indeed. Consider, for example, the assertion of Adlerblum: "A child who has a favorable start in a good kindergarten with a warm, perceptive teacher is . . . less likely to develop into the one out of 12 who (at the present rate) will some

---

[3] See Dorothy W. Baruch, "Mental-Health Practices at the Pre-School Level," *Mental Health in Modern Education,* 1955 Yearbook of the National Society for the Study of Education, Part II (Chicago, University of Chicago Press), Ch. 7, pp. 145-76.

day be a patient in a mental hospital." [4] While there may or may not be research evidence to support this rather strong view, it corresponds with the experience of the authors in their work with pre-primary children and teachers.

One of the advantages of a kindergarten understructure for the elementary years is that parents and teachers are enabled to establish, under less pressure than would exist later, a bond of mutual understanding and a basis for estimating the child's future progress in school. This has been discussed briefly in the chapter on reporting, but deserves re-emphasis here because of its implications for sound mental health in both the parent and the child, if not the classroom teacher as well. Beginning with the kindergarten level, the parent comes to see his child through the progress-reporting system in dimensions not otherwise open to him, and the adequacy of the system is therefore of crucial importance. A system geared to grade-level-expectancy standards and replete with the vocabulary of promotion and failure cannot possibly be so adequate, especially in the early years, as one in which the artificiality of grade requirements has been set aside.

With a successful and helpful kindergarten experience behind it, therefore, each class of beginning primary children may find it relatively simple to adjust to the requirements and the arrangements of a nongraded program. Nevertheless, the teachers must pay constant attention to the smaller as well as the larger details of pupil identification with the program. For example the class may need to be reminded again and again, as subtly as possible, that its correct classification is "primary." Whenever reference needs to be made to other children in the second and third grades, etc., it should preferably be done by the use of their teacher's name ("Miss Jones's class"). It would be helpful to explain the new system to the second-, third-, and intermediate-grade children and to request that they support the enterprise by use of the new "Primary" label. This is especially important in the case of the older brothers and sisters of primary children, who should perhaps receive occasional "pep talks" on the subject of their sibling's novel and enviable status as the first of the classes in the new plan.

In the beginning, it may appear to the staff that the elimination of grade levels is a losing fight. The habits of a century are not easy to shake, and adults and children alike are bound to slip. Probably the minor irritation of the vocabulary-and-labels problem assumes an artificial importance during this critical period, and the temptation increases to abandon effort and return to the habitual

---

[4] Evelyn D. Adlerblum, "Mental Hygiene in the Kindergarten," *NEA Journal*, *44* (February 1955), p. 80.

pattern. Often a teacher and class reach a point where progress seems evident, and then some event (such as the arrival of a new pupil, who brings with him his grade-level vocabulary and possibly his fears about "passing in June") arises to threaten the progress. Whenever transfers of children from class to class are made, a century of old habits somehow impresses itself upon the persons concerned in various obvious or mysterious ways, especially when a situation arises in which a child has clearly "lost a year's time." No matter how skillfully the change in status has been accomplished, some children will of course be at hand to taunt the affected child with the century-old gestures and comments describing failure.

Yet the observant and objective teacher will become aware of the slow but certain decline of such events and attitudes, and over a period of time she can reduce them to nearly zero by patient counseling, correcting, guiding, praising, and encouraging. Even in as short a time as three or four years principals have reported that the philosophy and the structure of nongraded class organization have become so well accepted that the children themselves straighten out the newcomers and their parents forget their earlier habits. When this point is reached, the staff can more fully divert its attention from the superficial problems of vocabulary and labels to the far more important business of truly individualizing the instruction in the nourishing environment which has been created.

A Challenge to Administrators and Supervisors

This chapter has dealt with the nongraded school at the level of practice, including ways of initiating and developing nongraded programs. Opening with the problems and the advice reported by administrators who are presently operating nongraded schools, it has suggested ways of preparing the administrators, the teachers, the parents, the community, and the children for the introduction of a nongraded plan. Out of this chapter and the ones preceding it, therefore, may have emerged a number of practical, operational concepts that have general applicability in situations where a change in school organization is being sought.

Clearly, the most important of these concepts is that resistance to the changeover to a nongraded program will more likely come from the teaching staff than from laymen. Clearly, too, this resistance will be greatest in the hearts and minds of those teachers for whom the individualization of instruction is still a hazy or doubtful goal. Grade-mindedness has left so deep a mark on the teaching profession that its by-products are everywhere, and it often blinds teachers to the real facts of professional life. The meaning of this situation for administrative and supervisory practice is very great.

It becomes evident, for example, that the administrator who sets out to establish a nongraded school must be prepared for many disappointments and set-backs along the way. Only a deep and abiding belief in the virtue of the goal can assure his survival at these moments. To reiterate a phrase from a previous page in the chapter, "The history of nongraded plans in this century is a story of the zealous dedication of individual leaders to an idea." Zeal belongs with conviction, and conviction grows from understanding.

Like a two-edged sword, the dedication of leaders (especially at the top of the hierarchy) involves certain hazards as well as protections. The protections include not only assured cooperation at the policy level and from top administration, but a stimulant toward system-wide adoption of the plan. It is no secret that a "pilot school," or a place where something "different" is being attempted, is often envied, resented, misunderstood, or resisted by other schools. Frequently it takes real courage to stand alone. In every city where a nongraded program has been initiated first in one or two schools on a trial basis, the principal and the teachers have been subjected to various pressures for their nonconformity. In most cases, the suspicions of others have gradually given way to acceptance, and the plan has spread to the other schools. In a few, however, the effort has been submerged in the currents of controversy. The principal of one such school wrote the authors to say that the most difficult block or problem he had to overcome, insurmountable at the time, was the total lack of any attempt to endorse the plan system-wide. It becomes obvious that the central administrative staff needs to bend its every effort, not only to support the pilot schools, but to spread the idea to the others.

The hazards mentioned above stem from the tendency of some leaders to become inextricably identified at the personal level with the causes to which they are dedicated. Sometimes a leader's enthusiasm for an idea such as the nongraded plan is so strong and so contagious that the idea spreads, more because of the affection or trust felt by the leader's colleagues for him than because of the intrinsic appeal of the idea itself. There is considerable evidence in the literature on leadership to support the thesis that followers will identify with a leader's ideas because of their identification with the leader as a person. In a recent yearbook of the National Society for the Study of Education,[5] for example, one of the basic

[5] *In-Service Education for Teachers, Supervisors, and Administrators,* Nelson B. Henry, ed., The Fifty-sixth Yearbook of the National Society for the Study of Education, Part I (Chicago, The University of Chicago Press, 1957).

principles expressed or implied is that change is more likely to occur in a school system when teachers identify the change process or the new procedure with a leader who has a record of getting things done and whose views are generally respected. It is also observed that teachers are likely not to identify with a leader whose reputation or record suggests that his ideas are not valued very much in the administrative hierarchy.[6]

It is important for leaders to be aware of this phenomenon. While an idea may be more widely espoused if a popular leader associates himself with it, it is potentially hazardous if the intrinsic merits of the idea are not fully explored and appreciated by themselves. If the idea seems good to teachers only because its proponent is their respected leader, there is always the possibility that the departure of the leader, or even a decline in his prestige, will result in the abandonment of the idea at a later date. This has, in fact, happened before. In the study of ungraded primary schools by Austin, the investigator came to feel that much "of the success of the gradeless idea rested on the shoulders of the enthusiastic leaders, and should they leave the schools the programs [are in danger of] reverting back to a regular graded school." [7] Since the record shows that this has occurred at least a half-dozen times in the past fifteen years, it behooves administrators to make certain (1) that they take pains to avoid too personal an identification with the plan and (2) that they make certain that most of the staff at least enthusiastically favors the plan on its own merits.

Coda: A Nongraded School Is Born

(*The following story is not literally true, although it combines elements from the actual experience of several groups of teachers and administrators. The authors are indebted to these pioneers for furnishing the data upon which the story has been based.*)

Probably the idea first entered Max Marshall's mind during the report card study. He had been Chairman of the Committee on Reporting that year, and this had given him a wonderful opportunity to do some serious thinking about the promotion policy, among other things. He recalls now how angry and frustrated he and his fellow committee workers were the night of the big uproar at the Board of Education meeting. That was the night the Citizens for Higher Standards came to challenge the recommendation, then

---

[6] *Op. cit.*, see in particular pp. 96 and 177.

[7] From a letter to one of the authors by Kent C. Austin, dated August 2, 1956.

under consideration by the Board, that a continuous-promotion policy be adopted. "There must be a better way to solve this problem," he remembers telling his wife that evening, after a blow-by-blow account of the fateful discussion.

And then, about three months later, all the pieces suddenly fell into place for Max Marshall. He was attending summer school at State, taking the last two courses for his Master of Education degree: the required course in measurement and an elective under Professor Sloane. It was a good feeling, after five years as an elementary school principal in Center City, to be finishing the degree work at last. Sloane's course on "Current Problems of Elementary Education" seemed like a logical one for pulling his graduate training together, and it had been most enjoyable up to July 12. That was the date of the summer conference, and Sloane had called off his class so that everyone might hear Dr. Thorne's lecture.

Thorne spoke straight to Marshall's purpose. It was almost as if Thorne had eavesdropped on the Committee on Reporting, or as if he had witnessed that school board fight, or even as if he had been sitting in the Roosevelt School office the past few months listening to Max's conversations with certain parents and teachers. Dr. Thorne knew the problems all right, and his proposal for their "solution" (he probably said "reduction," but you could tell he was sold on the idea) really made sense. Whether it was actually a great speech, or whether Max Marshall was simply very receptive, is now of no consequence: that was the day Marshall caught fire about nongraded elementary classes.

There were talks with Dr. Thorne, and Marshall was able to borrow the manuscript long enough to get it typed on stencils. There was the bibliography, each item of which had to be tracked down and digested. There were all those schools and people to write to. Suddenly the summer session was too short. Professor Sloane let Marshall change the topic of his course paper to one related to nongraded schools, so that some of his work in the library served a double purpose. Marshall's energy was channeled into the collection of as much information about nongraded classes as he could possibly obtain. The material from Appleton, Wisconsin, and Cabool, Missouri, arrived in time to be included in the paper and proved to be particularly helpful. Unfortunately, some excellent materials from Edmonds, Washington, and Coffee County in Georgia did not arrive until the day after his paper was turned in.

It was pretty close to Christmas before Marshall's search for information by mail had been essentially completed, but even before he returned to Center City from summer school he had collected enough evidence to support Thorne's enthusiasm for the nongrading of elementary classes. The periodical literature was rather thin and some of it was hard to find, but it was obvious from the tone of the letters he received that people were enthusiastic about their nongraded plans and wanted to encourage him. Most of the mimeographed materials they enclosed were also very enlightening and useful.

And so it was that Max Marshall found himself in Superintendent Smith's office on the Saturday morning before the preschool conference, chatting about his summer experience and sounding out his boss on the idea of nongraded classes. Max liked working for Smith, and he felt free to propose changes to him. He wasn't always able to win his point, but it seemed to Max that Smith was well informed and always objective in his analysis of a problem or a proposal. He could see at once that Smith knew about the nongraded plan and was favorably disposed toward it, but also that he saw it as a big step for a place like Center City to take.

The upshot was that Max was encouraged to study the idea with his staff and his P.T.A., and to report back to the superintendent in a few months (or wheneve. there was need for further discussion). Mr. Smith would find a way to alert the Board of Education to the fact that Roosevelt School would be studying the matter so that they would not be surprised if the news got around. These plans suited Marshall very well, indeed.

Preschool conference afforded several excellent opportunities for planting the seeds of the idea here and there. The traditional tea for parents of kindergarten children, held just after "early-bird" registration for the purpose of getting the parents and teachers together socially, was one chance Marshall would have for saying a few words to the mothers. Most of them, of course, were sending children to school for the first time, and so their interest and cooperation would both be high. The two kindergarten teachers, Mrs. Bailey and Jo Anne Green, met with Marshall on Monday to make last-minute plans for the tea, and they were joined by the invaluable Mrs. Hartwell, former president and now social chairman of the Roosevelt P.T.A. Marshall shared his plans with them in briefest detail, asking if they would approve the idea of setting up a study group or its equivalent to think during the year about a nongraded program. Jo Anne and Mrs. Hartwell took to the idea at once; Mrs. Bailey was agreeable, but Marshall made a mental note that she would probably need a little more convincing.

The tea was on Thursday. When Mrs. Hartwell introduced Max, she went a little overboard by saying, "Mr. Marshall has a wonderful new idea he wants to share with us, and he hopes we'll form a study group so that we can lay plans for an experiment a year from now." Marshall appreciated Mrs. Hartwell's enthusiasm, but did his best to retrieve the implied commitment. He pointed out his desire to enable teachers and parents, through cooperative effort, to work out still better ways of guiding children through the primary grades in order that their opportunities, especially for growth in reading skills, might be enhanced. He stated that the school would be asking for chances to discuss some plans and ideas about primary school organization "sometime this year," and urged any mothers with a special interest in the problem to make their names known to him or to Mrs. Hartwell.

The day before the tea, the Roosevelt teachers had met for what had come to be known as "local workshop," a full day for meetings and work sessions in one's own building. This was expected to be a big year, with class groups taking over one of the art rooms and also the newly created classroom where the old lunchroom used to be. This made for a total of 23 classrooms plus the kindergartens, and there were four new teachers in the building. Therefore Max had a lot of business to take up with his staff during local workshop. He did have a chance to tell briefly of his summer experiences at State, however, and he mentioned Dr. Thorne's talk and the study that he had been making of nongraded schools. He discovered to his surprise that Miss O'Neill, the new sixth-grade teacher, had also heard Dr. Thorne at the summer conference, and when she volunteered how much she had been impressed with the idea, it seemed to Max that the staff's faces reflected real interest. Jo Anne Green didn't say anything during the meeting, but when Max told the staff of his hopes to present a more complete description of the nongraded plan in the near future, he noticed that Mrs. Bailey whispered something to Miss Wragg, a second-grade teacher and a special friend of hers.

On Friday afternoon, another second-grade teacher came to see Mr. Marshall about a routine matter, and among other things she expressed concern because so many of the children she would have that year were apparently "below level" in reading. "I just hope I can have them out of the second readers by June" was her way of summarizing the problem.

"What difference would it make if you couldn't?" Max asked, in a semi-serious tone of voice.

"Well, I'd feel that I hadn't done my job well," was Miss Standish's reply, "and it wouldn't be fair to the third-grade teachers, either."

"That's the way we tend to feel about it when children are behind schedule," Max agreed. He then told Miss Standish some of the things that Dr. Thorne had said about grade expectations and their effect on teacher morale and efficiency. Their conference lasted over an hour; and Max could tell that Miss Standish was at least open-minded, possibly even enthusiastic, about nongrading.

He was pleased, because Miss Standish had prestige and influence with the staff.

It was five weeks before the new school year had settled down enough to permit further exploration of Max's plans. There were individual talks in which the idea of nongrading came up, but not until the second regular staff meeting did Max reopen the matter with the whole group. Then his plan emerged. He offered to conduct a series of voluntary study meetings on Mondays from 3:45 to 4:45, in which problems of promotion, grouping, reporting, and other aspects of pupil progress would be discussed. He agreed to make a library of pertinent readings available (magazine reprints, copies of Thorne's lecture, the materials received from Edmonds, Appleton, Coffee County, Cabool, and similar materials) and to report on his own studies of the problem. He suggested that the study group might be larger and more interesting if some of the parents were invited to join it, but this was not necessary if teachers preferred otherwise. He then asked the teachers for their reactions to the whole idea.

Miss Wragg was the first to speak. "Why couldn't we do this in our regular monthly meetings, instead of setting up extra afternoons for it?" Miss O'Neill, quite vocal though a newcomer, countered with the argument that it was a very complicated business, and she didn't see how there'd be enough time unless special arrangements were made. Jo Anne Green and Miss Standish expressed similar feelings, although Miss Standish admitted to misgivings over committing additional afternoon hours to school business. Mrs. Rutter, a fourth-grade teacher who had served for two years on the original Committee on Reporting, agreed with Miss Wragg and Miss Standish that time was precious, but she argued that the problem was an extremely important one. "It's time to get ourselves off dead-center on this promotion dilemma," she said. Miss Standish nodded her head in obvious agreement, and soon the group agreed to go ahead with the proposal of Monday meetings.

Marshall repeated that participation would be entirely voluntary and suggested that the first meeting be the Monday after next. He handed out copies of Thorne's speech for those who were interested, and told them that the other materials would be kept on a special shelf in the teachers' work room. On the parent participation question, which had been ducked by the teachers, he decided to sit tight.

Seven teachers came to the first meeting. Miss O'Neill was out with a cold, and Mrs. Rutter was a half-hour late because of a minor after-school accident involving one of her pupils. Miss Standish, Jo Anne Green, Miss Delancy (third grade), Miss Dalrymple (new teacher, first grade), and (to Max's surprise) both Mrs. Bailey and

Miss Wragg were there. Max had some "props" for his meeting, borrowed from a principal in Grosse Pointe, Michigan. One was a series of pictures showing the differences in pupil progress under graded and nongraded arrangements. Another was a similar chart, with flaps pasted at the grade-barrier points to dramatize the "wall effect" of grade lines. A third was a chart showing reading levels instead of grade levels, with detachable lines showing where the grade levels usually are found. These illustrations were highly interesting to the teachers, and in fact they dominated the discussion so much that the hour was gone before Max had found time to present his own report or to discuss certain aspects of Dr. Thorne's presentation. Max noticed that when Mrs. Rutter joined the meeting, Miss Delancy was the one who voluntarily explained the charts to Mrs. Rutter. She did a good job of it, too.

Max Marshall felt during the week that the meeting had gone well, but he was disturbed that only a third of his staff had been present. Apparently he did not notice that the charts, which were left in the teachers' room after the meeting, received a fair share of attention during the week. Not all of it was favorable, as he later discovered, but the discussions had had their effect: the following Monday there were thirteen teachers present at the second meeting. Besides Miss O'Neill, the newcomers included all but three of the primary teachers. Two big problems were discussed this time, one being "how do you report to parents in a nongraded program?" and the other being "how do children move from group to group if they get behind or ahead of the average?" Again, the hour proved to be too short a time, but it was definitely a good meeting.

Later in the week Mrs. Hartwell came in to discuss P.T.A. business, and she asked Max about his plans for the parents' discussion group. He told her that he hoped to get something started soon, and that the teachers were already engaged in a similar activity. He showed Mrs. Hartwell the charts, and also some of the reading materials available. Her keen interest led him to resolve that the inclusion of parents should not be delayed any further.

The following Monday, twelve teachers appeared. Max opened the meeting by expressing his genuine pleasure in the interest teachers had shown in the study group and by asking if the group felt ready to make some decisions about its future direction. Specifically, he asked them if they wanted to establish an agenda of questions to discuss, and whether they would like to think about his original question about parent participation.

Max was both surprised and pleased when Mrs. Bailey referred in friendly tones to the interest Mrs. Hartwell had shown in the idea of a study by kindergarten parents. She said, in effect, that she now felt comfortable enough about the nongraded idea to talk about it with parents, "especially the room mothers and people like that." Jo Anne Green immediately agreed, but felt that more than kindergarten parents should be involved.

At this point, Mrs. Dun, a third-grade teacher who had come for the first time, asked, "Does this mean you've already decided to have nongraded classes, and are trying to sell the parents on it?" This proved to be a helpful question, and it led to discussion of the difference between *studying* something and *deciding* something. The outcome was an agreement to invite Mrs. Hartwell, the eight kindergarten room mothers, and Mrs. Keeney, the P.T.A. president, to the following Monday's meeting for purposes of laying plans. Miss Wragg emphasized that the parents should be apprised that study, not decision-making, was the business at hand.

Mrs. Keeney and Mrs. Hartwell persuaded six of the room mothers to join them, and the following Monday the teachers' room was a busy place. This time there were about fifteen Roosevelt teachers on hand. Mr. Marshall opened the meeting by explaining why the parents had been invited, and by prearrangement Jo Anne Green mentioned briefly the charts and resources that were available to persons studying nongrading. Max maneuvered Miss Delancy into describing the charts more fully, and soon some of the other teachers were engaged in an impromptu panel discussion of nongrading, for the benefit of the mothers. At what seemed to him to be the right moment, Marshall asked the P.T.A. people if they thought the kindergarten parents would be interested in a series of meetings on this topic, and it was immediately apparent that they did. It was decided to refer the idea to the P.T.A. Executive Committee, with the recommendation that at least some of the meetings be scheduled when fathers could be present.

Max had been keeping Superintendent Smith in touch with the project, and now that a major milestone had been reached, he felt the need for more careful checking with him. In their conference, Smith reported that the board members had not objected when a casual reference to the Roosevelt School study group had been made. He suggested that Marshall present a brief report to the principals' staff meeting the following week, and he agreed to change the regular Monday meeting of the supervisory staff so that the reading consultant and the guidance director would be free to sit in on several of the Roosevelt meetings. Further, he expressed the hope that he himself could take part in some of the meetings.

Mr. Smith came through in more ways than he had promised. A chance meeting with Mrs. Keeney enabled him to give a verbal boost to the Roosevelt P.T.A.'s efforts, and since Mrs. Kennedy of the Center City P.T.A. Council was with her at the time, this led to expressions of interest in other P.T.A. groups. At the principals' staff meeting, Smith was especially skillful in the way in which he introduced Max's report, so that it looked to the other principals more like an expression of interest on the part of parents and teachers than like a pet project Max had cooked up. This was a touchy bunch, Max had found out, and it was best not to appear like a limelight-seeker.

Smith also had some ideas about press relations. He knew that Silas Bradbury, the local editor, would eventually hear about the study groups and that he might jump the gun on a news story. So he called on Bradbury, and after a brief explanation of the developing situation, asked if he'd like to assign a reporter to sit in on the meetings for a while in order to get background for the stories that *might* (he emphasized this) come out of them eventually. Smith capitalized on Bradbury's known interest in the continuous-promotion policy and on Bradbury's realization that his reporters a year ago had done an inadequate job on the wrangle involving the Citizens for Higher Standards. While he didn't say it, Smith more or less implied that perhaps Bradbury owed the schools a little better treatment the next time. Apparently Bradbury agreed.

The idea of inviting Dr. Thorne as the Central P.T.A. speaker in February must have originated with Miss Standish, who happened to be the P.T.A.'s corresponding secretary. At any rate, Max almost jumped out of his seat when Mrs. Keeney called to tell him Thorne was being invited. Several letters and one telegram later, Thorne was signed up. He would entitle his talk "Some School Problems We *Can* Do Something About," and it would deal with promotion and nonpromotion, meeting individual needs, helping the gifted, developing better readers, and so forth. Since Central P.T.A. involved all schools, this meeting was a perfect answer to Max's problem with the other principals. Roosevelt P.T.A. could drum up a real audience for Dr. Thorne by a telephone campaign, and the meeting would therefore serve as a good springboard to the study-groups plan. Furthermore, a date in February would give the Roosevelt teachers a little more time to consolidate their own thinking before parents became too heavily involved. Max knew that the teachers were likely to be more stubborn than parents about giving up their grade labels, and the extra time for teacher study would be helpful.

Throughout this period the reference library had been growing steadily. The teachers' work room happened to have a large bulletin board on the wall near the bookshelves, and this space was kept filled with the charts and other materials of interest. Pamphlets, graphs, and sample forms received from nongraded schools throughout the country were clipped or pasted on oak tag and displayed on some plastic book-stands Max found at the stationers. Bulkier materials were fastened in binders for easier handling.

The teachers in studying these materials became particularly aware of two features: nearly every nongraded school had developed graphic or tabular information on progress levels (especially in reading), and most of them furnished samples of their reporting forms. During one of the January staff meetings, it was agreed that the Roosevelt teachers would go over all of these materials and establish a separate collection for each category. Mrs. Rutter, a veteran on the reporting committee, agreed to be responsible for organizing the reporting materials, with the assistance of Miss Dalrymple, Mrs. Bailey, and Mrs. Dun. Another informal working "committee," headed by Miss Delancy and including Jo Anne Green and two first-grade teachers, agreed to organize the materials on progress levels.

A few days after the meeting in which the two working committees were established, Miss Wragg asked Max Marshall for an appointment. It was evident from her expression that she was none too happy about something. Max suggested that they talk during the afternoon period when her second-graders would be having an art lesson.

Miss Wragg came directly to her point. "I think it's only fair to tell you that some of us aren't happy about this primary school business. We think it's being rushed too fast, and there's not enough study of the negatives."

"The negatives?" Max's intonation invited Miss Wragg to elaborate.

"Yes, there are some bad things about it. This levels business will be much harder to keep track of, and parents will probably ask a lot more questions to find out just where their children stand, and it seems as if teaching will be much harder to plan if there aren't any grade standards we can depend on."

"Well, aren't these the questions we're trying to study?" Max inquired. "I hope it isn't true that we're rushing into this thing too quickly."

"I think we are rushing," Miss Wragg rejoined. "Otherwise why would Beatrice Rutter tell her committee what she did about having the report form worked out by next week?"

Max listened patiently as the basis for Miss Wragg's concern became more apparent. Mrs. Rutter, it seems, had given a pep talk to her committee about trying to get everything organized and surprising the staff with a recommended reporting form. Mrs. Bailey had interpreted this as a stampeding maneuver, and, of course, her close friend Miss Wragg had soon heard of her concern.

Max did his best to assure Miss Wragg that the matter would

not be rushed. On the matter of negatives, he invited her to "play the Devil's advocate" by organizing her doubts into a document for discussion.

A day or two later, the mail brought a document from Vestal, New York. It was the summary of a questionnaire sent by a group of teachers studying the nongraded school movement to forty-three school systems which were using, or formerly had used, the nongraded plan. About three and a half pages of the report were devoted to replies to the question, "What is bad about the nongraded plan?" Max immediately offered the report to Miss Wragg for her use in reviewing the negatives. Furthermore, he told her he would try to help in preparing such a list, since there were a number of questions in his own mind and this would help to organize them.

Within a week, Miss Wragg and Max had prepared a list of problems, in question form. For a title on the document, they agreed to "Can We Answer These Questions Satisfactorily?" Among the questions were: (1) Are reading levels merely a lesser evil than grade levels? (2) Would group instruction become impossible if every child were progressing at a different pace? (3) Will parents be dissatisfied if pupil progress is not geared to grade norms? (4) Will teaching become too difficult in a nongraded classroom?

The list was mimeographed, and given to teachers on the Friday preceding the next study meeting. Whether the list or the activities of the working committees had stimulated interest, Max was amazed to observe that every Roosevelt teacher was present on Monday. This was the first occasion of 100 per cent attendance, and it also turned out to be a good meeting. There was plenty of discussion pro and con, with the questions providing a general structure for the meeting. A number of the questions were apparently answered to the satisfaction of everyone, including those least enthusiastic about the plan. Some of the other questions, it was recognized, could not be answered until more information was available. Three or four of the problems appeared to be genuine roadblocks, with the "proponents" of nongraded classes hard-pressed to find a satisfactory answer.

At Miss Standish's suggestion, it was agreed that the questions not satisfactorily answered should be sent to Dr. Thorne, whose talk was scheduled for about two weeks later. It was also agreed that further communication with some nongraded schools about these specific questions would be desirable.

And so the weeks sped by, and the project gained momentum. Dr. Thorne's talk was well received by the parents as a whole, although there was quite a bit of attention paid to the reporting problem, and to what one parent called a "softening of school standards," during the question period. Seventy-three parents signed up that night for a "study series" to extend over the next several months; and with about fifty additional parents who had signed up through the kindergarten room mothers earlier, a good-sized group of interested people met four evenings. Attendance averaged about 85, not including the six teachers who had volunteered to serve as resource people for the "buzz groups."

At the staff level, the two working committees came up with progress reports that served as the basis for several lively meetings. The teachers found it easier to agree on the curriculum levels than upon the reporting system. In fact, the latter problem wasn't really resolved until the following September.

In early April, Max and three of the teachers motored to the nearest community in which a nongraded program was in operation. The trip was 382 miles each way, so they drove over on a Sunday and came back Tuesday night. The Board of Education paid their expenses. Although they felt that the trip hadn't allowed them enough time to do everything they had hoped, they were agreeably impressed with what they saw, and their hosts were more than generous with their time and ideas. The group reported to the other teachers in an informal panel discussion, which was tape-recorded; the following week the recording was played for the parent study group and Max used the opaque projector to show all the various forms and written materials they had picked up. While nothing especially new or unexpected had been learned during the visit, somehow the Center City people gained reassurance from the first-hand knowledge that the nongraded school plan was succeeding elsewhere.

With the end of the school year approaching, Max learned that one of the first-grade teachers would not be returning to teach in Center City next year because of a change in her husband's employment. In the process of recruiting a new primary teacher, Mr. Smith and Max both took special pains to inform candidates of the school's interest in nongraded classes and one of the criteria for selection of the new teacher was adaptability to, and a definite enthusiasm for this pattern of organization.

By the middle of May, the teaching staff and the parent study group were both convinced that the nongraded plan was worthy of adoption, and most of the presumed obstacles had been overcome. Miss Delancy's committee, joined by a group of parents, had worked up a statement of general goals for the primary curriculum and a statement describing the progress levels which were to replace grade levels. Mrs. Rutter's committee, augmented not only by some parents but also by a principal and a teacher from the Lincoln School in Center City, had worked out a tentative plan for reporting pupil progress. Max himself, with the help of Mrs. Keeney and

Superintendent Smith, had worked out a public-relations plan for obtaining public understanding. In the busy weeks that followed, formal or informal authorization was given, in order, by the teaching staff, by the Roosevelt School P.T.A., by the principals' staff, and by the Board of Education.

The plan called for the establishment of a first-year-primary group in the Roosevelt School beginning in the fall. In each of the two succeeding years, the plan would be moved upward into the next grade, until the entire primary program would be ungraded. It was agreed that any parent or teacher unwilling to participate during the trial period could request a transfer to another school, and that children or teachers so transferred would be penalized in no way. No teachers requested a transfer. The parents of three children made a transfer request, but subsequently changed heart when they learned that other parents were not similarly inclined.

On September 5, there were four new signs on the corridor walls. One of them said "Primary Classes, Rooms 6, 7, and 8." The others said "Miss Dalrymple, Primary"; "Miss Cotton, Primary"; and "Mrs. Reid, Primary." Some of the older children noticed the signs and talked among themselves, in a matter-of-fact way, about the "new plan without grades." The children who entered Rooms 6, 7, and 8 passed by the signs without any noticeable change in blood pressure or pulse rate. Inside, they settled down to the serious business of learning. A knowing parent or two, mindful of the meaning of the signs and with a mild sense of excitement, peeked through the door glass to see if all was well.

Down the corridor in his office, Max Marshall was so busy summarizing the opening-day attendance statistics that the significance of the moment escaped him.

But a nongraded school had been born. And there wasn't a cigar in sight!

The story of Center City has here been painted in rather bright colors. One may rightfully wonder if changes in school procedure could be accomplished normally with so little struggle. We would be the first to agree that this is a fair question, and that often the road to a nongraded program will be an uncomfortable and even perilous one. Yet we believe that our story is by no means sugarcoated or unrealistic, and that it could be duplicated in literally thousands of American school situations.

The characters in our story were sincere and intelligent teachers, blessed with good leadership, and working within the friendly climate of strong home-school relationships built up over many years. They were enabled gradually *to understand and to believe in* the nongraded organization as one means of reducing the problems that had been disturbing them for a long period of time. They were caught up in the spirit of an exciting idea, and they allowed themselves to explore it at least. They drew without embarrassment upon the resources and ideas offered generously by other professional people whose experiences had been different from and in some ways richer than their own. They asked questions openly and they considered the answers objectively. They shared the workload of their study, including service to the parent study group, willingly and in a cooperative spirit. Is it unrealistic to believe that a great many teachers would behave in much the same way if given the opportunity?

For Further Reading

Bahner, John M. "An Analysis of an Elementary School Faculty at Work: A Case Study." Unpublished doctoral dissertation, Chicago, University of Chicago, 1960.

Reports the experiences of the school staff in Englewood, Florida, where significant curriculum-improvement activities and efforts at school reorganization proceeded simultaneously.

Downey, Lawrence. "Direction Amid Change," *Phi Delta Kappan* (February 1961), 186-91.

An excellent discussion of the reorganization process in schools, and the factors to be taken into account.

Lippitt, Ronald, Jeanne Watson, and Bruce Westley. *The Dynamics of Planned Change: A Comparative Study of Principles and Techniques.* New York, Harcourt, Brace & World, Inc., 1958.

Chapter 2, "Diagnostic Orientations Toward Problems of Internal Relationships," includes discussions of the internal distribution of power, the internal mobilization of energy, and internal communication. Chapter 3 deals with external relationships. Chapter 4, "Motivation of the Client System," discusses "change forces" and "resistance forces." Chapter 6 describes seven phases of planned change (development of need; establishing a change relationship; working toward change: diagnosing or clarifying the problem, examining alternative routes and goals, and transforming intentions into actual change efforts; generalizing and stabilizing change; and terminating relationships with any outside "change agent" involved). Subsequent chapters describe the specific techniques used by the change agent. In Chapter 10 there is a discussion of "changeability within the system" together with comment on the problems of doing research on planned change.

9. THE NONGRADED SCHOOL

TODAY AND TOMORROW

In education, we know much better than we do. We have yet to create the best school of which we are capable. But fortunately we have our visions. As soon as one vision is translated into reality, it is replaced by others, and each seems better than the last. To close the gap between reality and our best visions is a great task of human engineering, the mission that challenges every educator who wants to make good schools better.

There is a past, a present, and a future to be taken into account in school improvement. Unless educators know where they have been, they cannot judge the relevance of where they are going. Unless they know where they are, they cannot properly appraise the skills required to get where they want to be.

The elementary school we have is largely a product of the past. It represents the outcome of previous efforts to translate educational views into the solid substance of a school. Similarly, the school of tomorrow will reflect educational views of today. To project the school which we could have, we must understand both the school we have and the thinking behind suggestions for improvement in it. This concluding chapter first points to discrepancies between the graded elementary school and certain aspects of contemporary educational thought. It then suggests some improvements which will lead to the better school of tomorrow.

The School We Have and the School We Could Have

The graded school, brought into existence more than one hundred years ago in Quincy, Massachusetts, was not completely new. But it was a unique synthesis of features that characterized other schools, and it represented the ideas of thoughtful men of the time. The men who created the Quincy Grammar School prophesied that it would set the pattern of American schools for fifty years to come. They erred only in being conservative. The graded school became not a landmark but a shrine, growing more venerable over a century of school-keeping.

It must be appreciated that the nineteenth-century graded school was a significant creative effort appropriate for its time. It permitted the convenient classification of unprecedented numbers of pupils pouring into the schools during the second half of the century. It encouraged the division of knowledge into segments to be taught at the various grade levels. Consequently, it simplified the task of preparing needed teachers quickly; teachers simply were taught what they were themselves to teach in a given grade. Man's zeal for efficiency was challenged and he met the challenge vigorously. Soon an enterprise of gigantic proportions was functioning with amazing efficiency while continuing to expand at an astonishing rate. That so many people agreed so quickly and so generally on distinct learning tasks for each grade level is truly amazing.

But not all people agreed. There were those who saw in such a system not efficiency but regimentation. Some spoke out against what appeared to them to be a denial of individual uniqueness and an appeal to mass conformity. A few acted. Here and there innovations appeared in school organization, innovations that encouraged individual rather than uniform rates of pupil progress. But the innovators moved or retired or died, and with them went the products of their creativity. Their works, however, became data to be reckoned with in more propitious times.

The twentieth century brought these more propitious times. Long-standing concern for the individual led to scientific study of the individual. Basic likenesses in the needs, drives, and associations of human beings were reaffirmed. But now the differences in capacity, temperament, interest, energy, and creativity were documented. Educators began to realize the infinite variety of routes to individual accomplishment and satisfaction and the varied settings needed to realize human potentialities. Some regarded learning more as a process of intellectual inquiry than the possession of a classified body of facts and ideas.

School practices underwent change. Recognizing the differences in reading attainment among children in a given grade at any moment, some teachers divided their classes into several groups, each group using different reading materials and receiving separate instruction. Recently, in fields such as science and social studies, a few publishing houses have been producing two sets of textbooks, each covering the same material but at different levels of readability. Some school systems changed their marking and reporting practices. Instead of marking pupils on the basis of child-to-child competition (A to the top 5 per cent, B to the next 20 per cent, and so on), they marked them on individual progress and effort in relation to previous performance and the teachers' estimates of ability. Thus, a child of very low ability might well receive an A because of his progress or serious effort.

Such changes were not generally acclaimed by either teachers or parents. High-school teachers, in particular, were often confused about the real meaning of new marking procedures in the elementary schools and protested that what they saw was an abandonment of grade standards. Parents were bewildered and frequently angered over the seeming contradiction between good marks all year and nonpromotion for certain children at the end of the year. They regarded with suspicion the discovery that their Billy was assigned easier readers than the neighbors' Susie who was in the same class and grade.

Perhaps even more confused and bewildered were some of the elementary-school teachers, caught up in what were more than seeming contradictions. Daily facing the facts of gross differences among pupils of the same age and grade, they nonetheless felt obliged to observe grade levels and what the graded system of school organization implied. Exhorted in preservice and in-service classes to differentiate instruction, they felt thwarted by grade-level expectations.

By 1950, schools and school systems across the country had virtually run the gamut of experimentation with marking systems, new methods of reporting to parents, modification of promotion practices, and so on. Few of the innovations were considered satisfactory for long. A considerable body of research pointed clearly to the fact that nonpromotion of low achievers rarely accomplishes what is intended. Nonpromoted children frequently suffer socially and emotionally. Achievement standards for all children tend to be lowered when nonpromotion rates are high.

Advocates of higher achievement standards often do not see that what appears to be an obvious remedy for the slow learner—repetition of the grade—actually compounds his problems. To these persons, newer practices based on recent research findings and theories of personality appear to run counter to the improvement of standards of achievement.

The authors believe that modern instructional procedures should and can promote both high educational standards and sound personality development for every child enrolled in the elementary school. There need be no incompatibility between the two.

We believe that a harmonious relationship between high educational standards and the development of individual human potentiality can be achieved best in a nongraded elementary school. We do not believe, however, that the establishment of nongraded schools will automatically establish this harmonious relationship. Nongraded structure simply creates the setting in which instructional practices clearly reflecting modern theories of sound mental health and personality development may find a hospitable reception. Nongraded structure also creates the setting in which each child may progress at his individual rate of speed and in his unique way. The authors equate high educational standards with children's progressing in the manner best suited to their attainments and potentialities. True standards arise from within the learning process; they are not found outside of it.

What we propose is neither new nor revolutionary. Since the late decades of the nineteenth century innovators seeking to facilitate varied rates of pupil progress have found it necessary or desirable to modify graded structure. During the past two or three decades many schools and school systems have been moving toward the nongraded viewpoint. Today hundreds have nongraded plans in operation and others are considering such a move.

What we propose, however, is much more than the mere elimination of grade lines. In fact, the removal of grades merely sets the stage for the creation of an elementary school which will encourage high educational standards along with the full development of the individual. The school we envision does not yet exist but could. It would represent a creative synthesis of the advances made by the nongraded schools of today and the new ideas which their experience suggests.

Practices in Nongraded Schools [1]

Actual change in schools lags behind proposals for educational reform. The nongraded concept is not new, as was pointed out in Chapter 3. In fact, some very early schools in the United States

---

[1] The data on educational practices in nongraded schools presented here and on subsequent pages are drawn from the authors' surveys, visits to nongraded schools, analyses of handbooks and reports prepared by personnel in nongraded schools, and extensive correspondence with persons involved in the nongraded school movement. For further reading, see particularly Robert H. Anderson and John I. Goodlad, "Self-appraisal in Nongraded Schools: A Survey of Findings and Perceptions," *Elementary School Journal*, 62 (February 1962), pp. 261-69; and John I. Goodlad and Robert H. Anderson, "Educational Practices in Nongraded Schools: A Survey of Perceptions," *Elementary School Journal*, 63 (October 1962), pp. 33-40.

were characterized by the fundamental premise of nongrading: continuous, unbroken progress from learning task to learning task for each child. However, nongraded schools as departures from the graded schools we know and have known date back to very recent decades. And only in recent years has the movement grown to such proportions as to warrant an analysis of existing practices.

All but a handful of today's nongraded schools came into existence after 1950. One study estimated that 6 per cent of the elementary schools in the United States possessed some nongrading in 1956.[2] This probably is a generous estimate. An interesting finding of the study is an expectation for some nongrading in 26 per cent of elementary schools by 1966.[3] Although this, too, appears to be a high estimate, the sharply upward character of the prediction corresponds closely with the authors' observations.

From a few scattered schools in the 1940's and early 1950's the nongraded school movement is now surging ahead with a wholesale adoption of the plan in many large cities. Consequently, it is almost impossible to report accurate statistics, especially when there is still considerable disagreement and misunderstanding with respect to the precise nature of a nongraded school. The difficulty in reporting is compounded by the fact that some survey respondents cannot separate fact from fiction; that is, they do not always separate data on schools in existence from expectations for schools yet to be nongraded.

The rapid increase in the number of schools called nongraded, the lack of agreement on definition, and the variety of practices being carried on under the nongraded label show clearly the need for a description and analysis of existing practices. Subsequent generalizations are derived from the authors' surveys and firsthand observations.

In perhaps four out of five cases school personnel moved into nongrading in an attempt to provide uninterrupted progress and a flexible placement for pupils. They frequently use the words "better provision for individual differences" in describing the nongraded school. Interestingly, few nongraded schools seem to have been created to bring about fundamental curriculum reform. Perhaps this is to be expected, since nongrading is seen primarily as an organizational and not a curricular innovation.

The feature most frequently characterizing nongraded schools at the time of their inception is a "levels" scheme of organizing the

---

[2] *The Principals Look at the Schools,* a working paper prepared for the Project on the Instructional Program of the Public Schools (Washington, D.C., National Education Association, 1962), p. 40. Estimates in this report were the results of extrapolating, using small-sample technique.

[3] *Ibid.*

skill areas of the curriculum. Since nongrading is found most frequently in the primary unit, replacing the first three grades, it is not surprising to find that reading is the field most commonly defined by levels. Sometimes children are assigned to and moved from classes according to levels. More often the levels serve as a device for grouping and advancing pupils within classrooms.

Within a few years after abandoning a graded structure, the faculty of at least one nongraded school in three confronts the need for curriculum reform. The subjects most commonly identified for restudy early in a school's development of nongrading are reading and arithmetic, for these two subjects lend themselves most readily to the identification of a precise progression of skills or concepts and of textbooks to accompany the levels. Later, school faculties turn to science and social studies as subjects for curricular study. The evidence suggests, then, that school people tend to see nongrading initially as an organizational device. Once they have departed from graded structure, however, they turn increasing attention to the more fundamental problem of curriculum reform.

Within three or four years of entering into nongrading, at least one faculty group in two becomes dissatisfied with or involved in revising some aspect of pupil evaluation. During this time, about half of the nongraded schools introduce conferences with parents, as either substitutes for or additions to the report-card method of communicating with the home about children's progress. There is ample evidence, also, to show that teachers in nongraded schools become dissatisfied with the narrow range of evaluation programs in our schools. Educators talk much about encouraging problem-solving and creative behavior but test little more than the possession of specific information.

Nongraded schools today appear to be marked by a search for more satisfying procedures in almost all realms of endeavor. Bahner, for example, speaks of nongrading as an unshackling device.[4] In his four years as principal of Englewood Elementary School in Florida, during which the school moved from grading to multi-grading, multi-aging, and nongrading, teachers became dissatisfied with curricular rigidity, classroom grouping practices, and evaluation procedures. Staff members became aware of so many inter-related inadequacies in school practices that even their remarkable steps forward often seemed to them to be discouragingly slow. Skillful leadership was called for in maintaining perspective.

Nongraded schools appear not to have adopted a uniform set

---

[4] John M. Bahner, "An Analysis of an Elementary School Faculty at Work," unpublished doctoral dissertation (Chicago, University of Chicago, 1960).

of characteristics. They appear, rather, to be somewhat individualistic with respect to the innovations developed after entry into nongrading. This is particularly true of nongraded schools that did not begin with a levels plan of curriculum organization. In fact, schools that began with the levels approach appear to be preoccupied with it years after its inception.

Nongrading in a school or school district is rarely accompanied by a systematic scheme for evaluating the effectiveness of the plan. Attempts to change school practices rarely include means for appraising the results of change. Furthermore, long-established practices are usually accepted because they exist, rather than because they have proved superior. A research orientation to school practice and minimal financial support for research are more akin to dreams than attainable goals for the immediate future. Nongrading, then, like most other educational practices, stands or falls on its logical relationship to general bodies of appropriate data (such as those cited earlier in this volume) and the experience of those who have worked with it.

The vast majority of educators who have worked with nongrading are enthusiastic about it. Some of them speak of higher achievement among pupils in nongraded schools, a reduction of discipline problems, a greater challenge for the gifted, the removal of the nonpromotion stigma for the slow, a more positive classroom atmosphere, and so on. Negative reactions from teachers and administrators actually conducting nongraded schools are hard to find. Similarly, surveys report positive reactions from parents, 83 to 96 per cent responding favorably.

A significant proportion of educators involved in nongrading view graded expectations among professional and lay persons alike as the most important obstacle blocking smooth implementation and development of nongraded schools. Graded schools have been with us through several generations of parents and teachers. Content, textbooks, teaching-learning activities, achievement tests, promotion policies, and reporting practices are geared to both the concept and the practice of grading. A vocabulary of nongrading has not yet been developed. Attempts to describe the specifics of nongrading are couched almost inevitably in the language of grading: the primary unit embraces "the first three grades of the graded school," your child would be "in the sixth grade of a graded school," your child is reading "at a fourth-grade level." And since a common vocabulary for describing general problems and practices of school organization has not yet been developed,[5] confusion reigns.

---

[5] John I. Goodlad and Kenneth J. Rehage, "Unscrambling the Vocabulary of School Organization," *NEA Journal, 51* (November 1962), pp. 34-36.

Educators planning to develop nongraded plans are not helped much by visits to schools calling themselves nongraded. Often the practices observed do not correspond to previously conceived visions of nongrading. There is great need at this time, then, for an analysis of what nongraded schools are and are not, and of what they can and cannot do. We seek to provide such an analysis on the succeeding pages.

The Nongraded School Movement Today: An Analysis [6]

The authors' studies of the nongraded school movement to date reveal two major misunderstandings. The first is the failure to understand that nongrading is a scheme for organizing schools *vertically*. It does not account for the many problems of organizing schools horizontally. The second is the false assumption that a scheme of school reorganization automatically changes other educational practices. Nongrading, like any other organizational scheme, only creates an opportunity for change—a special kind of opportunity, admittedly. The form and substance of education in a nongraded school depend on the same human energy and ingenuity that modify school practices generally.

Vertical school organization is designed to serve the necessary school function of moving pupils upward from the time they enter the school unit until the time they leave. There are two polar, alternative structures for doing this: the graded and the nongraded systems. Between these two systems lies a modification of grading known as multi-grading. In a multi-graded classroom, pupils are classified for instruction in as many as three different grades. Consequently, a pupil may be enrolled simultaneously in the fourth grade for reading, the third grade for arithmetic, and the fifth grade for science.

Horizontal school organization serves the function of allocating pupils to available teachers. There are many alternative ways of

---

[6] Some of what follows is based upon a more extensive analysis of over-all school organization by John I. Goodlad, prepared for *Planning and Organizing for Teaching,* a publication of the Project on the Instructional Program of the Public Schools (Washington, D.C., National Education Association, 1963). See also John I. Goodlad, "Individual Differences and Vertical Organization of the School," *Individualizing Instruction,* 1962 Yearbook of the National Society for the Study of Education, Part I (Chicago, University of Chicago Press), pp. 209-38; Robert H. Anderson, "Organizing Groups for Instruction," *Ibid.,* pp. 239-64; John I. Goodlad, "Toward Improved School Organization," *Elementary School Organization,* Yearbook of the Department of Elementary School Principals (Washington, D.C., National Education Association, December 1961), pp. 61-127.

doing this. Students in a school may be grouped horizontally according to their assumed or appraised homogeneity in ability, achievement, interests, or study habits—or they may be grouped quite heterogeneously. Likewise, they may be assigned to one teacher for all subjects or to a different teacher for each subject. Sometimes students are assigned as a group to a team of teachers who then subdivide this large group into instructional groups of varying sizes. The resulting scheme of horizontal organization is called cooperative, associated, or team teaching. But neither team-teaching nor any other kind of horizontal organization is an alternative for or necessary concomitant of nongrading.

Grading as a vertical plan of school organization takes on substance not because of grade labels but because of learning requirements and expectations for each grade. Pupils progress upward by covering the content and materials designated for each grade. Unusually rapid or slow progress is recognized by accelerating the pupil—moving him upward ahead of schedule—or by retaining him in the grade for a longer period of time, usually a year.

The serenity of teachers responsible for determining this progression of pupils through the grades is upset when they gain insight into gross individual differences among learners. Not just a few but many pupils deviate markedly upward and downward from grade norms. In fact, less than 15 per cent of a class usually is at grade level in all subjects. (See Chapter 1.) Furthermore, most children advance on a broken front, their achievement in three or four subjects scattered across as many grade levels.[7] The picture of inter-individual and intra-individual trait differences increases in complexity when behaviors in addition to academic achievement are examined.

Frustrated in the effort to fit gross variability among pupils of a class into the relatively narrow limits of a grade, many teachers turn eagerly to some more flexible "casing" or structure. They find in multi-grading both a comforting link with grading and some of the flexibility desired. It is surprising that school people, dissatisfied with the organizational structure they have and yet reluctant to depart radically from convention, have not turned more often to multi-grading.

Other educators have been tempted by the still greater flexibility of nongrading. But, with grade labels abolished, they find that the substance of grading remains: graded content, graded

---

[7] For a revealing picture of class heterogeneity on reading subtests *after classes had been set up homogeneously according to grade equivalents in reading,* see Irving H. Balow, "Does Homogeneous Grouping Give Homogeneous Groups?" *Elementary School Journal, 63* (October 1962), pp. 28-32.

materials, graded tests, graded children, graded parents, and graded teachers. After over a century of tradition expectations are not removed by creating a new name.

Those caught up in this change must now define new substance to replace the old, substance which will provide a tangible basis for pupils' progress. Here begins the most difficult work of all. It is not surprising that many school people develop at this point a detailed description of supposed levels of difficulty in such tangible fields of endeavor as reading and arithmetic. Nor is it surprising that this description often takes the form of a sequence of materials, especially textbooks in a publisher's series. And so is born the "levels" plan of nongrading.

This pattern of nongrading has been the target of much criticism. "Twelve, or twenty, or thirty-two reading levels," say the critics, "have replaced three grade levels." However, there appears to be nothing inherently damaging or dangerous in identifying a hierarchy of specific learnings within a larger unit of learning. In fact, this kind of curricular analysis appears to be a step in the right direction. Programing learning for automated instruction, for example, rests on the premise that content can and must be broken down into a series of sequential specifics. And, certainly, the short intervals between levels provide considerable flexibility in seeking to differentiate the instruction and upward progress of pupils varying widely in attainment. This kind of flexibility is in tune with one of the central concepts of the nongraded school.

None the less, there are at least two shortcomings in the levels plan of nongrading as it has emerged to date. The first is the common practice of setting up homogeneous classes based on levels. Whatever the arguments for doing this, good or bad, such an interclass plan of grouping is as much a scheme of horizontal school organization as it is a nongraded "levels" plan of vertical school organization. To call it a nongraded plan, therefore, is to misname it. It is both a nongraded levels plan and a plan of achievement grouping. Whatever the resulting assets or liabilities of such a scheme of school organization, its effects must be attributed, wherever they can be identified, to both the vertical (nongrading) and the horizontal (achievement grouping) dimensions. This rarely has been done in either the self-appraising testimonials or research reports on so-called nongraded schools now available in the literature.

The second major shortcoming of levels plans stems from difficulties inherent in curriculum analysis. Curriculum plans, with a few notable exceptions, provide detailed descriptions of content to be taught, but few clues to the concepts, principles, or values underlying this content and giving it cohesion. Curriculum specialists, since before the advent of nongraded schools, have urged that concepts, skills, principles, generalizations, and methods of inquiry inherent in fields of knowledge be identified and used as longitudinal elements around which to organize specific topics for study. (See Chapter 5.) Some progress in this direction has been made.[8] But the idea remains more a hope for the future than achieved reality.

Lacking curriculum guides with these fundamental organizing elements identified, then, educators moving into nongrading often do the next best thing: they seek to identify a progression of specific learnings based on order of difficulty. This is to put the cart before the horse. There can be no real sequence without the presence of a continuous element which is repeated and further developed with each fresh addition of subject matter. None the less, the effort is understandable and, in part, commendable. It is when the resulting levels of attainment are set as arbitrary hurdles or criteria for homogeneous interclass grouping that fundamental distortion of the nongraded concept occurs.

An encouraging note, mentioned earlier in this chapter, is that persons involved in nongrading, once having embarked on school reorganization, frequently see the need for curriculum reform. They see that the longitudinal, sequential curriculum they need and the concept of continuous vertical progress inherent in nongrading are compatible. Hopefully, the current interest in both may very well stimulate the simultaneous improvement of curricula and school organization.

Research Design and Findings

An over-all plan of vertical school organization such as grading or nongrading is a gross, in contrast to a sensitive, educational technique. Grading facilitates the placement of subject matter, the orderly progression of masses of pupils through it, and the establishment of normative standards for comparing schools and students. Grading sets a certain tone, a way of thinking about and looking at school practices. The presence of grades and the expectations accompanying grade standards may even set the tone for classroom instruction. *But the graded system does not arbitrarily predetermine the conduct of the learning-teaching process.*

Similarly, nongrading sets a tone, a way of thinking about and

---

[8] See Dorothy M. Fraser, *Current Curriculum Studies in Academic Subjects,* a report prepared for the Project on the Instructional Program of the Public Schools (Washington, D.C., National Education Association, 1962).

looking at school practices. The absence of grades may open up avenues to the longitudinal reordering of subject matter and to the pursuit of more absolute measures of pupil progress. The absence of grades may even affect the tone of classroom instruction. *But the nongraded system does not arbitrarily predetermine the conduct of the learning-teaching process.*

Since vertical school organization is a gross, facilitating device, there is little likelihood that changes in organizational design alone will be directly reflected in changes in the learning output of pupils. Failure to recognize this fact is probably the most significant weakness of research designed to appraise the effects of nongraded schools.

The second major deficiency of research into the effects of non-grading results from a failure to recognize that the nongraded school is a vertical and not a horizontal plan of school organization, a misunderstanding identified earlier. Nongraded schools using the levels approach frequently adopt, also, a horizontal scheme of inter-class grouping based on these levels. Many researchers either assume that this interclass grouping arrangement is a characteristic of nongrading or ignore its presence completely in the research design. Consequently, there is no way of knowing whether any significant differences in pupils' accomplishments are a product of differences in the vertical school organization (grading or non-grading) or in the horizontal school organization (patterns of interclass grouping).

The two deficiencies in research design identified above have characterized most studies of the effects of school and classroom organization.[9] Similarly, most of these studies have used a narrow conception of pupil attainment as a criterion. The very nature of standardized achievement tests creates a unique problem in seeking to appraise graded and nongraded schools. Such tests are standardized on the basis of the grade-by-grade performance of pupils. In many nongraded plans, pupils move through the school at different rates of speed. With what grade norms should the performance of slow- or fast-moving nongraded pupils be compared? Let us imagine, for example, a situation in which bright pupils have moved through a six-year, nongraded elementary school in only five years. These pupils are now in the seventh grade of a graded junior high school. Should their performance be compared with fellow seventh-graders who are, on the average, a year older or with sixth-graders of the same age? And, if compared to and found

---

[9] John I. Goodlad, "Classroom Organization," *Encyclopedia of Educational Research,* third edition, edited by Chester W. Harris (New York: The Macmillan Co., 1960), pp. 221-26.

no better than their older, seventh-grade classmates, what positive weight should be given to the fact that these products of nongraded schools were exposed for fewer years to the schoolwork on which the achievement comparisons are based?

Studies that fail to account for the problems of research design analyzed above—and almost all studies into the effects of various patterns of school organization are characterized by one or more of the deficiencies enumerated—are worse than useless. The findings of such studies can be dangerously misleading. This fact strikes home when we realize that most persons interested in the findings are likely to be even less aware of the limitations in research design than the persons who are perpetuating the research errors.

One California study affords a classic example of several problems in research design enumerated above.[10] The Board of Trustees of the school district decided, on recommendation of the superintendent, to initiate a three-year pilot program using what the Board called "the ungraded primary." Two schools were selected for the experiment. The principals of these schools explained the proposed program to the P.T.A. and, subsequently, to the primary teachers.

Personnel in the school district described their ungraded primary schools as "a system of attempting to group primary children by means of reading achievement." Here we have the familiar confusion of vertical with horizontal school organization. The grouping pattern in the experimental schools was the only factor distinguishing them from the control schools. Therefore, any significant differences between pupils in control and experimental schools, if at all attributable to school organization, must be laid at the door of the horizontal scheme of grouping, *not nongrading*.

The control and experimental schools were compared with respect to reading achievement and, for reasons that are quite obscure to us, attendance and classroom social structure. No significant differences were found, although a few minor ones favored the control or graded schools.

By the end of the "experiment" teachers in the experimental school still did not realize, apparently, that the most significant organizational aspect of their schools was the plan of achievement grouping and not the nongraded vertical reorganization. Their wording is significant: "Because of the measured findings in the pilot study we find that *grouping by reading achievement* [italics

---

[10] The authors have chosen to withhold the identity of the school district involved. At the conclusion of the work described here, members of the administrative and supervisory staff became aware of some of the deficiencies involved and consulted one of the authors for further analysis. All direct quotes are from duplicated documents sent to the authors.

ours] has not produced significant differences in peer relationships between children. *This grouping* [italics ours] has not produced significant differences in reading achievement. . . ." And then, still not realizing the significance of their own previous wording and quite unaware of the fact that they *had not yet even tried nongrading*, they concluded, "We would suggest at this time that the present ungraded program not be adopted as a general pattern of organization in the School District."

A study by Buffie [11] compared existing nongraded schools with graded schools. Neither type of school was considered part of an "experiment." After matching four graded schools from Community G with four nongraded schools from Community N, he compared two groups, each containing 117 children who had been enrolled continuously. All significant differences and all trends in the two areas measured—mental health and academic achievement—favored the nongraded children.

Advocates of nongrading are urged to treat these results with caution. Even in Buffie's comparatively careful study, we do not know the precise nature of the features differentiating the two types of schools. As stated earlier, school organization is such a gross device that we must be careful in assuming that any change in it will *by itself* influence pupil accomplishment significantly.

As this volume goes to press, we know of only one carefully controlled experiment seeking to isolate the effects of organization alone. This is the study of Hillson and his associates, now only partially completed.[12] All first-grade students entering a selected elementary school were randomly assigned to either nongraded experimental ($N = 26$) or graded control ($N = 26$) groups. All teachers, whether assigned to experimental or control groups, were selected on the basis of their excellence in teaching.

The essential difference between the experimental and control groups was the system of vertical progression in reading. Pupils in the control group were placed in one of three *reading level groups* within a conventional graded program, and their instruction was adapted to the assumed achievement level of each group. A child was always assigned to one of the three reading groups of his grade level. Thus a second-grade child was never assigned to one of the three first-grade or third-grade groups. By contrast, pupils in the experimental group were permitted to move upward

---

[11] Edward G. Buffie, "A Comparison of Mental Health and Academic Achievement: The Nongraded School vs. the Graded School," unpublished doctoral dissertation (School of Education, Indiana University, 1962).

[12] Maurie Hillson, J. Charles Jones, J. William Moore, and Frank van Devender, "A Controlled Experiment Evaluating the Effects of a Nongraded Organization on Pupil Achievement" (8 pp. verifax, Bucknell University).

through the levels plan as rapidly as their performance suggested.

It is fascinating to note that the definition of the *graded* control groups resembles to no small degree the description of *nongrading* so often presented, quite erroneously, by researchers less knowledgeable about the nature of school organization. Hillson and his associates stand almost by themselves in their clear-cut understanding of nongrading as a vertical pattern of school organization and not as an inter- or intraclass plan of horizontal grouping.

After one and a half years (the midway point in the study) the nongraded experimental group exceeded the graded group in the Lee Clark Reading Test and the Paragraph Meaning and Word Meaning tests of the Primary Battery of the Stanford Achievement Test at .01, .01, and .06 levels of significance, respectively.

The findings of a study by Carbone [13] contrast sharply with the findings of Hillson and his associates. Carbone compared 122 graded with 122 nongraded pupils with respect to achievement, mental health, and the instructional practices of their teachers. He found that graded pupils scored significantly higher (.01 level of significance) than nongraded pupils on the Iowa Tests of Basic Skills, and on one (social participation) of five factors on the California Test Bureau's Mental Health Analysis. There were no significant differences between graded and nongraded pupils on the other four mental health factors. Although there were differences and similarities in instructional practices, no significant patterns of difference between graded and nongraded schools were identified. On the Semantic Differential, graded pupils tended to describe their teachers as little, loud, boring, hard, dull, rough, sour, stiff, and bad. Nongraded children tended to describe their teachers as bright, smooth, sweet, relaxed, big, quiet, interesting, soft, and good.

Organizational features separating graded from nongraded schools were not identified. The nongraded schools were listed as nongraded, however, in the Appendix of an earlier edition of this volume.[14] But we included in that list any school that chose to classify itself as nongraded: "a school with labels removed from two or more grades." There is no way of knowing what other organizational features—such as, perhaps, horizontal grouping by reading levels—might have been included.

Carbone took considerable care in selecting pupils and instruments. The control and experimental schools took on the names of

---

[13] Robert F. Carbone, "Achievement, Mental Health, and Instruction in Graded and Nongraded Elementary Schools," unpublished doctoral dissertation (Department of Education, University of Chicago, 1961).

[14] John I. Goodlad and Robert H. Anderson, *The Nongraded Elementary School* (New York, Harcourt, Brace & World, Inc., 1959).

differing patterns of vertical school organization. But we don't really know the meaning of the nongraded label. In what way did the sample of graded schools differ from the sample of nongraded schools *with respect to vertical organization?* The study of Hillson and his associates sets forth the first ingredient of research studies purporting to appraise graded and nongraded schools: there must be clear and acceptable definitions of grading and nongrading as patterns of vertical organization, and the samples of graded and nongraded schools must satisfy the definitions.

We have emphasized research design over research findings with respect to nongraded schools because the improvement of research is by far the more important problem. Studies comparing graded and nongraded schools, taken as a group, are inconclusive. They will continue to be inconclusive until these weaknesses are corrected. In this respect, such studies have much in common with all other research on school organization. However, the first problem identified—that of the gross character of school organization—defies easy resolution.

The research needed requires that conceptual models be developed so as to differentiate nongraded from graded schools. Such models consist of descriptive statements which serve to separate the two types of schools. We visualize two pairs of models. The first pair involves organization, each set of statements differentiating the upward progression of pupils in the graded plan from the upward progression of pupils in the nongraded plan. The second pair involves curriculum and instruction. This kind of model is more speculative. Constructing such a model for nongrading calls for the logical extension of principles underlying nongrading as an organizing device into other aspects of schooling that pertain to the vertical progression of pupils.

Throughout this volume, we have maintained that nongrading is an organizational device pertaining only to the vertical progression of pupils and not to their horizontal assignment to classes and teachers. We hold to our position. But we have also maintained that nongrading creates an opportunity for educational change, an opportunity for teachers to depart from certain rigidities associated with the graded system. We are not impressed with the nature and extent of the departure from tradition so far evident in nongraded schools. We think this is because educators have relied too heavily on the educational advantages thought to be natural concomitants of organizational flexibility. They have not been sufficiently insightful and vigorous in pushing toward changes which nongrading suggests but does not effect. And this, we think, results from the fact that advocates of nongraded schools have have been timid in suggesting next steps.

218

We do not pretend to be able to formulate a conceptual model of curriculum and instruction for nongraded schools. A complete, final, and fixed model is neither feasible nor desirable. Tomorrow's nongraded school will be an evolving venture. However, in the next and final section we advance some desired characteristics of nongrading which educators may find useful both for implementing and for appraising nongraded schools.

Tomorrow's Nongraded School

Organizational Aspects

Nongrading is a vertical pattern of school organization. This we have said repeatedly. A vertical pattern of school organization serves to move pupils upward from the time they enter school to the time they leave it.

The nongraded school serves a set of values with respect to this vertical progression of pupils. These values, as we see them, are embedded in the following statements that describe several major organizational aspects of nongrading. These values are quite different from the values supporting graded organization. Educators who do not accept the values stated below are advised not to move into the nongraded plan. Educators who accept these values *and* grading are reminded of the inconsistency between the two. The graded system can be adapted to encompass the following characteristics only by modifying it to the point where the system becomes essentially nongraded in fact if not in name.

The nongraded school provides for the continuous, unbroken, upward progression of all pupils, the slowest and the most able. No arbitrary repetition of work is imposed. Hence, nonpromotion is not used.[15] Gaps are not imposed by acceleration through the system. Consequently, "skipping" has neither a place nor a meaning. The teacher makes a decision, based on a diagnosis of the individual child, whether to reinforce learning through increased emphasis on similar learnings or whether such reinforcement is superfluous.

This concept of continuous progress is reflected when teachers set up instructional groups *within the classroom* after children have been assigned to teachers within the nongraded plan. Teachers, not a predetermined grade standard, must determine the range of pupil variability. An arbitrary slicing of work expected for the grade into three or four categories of assumed difficulty should not

---

[15] John I. Goodlad, "To Promote or Not to Promote? Several Answers: Short-Term and Long-Term," *Toward Effective Grouping* (Washington, D.C., Association for Childhood Education International, 1962), pp. 34-38.

be the basis of the grouping. The abilities of the children enrolled, then, not the arbitrary designation of grade-level expectancy, determine vertical pupil placement. In the nongraded school learning tasks selected for the most able children assigned to a room usually will be years, not months, in advance of work selected for the least able. (This will be true even when children are assigned initially to classrooms on the basis of an assumed academic homogeneity—a procedure which may or may not accompany nongrading, as we have said before.) Furthermore, years of difficulty may separate two or more areas of activity for *one child*.

This organizational feature of nongrading described above is the one so carefully differentiated by Hillson and his associates in the graded control and nongraded experimental classes described earlier.

The nongraded school provides for the irregular upward progression that is characteristic of almost every child. This irregular progression is covered partly in the first characteristic of nongrading stated above and partly in the third stated below. Children do not advance evenly, a year of graded accomplishment for a year of living and schooling. They spurt and stop, regress and advance in both their general and their specific development. Classes in the nongraded school are set up to recognize and account for wide ranges of accomplishment so that even very long lags or very gross spurts on the part of pupils still fall within normal expectancies for the group.

In the graded pattern of school organization, children frequently are retained or nonpromoted when they progress only two or three months for nine months of schooling. The standard is the grade level and gross deviation from it corrodes the very concept of grading. If these retained children spurt at some later time, it does not seem reasonable to reassign them to the rooms of their former classmates. After all, these retained children have not been exposed to the work of the next grade. And so the nonpromoted children remain a full year of time behind, usually permanently, even when their achievement equals or exceeds that of at least several promoted agemates. They are punished simply because the timing of their development does not fit the school schedule, with its cycle of promotions and nonpromotions. Promotion and nonpromotion, the adjustment mechanisms of grading, do not allow for the natural irregularity of pupil progression. (See Chapter 2.)

The nongraded school provides several alternative vertical classroom placements for every child at any time, no one of which denotes nonpromotion or skipping. This accounts for the flexibility so often attributed to nongraded schools but as yet only crudely developed in them. It is a criterion that simply is foreign to and incompatible with any reasonable interpretation of grading as a concept of vertical school organization.

Many educators feel the classroom placement of children should be determined by their academic, social, physical, and emotional development and by the characteristics of the teachers. The last several decades have witnessed little progress in the development and use of these criteria. Schools continue to use a narrow definition of academic attainment or to depend on some predetermined criterion of age or grade to make placement decisions automatically. Techiniques for appraising the range of criteria to which some schools are committed are unlikely to emerge until educators demonstrate a need for them. The alternative placement concept of nongrading creates such a need.

We recommend the use of overlapping classroom habitats as a device for attaining the flexibility intended in nongrading. This is a deceptively simple recommendation. The range of pupil attainment *in anything* represented by third-grade class very much overlaps the range represented by second- and fourth-grade classes and to some degree overlaps the range represented by first- and fifth-grade classes. A third-grade class, then, contains pupils achieving at five (or more) grade levels. The use of overlapping classroom habitats in nongrading simply recognizes this fact.

For teachers in graded schools to meet these pupil realities is to deviate from the expectancies of grading. Teachers must deviate from the system in seeking to overcome its defects. To expect them to do this is to expect a great deal. The nongraded plan, on the other hand, presents the meeting of these realities as standard, not deviate, teacher behavior.

Take as an example a nongraded primary unit of six classes replacing two first-grade, two second-grade, and two third-grade classes. In these six classes there are children functioning academically but perhaps not socially at fourth and fifth grades. Similarly, there are children functioning at nursery-school and kindergarten levels in aspects of their behavior. To skip the advanced pupils into higher grades and to keep the slow ones out of school until they meet first-grade standards are not adequate solutions. Instead let us assume that vertical school structure should at least encourage instructional provision down to kindergarten level and up to fifth-grade level within the three-year span of the primary grades.

Figure 17 illustrates the difference between graded and nongraded vertical structures in accounting for the spread of individual differences normally encountered in the first three years of schooling. The graded classes, two at each grade level, provide for the first three grades of the elementary school. The nongraded classes, each overlapping at least two other classes to some degree, provide for the anticipated range of six years of schooling, kindergarten through grade five. Remember that the anticipated range of attainment is conservative; actually, some children would perform at

Figure 17

X Range of accomplishment among pupils in the first three years of school, computed in grades

KINDER-GARTEN	GRADE 1	GRADE 2	GRADE 3	GRADE 4	GRADE 5

Y Range of accomplishment expected in six graded classes embracing grades one through three

GRADE 1	GRADE 2	GRADE 3

GRADE 1	GRADE 2	GRADE 3

Z Range of accomplishment expected and provided for in six nongraded classes embracing the first three years of schooling

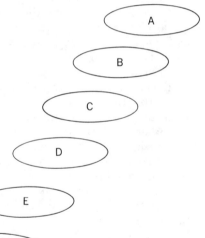

Comparison of six graded classes and six overlapping nongraded classes in providing for the individual differences found in the first three years of schooling.

X represents a conservative estimate of the range of general achievement found in the first three "grades."

Y shows the inadequate provision for this spread in the typical graded school; children at the extremes are not easily accounted for in the organizational plan.

Z shows the greater spread in attainments that might be accommodated in six multi-age nongraded classes. Note: Z represents only one of many possibilities; groups could be more or less overlapped, if desired.

nursery-school level and others would perform at seventh- or eighth-grade level in at least one major aspect of behavior.

Each nongraded class provides for a spread of several years in attainment from top to bottom child. In the nongraded plan, then, there are several alternative placements for each child at any time. The larger the school, the greater the number of such alternative placements.

We contend that, at present, teachers are the best judges of where a child should be placed. Teachers, more than anyone else, possess the information needed in determining the most appropriate educational habitat for each child. They are the general practitioners who must make the diagnoses, using the best evaluation procedures that are available. Resourceful teachers will use several criteria, rather than the usual criterion of achievement, in determining the most appropriate placement of a child.

Throughout this discussion of nongrading as an organizational device, we have kept strictly away from the question of interclass horizontal organization. There is nothing in nongrading that necessitates or even suggests any specific pattern of interclass grouping. Nongrading is designed to encompass the stark realities of individual differences. Nongrading is in no way intended to reduce the range of individual differences with which teachers must cope. The authors support cooperative and team teaching as the most promising ways of organizing schools horizontally. The ideal school, then, from an organizational standpoint, is one that practices nongrading vertically and team teaching horizontally.

Curriculum and instruction

The research of Hillson and his associates suggests, other things being equal, that nongrading as a device for vertical organization of the school increases the attainment of pupils. We hope, of course, that similar studies will support these tentative conclusions. As we stated earlier, however, we consider nongrading to be a gross, rather than a sensitive, educational technique. Further, we consider nongrading to be an enabling or facilitating device. Consequently, the advantages of pupils in a nongraded school are likely to be the product of curricular and instructional, rather than organizational, changes.

In our judgment the nongraded school is so unshackling a concept that many instructional changes are likely to result from adopting it. We are prepared to identify two characteristics of curriculum and instruction which appear to be almost necessary concomitants of nongrading as a plan of vertical school organization. *First, the nongraded school forces the development of longitudinal patterns of curriculum organization. Second, the nongraded school demands that textbooks be distributed on almost an individualized basis.* Each class receives four of this book, five of that, eight of another, seven of still another, and so on, instead of thirty identical books for each subject. Further, a dynamic system of nongrading virtually demands a centralized school library.

In Chapter 5 we explored a longitudinal concept of the curriculum which appears to be compatible with nongrading as a vertical concept of school organization. There is no need to reiterate the point of view expressed there. We wish to add only that the academic disciplines are being reorganized along lines that parallel our proposed reorganization of the school's vertical structure. Academic subjects organized so as to emphasize fundamental methods of inquiry, concepts, principles, and generalizations and schools organized so as to emphasize the continuous progress of pupils belong together. For tomorrow we visualize a nongraded pattern of vertical school organization and a nongraded curriculum together providing continuous pupil progress from kindergarten through college.

High-level learning is a process of finding relationships among miscellaneous pieces of data, of testing principles against the facts of new experience, and of applying generalizations to a variety of situations. What was chaotic and meaningless becomes ordered and meaningful. The school's curriculum must promote such learning.

This kind of learning develops over long periods of time. The student does not understand the number system after merely learning to count in the primary grades. But he makes a beginning. He does not fully learn at any one moment the significance of the principle that when and where one lives affect the problems of living that one faces. But he makes a beginning and builds on that beginning, increasing his understanding with each new intellectual synthesis. His learning in any field is both developmental and continuous. It is not a matter of "covering" this topic today and that one tomorrow, of stopping in June and beginning again in September.

The curriculum embraces both a learner and something to be learned. Whether teachers should teach children or subject matter is a ridiculous topic for adult debate. They teach both. The children they teach, we have seen, differ widely at each moment in their understanding of what is to be learned. These differences take on a special meaning when they are considered in terms of the developmental and continuous nature of learning. What is to be learned must be viewed as longitudinal threads—concepts, skills, and values—running throughout the entire length of the school's program. Children progress along these threads at differing rates of speed. At any one time, they differ markedly in their understanding of given concepts, their proficiency in certain skills, and their appreciation of values and attitudes.

What is studied at each moment should, indeed, have value in its own right; the fact or the idea should be worth grasping. But the fact or the idea should have value beyond this: it should promote a deeper understanding of important concepts or principles.

When learning is viewed simply as the covering of topics, the relationship between the increase of understanding by the learner and the increase in the complexity of the concept is concealed or obliterated. Prescribing the subject matter for each grade level tends to shift the focus from developmental, long-term learning to an ineffective stop-and-go kind of learning. Topics listed as suggested means to important ends become ends in themselves. Too often the child comes to view learning as a process of consuming and digesting the miscellaneous topics listed for his grade.

But when learning is seen as increased understanding of basic concepts or principles, a longitudinal view is provided. Concepts of number, color, or space take on long-term significance. Grade-level prescriptions become inappropriate. The child studies a topic not because it is specified for the fifth grade but because it carries him one step further in understanding the concept to which it relates.

Learners of widely differing capacities and attainments proceed at varying rates of speed along curricular threads running the entire length of the school's program. Learning now becomes a longitudinal or developmental process, each child proceeding irregularly, but never according to the prearranged stop-and-go of grade barriers. Each learner achieves his own unique insights as he proceeds.

The nongraded school encourages this kind of sequential learning, this kind of pupil progress. The nongraded school does not *create* harmony among the learner, the subject matter, and the processes of learning. But it does provide a framework within which such harmony may be more readily seen and achieved. The nongraded school is the school we could have if insights from research on learning and human development were applied.

Throughout these pages we have argued the case of the nongraded form of school organization. We have done so, however, not because we are convinced that this structure will automatically provide the ideal learning environment. Rather, we see the creation of nongraded schools as a way of approaching problems of the school's function, curriculum organization, and classroom instruction.

It has become apparent that the nongraded school is no panacea. Such a school makes the conduct of education no easier. But the process of nongrading lays bare long-standing educational problems. A compatibility between the nongraded structure and continuous pupil progress, longitudinal curriculum development, and integrated learning becomes obvious. Having glimpsed the nature of this compatibility, educators must then face up to the arduous process of bringing it to life.

The nongraded school is not for those who would stop with a little organizational reshuffling. It is for those educators who would use present-day insights into individual differences, curriculum, and theories of personality, and who would commit themselves to a comprehensive revision of education.

COMPREHENSIVE BIBLIOGRAPHY

Individual Differences and Pupil Grouping

Aaron, I. E. "Patterns of Classroom Organization," *Education*, **80** (May 1960), 530-32.

———, and others. "Fourth Grade Teachers Experiment with Cross-Class Grouping in Reading Instruction," *Elementary English*, **30** (May 1959), 305-07.

Anderson, R. C. "The Case for Non-graded, Homogeneous Grouping," *Elementary School Journal*, **62** (January 1962), 193-97.

Association for Childhood Education International. *Toward Effective Grouping*. 1962 Membership Service Bulletin No. 5-A. Washington, D.C., The Association, 1962.

Austin, Texas, Woodridge School, *Grouping, Marking and Reporting to Parents*. Austin, Texas, University of Texas, 1950.

Bahner, J. M. "Grouping Within a School," *Childhood Education*, **36** (April 1960), 354-56.

Balow, I. H. "Does Homogeneous Grouping Give Homogeneous Groups?" *Elementary School Journal*, **63** (October 1962), 28-32.

Bennett, E., and others. "Schools Can Change Grouping Practices," *Childhood Education*, **30** (October 1953), 64-68.

Bettelheim, B. "Segregation: New Style," *School Review*, **66** (Autumn 1958), 251-72.

Blakemore, G. L. "Individualizing Education in the Elementary School," *The Daily Advertiser*. Wagga Wagga, N.S.W., Australia, Job Printing Department, 1955.

Brinkman, A. R. "The Tarrytowns Try Balanced Grouping," *Elementary School Journal*, **59** (March 1959), 320-23.

Brown, G. I. "Which Pupil to Which Classroom Climate?" *Elementary School Journal*, **60** (February 1960), 265-69.

Burr, M. Y. *A Study of Homogeneous Grouping In Terms of Individual Variations and the Teaching Problem*. New York, Bureau of Publications, Teachers College, Columbia University, 1931.

Carle, D. S. "A Program of Pupil Progress Through the Primary Grades," *National Elementary Principal*, **26** (December 1946), 15-18.

Carlson, W. H. "Interage Grouping," *Educational Leadership*, **15** (March 1958), 363-68.

Central New York School Study Council. *Toward a More Flexible Elementary School Curriculum*. Syracuse, Syracuse University Press, 1949.

Chase, E. S. "An Analysis of Some Effects of Multiple-Grade Grouping in an Elementary School." Unpublished doctoral dissertation, University of Tennessee, August, 1961.

Chase, F. S. "The Schools I Hope to See," *NEA Journal*, **46** (March 1957), 164-66.

Chase, W. L. "Individual Differences in Classroom Learning," *Social Studies in the Elementary School*, 163-68. Fifty-sixth Yearbook of the National Society for the Study of Education, Part II. Chicago, University of Chicago Press, 1957.

Clark, J. R. "Promising Approach to Provision for Individual Differences in Arithmetic," *Journal of Education*, **136** (December 1953), 94-96.

Conference on Reading, University of Chicago. Harris, A. J. "Reading Materials for Different Patterns of Grouping for Instruction," *Materials for Reading*, H. M. Robinson, ed., 36-48. Chicago, University of Chicago Press, 1957.

————. Powell, H. R. "Specific Patterns of Classroom Organization," *Promoting Maximal Reading Growth Among Able Learners*, H. M. Robinson, ed., 162-65. Chicago, University of Chicago Press, 1954.

————. Thimblin, L. M. "Adapting the School and Class Organization to the Varying Needs in Kindergarten Through Grade III," *Promoting Maximal Reading Growth Among Able Learners*, H. M. Robinson, ed., 51-54. Chicago, University of Chicago Press, 1954.

Conference on Reading, University of Pittsburgh. Mainwiller, C. E. "Extent and Nature of the Problem of Individual Differences," *Providing for the Individual Reading Needs of Children*, G. A. Yoakam, ed., 21-24. Pittsburgh, University of Pittsburgh Press, 1953.

————. Sheldon, W. D. "The Place of the Classroom Teacher in Handling Individual Differences in Reading," *Providing for the Individual Reading Needs of Children*, G. A. Yoakam, ed., 25-33. Pittsburgh, University of Pittsburgh Press, 1953.

————. Strickland, R. "Providing for Individual Differences Through Differentiated Material," *Providing for the Individual Reading Needs of Children*, G. A. Yoakam, ed., 119-27. Pittsburgh, University of Pittsburgh Press, 1953.

————. Wynn, W. T. "How to Teach a Class Grouped for Differentiation in Basal Reading," *Providing for the Individual Reading Needs of Children*, G. A. Yoakam, ed., 128-37. Pittsburgh, University of Pittsburgh Press, 1953.

————. Yoakam, G. A. "Problems Involved in Differentiating Materials to Provide for the Individual Reading Needs of Children," *Providing for the Individual Reading Needs of Children*, G. A. Yoakam, ed., 97-104. Pittsburgh, University of Pittsburgh Press, 1953.

————. Yoakam, G. A. "Problems Involved in Providing for the Individual Needs of Children," *Providing for the Individual Reading Needs of Children*, G. A. Yoakam, ed., 11-20. Pittsburgh, University of Pittsburgh Press, 1953.

Cook, W. W. "Classroom Methods: The Gifted and the Retarded in Historical Perspective," *Phi Delta Kappan*, **39** (March 1958), 249-55.

Cummins, E. W. "Grouping: Homogeneous and Heterogeneous." *Educational Administration and Supervision*, **44** (January 1958), 19-26.

Daniels, J. C. "Effects of Streaming in the Primary School," *British Journal of Educational Psychology*, **31** (February 1961), 69-78.

Davis, M. D. *The Variability of Children of Different Ages and Its Relation to School Classification and Grouping*. Albany, University of State of New York, 1937.

Ekstrom, R. B. "Experimental Studies of Homogeneous Grouping: A Critical Review," *School Review*, **69** (Summer 1961), 216-26.

Foshay, A. W. "Interage Grouping in the Elementary School." Unpublished Ed.D. project, Teachers College, Columbia University, 1949.

Frazier, A. "Needed: A New Vocabulary for Individual Differences," *Elementary School Journal*, **61** (February 1961), 260-68.

Goodlad, J. I. "Classroom Organization," *Encyclopedia of Education Research*, third edition, 221-26. New York, Macmillan Co., 1960.

————. "Individual Differences and Vertical Organization of the School," *Individualizing Instruction*, 209-38. Sixty-first Yearbook of the National Society for the Study of Education, Part I. Chicago, University of Chicago Press, 1962.

————. "The Increasing Concern for Effective Teacher Utilization," *The High School in a New Era*, F. S. Chase and H. A. Anderson, eds., 133-45. Chicago, University of Chicago Press, 1958.

————. "In Pursuit of Visions," *Elementary School Journal*, **59** (October 1958), 1-17.

"Grouping," *Childhood Education*, **36** (April 1960), 350-73 (entire issue).

"Grouping: Promising Approaches," *Educational Leadership*, **18** (April 1961), 410-34 (issue feature).

Hamilton, W., and W. Rehwoldt. "By Their Differences They Learn," *National Elementary Principal*, **37** (December 1957), 27-29.

Heffernan, H. "Grouping Pupils for Well-Rounded Growth and Development," *California Journal of Elementary Education*, **21** (August 1952), 42-50.

Henry, N. B. (ed.). *The Dynamics of Instructional Groups*. The Fifty-ninth Yearbook of the National Society for the Study of Education, Part II. Chicago, University of Chicago Press, 1960.

———— (ed.). *Individualizing Instruction*. The Sixty-first Yearbook of the National Society for the Study of Education, Part I. Chicago, University of Chicago Press, 1962.

Hildreth, G. "Individual Differences," *Encyclopedia of Educational Research*, W. S. Monroe, ed., 564-71. New York, Macmillan Co., 1950.

Lawson, D. E., "An Analysis of Historic and Philosophic Considerations for Homogeneous Grouping," *Educational Administration and Supervision,* **43** (May 1957), 257-70.

Lee, J. M. "Individualized Instruction," *Education,* **74** (January 1954), 267-71.

Loomis, M. J. "Grouping for Individualized Instruction," *NEA Journal,* **48** (September 1959), 17-18.

Mann, M. "What Does Ability Grouping Do to the Self-Concept?" *Childhood Education,* **36** (April 1960), 357-60.

Mitchell, V. M. "Analysis of the Grade Expectancies and the Actual Achievements of Fourth, Fifth, and Sixth Grade Pupils," *Teachers College Record,* **31** (November 1959), 21-22.

Mitchum, P. M., and A. G. Richardson. "Problems in Organizing the School Program to Achieve Balance," 126-61, *Balance in the Curriculum,* 1961 Yearbook, Association for Supervision and Curriculum Development, N.E.A.

National Society for the Study of Education. *The Grouping of Pupils.* Thirty-fifth Yearbook, Part I. Bloomington, Illinois, Public School Publishing Co., 1936.

Otto, H. J. "Elementary Education—III, Organization and Administration," *Encyclopedia of Educational Research,* W. S. Monroe, ed., 367-82. New York, Macmillan Co., 1950.

———. "Grouping Pupils for Maximum Achievement," *School Review,* **67** (Winter 1959), 387-93.

———. "Internal Organization of Schools and School Systems," *Review of Educational Research,* **16** (October 1946), 321-33.

Painter, H. W. "Meeting Individual Differences Through the Language Arts," *Elementary English,* **31** (February 1954), 85-91.

Parker, J. C., and D. H. Russell. "Ways of Providing for Individual Differences," *Educational Leadership,* **11** (December 1953), 168-74.

Petty, M. C. *Intra-class Grouping in the Elementary School.* Austin, Texas, University of Texas, 1953.

Polglaze, R. "Guide for Grouping," *Clearing House,* **36** (September 1961), 51-53.

Polkinghorne, A. R. "Grouping Children in the Primary Grades," *Elementary School Journal,* **50** (May 1950), 502-08.

———. "Parents and Teachers Appraise Primary Grade Grouping," *Elementary School Journal,* **51** (January 1951), 271-79.

Punke, H. H. "Ability Grouping as Individual-Group Relationship," *Phi Delta Kappan,* **43** (June 1962), 411-14.

Roff, R. "Grouping and Individualizing in the Elementary School," *Educational Leadership,* **15** (December 1957), 171, 174-75.

Russell, D. H. "Inter-class Grouping for Reading Instruction in the Intermediate Grades," *Journal of Educational Research,* **39** (February 1946), 462-70.

Shane, H. G. "Grouping in the Elementary School," *Phi Delta Kappan,* **41** (April 1960), 313-19.

Smitter, F. "The Pros and Cons of Grouping," *Reading Teacher,* **7** (December 1953), 74-78.

Strevell, W., and P. Oliver. "Grouping Can Be Flexible Within the Class-room," *Nation's Schools*, 59 (February 1957), 89-91.

Thelen, H. A. "Classroom Grouping of Students," *School Review*, 67 (Spring 1959), 60-78.

Thomas, E. M. "Grouping in the Classroom," *Childhood Education*, 30 (October 1953), 69-71.

Torrance, E. P. "Can Grouping Control Social Stress in Creative Activities?" *Elementary School Journal*, 62 (December 1961), 139-45.

Turner, E. M. *Child Within a Group*. Stanford, California, Stanford University Press, 1947.

Waetjen, W. "Is Learning Sexless?" *NEA Journal*, 51 (May 1962), 12-14.

Wagner, G. W. "What Schools Are Doing in Grouping Children for Reading," *Education*, 78 (January 1958), 309-12.

Wahle, R. P. "Methods of Individualization in Elementary School," *Educational Leadership*, 17 (November 1959), 74-79.

Washburne, C. W. "Adjusting the Program to the Child," *Educational Leadership*, 11 (December 1953), 138-47.

Wilhelms, F. T. "Grouping Within the Elementary Classroom," *NEA Journal*, 48 (September 1959), 19-21.

Wilkinson, D. H. "Individuality: Basic Concept in Educational Theory and Practice," *Peabody Journal of Education*, 31 (May 1954), 359-70.

Williams, R. J. *Biochemical Individuality*. New York, John Wiley and Sons, Inc., 1956.

———. "Individuality and Education," *Educational Leadership*, 15 (December 1957), 144-48.

Wilt, M. E. "Another Way to Meet Individual Differences," *Elementary English*, 35 (January 1958), 26-28.

Wrightstone, J. W. "Class Organization for Instruction," *NEA Journal*, 46 (April 1957), 254-55.

———. *Class Organization for Instruction*. What Research Says to the Teacher, No. 13. Washington, D.C., Department of Classroom Teachers and American Educational Research Association, National Education Association, May 1957.

Promotion Policies and Practices

"Accelerating the Academically Talented," *NEA Journal*, 49 (April 1960), 22-23.

Akridge, G. H. *Pupil Progress Policies and Practices*. New York, Bureau of Publications, Teachers College, Columbia University, 1937.

Anfinson, R. D. "School Progress and Pupil Adjustment," *Elementary School Journal*, 41 (March 1941), 507-14.

Aronow, M. S. "Some Figures on Promotion," *High Points*, 35 (December 1953), 5-12.

Arthur, G. "A Study of the Achievement of Sixty Grade I Repeaters as Compared with that of Non-repeaters of the Same Mental Age," *Journal of Experimental Education*, 5 (December 1936), 203-05.

Association for Childhood Education International. *The Primary School: Stop! Look! Evaluate!* Bulletin No. 61. Washington, D.C., The Association, 1952.

Ayres, L. P. *Laggards in Our Schools.* New York, Charities Publication Committee, 1909.

Caswell, H. L. *Non-promotion in Elementary Schools.* Nashville, Division of Surveys and Field Studies, George Peabody College for Teachers, 1933.

Coffield, W. H. "A Longitudinal Study of the Effects of Nonpromotion on Educational Achievement in the Elementary School." Unpublished doctoral dissertation, State University of Iowa, 1954.

————, and P. Blommers. "Effects of Non-promotion on Educational Achievement in the Elementary School," *Journal of Educational Psychology,* **47** (April 1956), 235-50.

Cook, W. W. *Grouping and Promotion in the Elementary School.* Series on Individualization of Instruction, No. 2. Minneapolis, University of Minnesota Press, 1941.

————. "Some Effects of the Maintenance of High Standards of Promotion," *Elementary School Journal,* **41** (February 1941), 430-37.

Dean, S. E. "Pass or Fail? A Study of Promotion Policy," *Elementary School Journal,* **61** (November 1960), 86-90.

Elsbree, W. S. *Pupil Progress in the Elementary School.* New York, Bureau of Publications, Teachers College, Columbia University, 1943.

Farley, E. S. "The Influence of Grading and Promotion Policies Upon Pupil Development," *National Elementary Principal,* **16** (July 1937), 268-74.

————. "Regarding Repeaters: Sad Effects of Failure Upon the Child," *Nation's Schools,* **18** (October 1936), 37-39.

Goodlad, J. I. "To Promote or Not to Promote? Several Answers: Short-Term and Long-Term," *Toward Effective Grouping,* Association for Childhood Education International, Washington, D.C., 1962, 34-38.

————. "Research and Theory Regarding Promotion and Non-promotion," *Elementary School Journal,* **53** (November 1952), 150-55.

————. "Some Effects of Promotion and Nonpromotion Upon the Social and Personal Adjustment of Children," *Journal of Experimental Education,* **22** (June 1954), 301-28.

Gordon, J. B. "Mental-Hygiene Aspects of Social Promotion," *Mental Hygiene,* **34** (January 1950), 34-43.

Hall, W. F., and R. Demarest. "Effect on Achievement Scores of a Change in Promotional Policy," *Elementary School Journal,* **58** (January 1958), 204-07.

Harris, F. E. *Three Persistent Educational Problems: Grading, Promoting and Reporting to Parents.* Lexington, Kentucky, Bureau of School Services, University of Kentucky, 1953.

Hartsig, B., and L. Langenbach. "Studies of Three Children Who Have Been Retained a Grade in School," *California Journal of Elementary Education,* **21** (August 1952), 51-63.

Heffernan, H., and associates. "What Research Has to Say About Nonpromotion," *California Journal of Elementary Education,* 21 (August 1952), 7-24.

Jones, J. A. "Grading, Marking, and Reporting in the Modern Elementary School," *Educational Forum,* 19 (November 1954), 45-54.

Jones, J. J. "Recent Trends in Promotional Theory," *Progressive Education,* 33 (January 1956), 5-6, 15.

Kitch, D. E. "Does Retardation Cause Dropouts?" *California Journal of Elementary Education,* 21 (August 1952), 25-28.

Klene, V., and E. P. Branson. "Trial Promotion Versus Failure," *Educational Research Bulletin,* Los Angeles City Schools, 8 (January 1929), 6-11.

Kowitz, G. T., and C. M. Armstrong. "The Effect of Promotion Policy on Academic Achievement," *Elementary School Journal,* 61 (May 1961), 435-43.

Kumpf, C. H. "Social Promotion . . . A Misnomer?" *National Elementary Principal,* 40 (May 1961), 35-37.

Le Baron, W. A. "Some Practical Techniques in Developing a Program of Continuous Progress in the Elementary School," *Elementary School Journal,* 46 (October 1945), 89-96.

Lennon, R. T., and B. C. Mitchell. "Trends in Age-Grade Relationships: A Thirty-five Year Review," *School and Society,* 82 (October 1955), 123-25.

Lobdell, O. "Results of a Nonpromotion Policy in One School District," *Elementary School Journal,* 54 (February 1954), 333-37.

Luther, G. H., and J. C. Adell. "A Survey of Current Practices in Large Cities of the United States Relating to Annual and Semi-annual Promotion, Age of Entry into Kindergarten and First Grade and Promotion Policies," Bureau of Educational Research, Bulletin No. 52. Cleveland, Ohio, Cleveland Public Schools, 1953. Mimeographed.

Myers, V. C. "The Child Who Fails," *Education,* 57 (January 1937), 306-09.

National Education Association. *Pupil Promotion Policies and Rates of Promotion,* Educational Research Service Circular No. 5, 1958.

Oaks, R. E. "Put Promotion in Its Place," *Childhood Education,* 23 (November 1946), 133-36.

O'Neill, J. H. "Who Really Fails?" *Catholic School Journal,* 51 (January 1951), 15.

Otto, H. J. "Grading and Promotion Policies," *NEA Journal,* 40 (February 1951), 128-29.

————. *Promotion Policies and Practices in Elementary Schools.* Minneapolis, Minnesota, Educational Test Bureau, Inc., 1935.

————, and E. C. Melby. "An Attempt to Evaluate the Threat of Failure as a Factor in Achievement," *Elementary School Journal,* 35 (April 1935), 588-96.

"Promotion Policies in Our Schools—A Symposium," *NEA Journal,* 49 (April 1960), 15-21.

Ridgway, R. ". . . And One To Grow On," *Educational Leadership,* 17 (February 1960), 313-17.

Russell, D. H. "Influence of Repetition of a Grade and of Regular Promotion on the Attitudes of Parents and Children Toward School," *California Journal of Elementary Education,* **21** (August 1952), 29-41.

Sandin, A. A. *Social and Emotional Adjustments of Regularly Promoted and Non-promoted Pupils.* New York, Bureau of Publications, Teachers College, Columbia University, 1944.

Saunders, C. M. *Promotion or Failure for the Elementary School Pupil?* New York, Bureau of Publications, Teachers College, Columbia University, 1941.

Shane, H. G. "The Promotion Policy Dilemma," *NEA Journal,* **42** (October 1953), 411-12.

———. "Promotion Practices Follow Sound Psychological Principles," *Nation's Schools,* **49** (June 1952), 59-60.

Schumann, M. G. "Parent Pressure for Promotion: Is This Your Problem Too?" *Minnesota Journal of Education,* **38** (March 1958), 33.

Solheim, A. K. "Shall a Child Be Retained in a Grade?" *Minnesota Journal of Education,* **41** (March 1961), 34.

Steadman, E. R. "Fifteen Who Were Not Promoted," *Elementary School Journal,* **59** (February 1959), 271-76.

Stringer, L. A. "Promotion Policies and Mental Health," *National Elementary Principal,* **37** (April 1958), 32-36.

Templin, R. S. "A Check-up of Non-promotions," *Journal of Education,* **123** (November 1940), 259-60.

Topp, R. F. "You Cannot Always Do It If You Try!" *Elementary School Journal,* **54** (December 1953), 230-34.

Washburne, C. W. "Promotion Versus Non-promotion," *Proceedings of Schoolmen's Week,* 81-92. Philadelphia, University of Pennsylvania Press, 1953.

Wentland, C. R. "Individual Differences and School Promotion," *Elementary School Journal,* **52** (October 1951), 91-95.

Williams, C. W. "Acceleration: Some Considerations," *Educational Leadership,* **18** (March 1961), 351-55.

Reporting Pupil Progress to Parents

American Association of School Administrators. *Appraisal and Promotion Procedures in Urban School Districts, 1955-56.* Educational Research Service Circular No. 8, 1956. Washington, D.C., The Association.

Anderson, R. H., and E. R. Steadman. "Pupils' Reactions to a Reporting System," *Elementary School Journal,* **51** (November 1950), 136-42.

Association for Childhood Education International. *Reporting on the Growth of Children.* Washington, D.C., The Association, 1953.

Association for Supervision and Curriculum Development. *Reporting Is Communicating: An Approach to Evaluation and Marking.* Washington, D.C., The Association, 1956.

Ayer, F. C. *Practical Child Accounting* (revised edition). Austin, Texas, The Steck Company, 1953.

Barclay, D. "What Should Report Cards Report?" *The New York Times Magazine* (October 21, 1958), 56, 58.

———. "When Teachers Grade Home Life," *The New York Times Magazine* (November 24, 1957), 69.

Barnes, M. W., and G. Rogers. "Report Cards Should Be Designed To Be Outmoded," *Nation's Schools,* **52** (October 1953), 54-56.

California Journal of Elementary Education, **24** (November 1955), entire issue, "Reporting Pupil Progress," 128 pages.

Camp, L. T. "Three-Way Conferences Assist Lay Participation," *Educational Leadership,* **15** (April 1958), 418-21.

Capehart, B. E. "Reports to Parents," *Nation's Schools,* **50** (December 1952), 43, 70.

De Pencier, I. B. "Co-operative Planning and Report Cards," *Elementary School Journal,* **53** (January 1953), 254-57.

———. "Trends in Reporting Pupil Progress in the Elementary Grades, 1938-1949," *Elementary School Journal,* **51** (May 1951), 519-23.

D'Evelyn, K. E. "Good Techniques for Conferencing," *Childhood Education,* **32** (November 1955), 119-21.

———. *Individual Parent-Teacher Conferences.* New York, Bureau of Publications, Teachers College, Columbia University, 1945.

Douglass, H. R. "Why Visit the Homes?" *National Elementary Principal,* **37** (September 1957), 242-43.

Ebel, R. L. "How to Explain Standardized Test Scores to Your Parents," *School Management,* **5** (March 1961), 61-64.

——— (ed.). "Inventories and Tests," *Education,* **81** (October 1960), 67-99.

"Educational Measurement—Interpreting and Using the Results," *National Elementary Principal,* **41** (November 1961), 6-38 (issue feature).

"Educational Measurement—Purposes and Techniques," *National Elementary Principal,* **41** (September 1961), 8-41 (issue feature).

Fitzpatrick, E. A. "Teacher-Parent Conferences," *Catholic School Journal,* **58** (April 1958), 38.

Freehill, M. F. "About That Report," *NEA Journal,* **40** (September 1951), 393-94.

Goodykoontz, B. "A Report on Report Cards," *Education Digest,* **21** (December 1955), 11-13.

Haas, R. "Experiment in Changing Reporting Practices," *Educational Leadership,* **11** (May 1954), 491-94.

Halliwell, J. W. "Report on Individualized Reporting," *Elementary School Journal,* **61** (April 1961), 394-99.

Hardy, C. "Communicating with Parents by Letter," *National Elementary Principal,* **37** (September 1957), 233-38.

Harris, F. E. *Three Persistent Educational Problems: Grading, Promoting, and Reporting to Parents.* Lexington, Kentucky, Bureau of School Service, University of Kentucky, 1953.

Heffernan, H., and L. E. Marshall. "Reporting Pupil Progress in California Cities," *California Jonrnal of Elementary Education,* **24** (November 1955), 67.

Herrick, V. E. "Promoting and Reporting Practices," *Encyclopedia of Educational Research*, third edition, 438-39. New York, Macmillan, 1960.

Heye, M. "The Testing Program in the Ungraded Primary," *School and Community*, **47** (October 1960), 14.

Hymes, J. L. *Effective Home-School Relations*. Englewood Cliffs, New Jersey, Prentice-Hall, Inc., 1953.

Jones, J. A. "Grading, Marking, and Reporting in the Modern Elementary School," *Educational Forum*, **19** (November 1954), 145-54.

Krugman, J., and J. W. Wrightstone. *A Guide to the Use of Anecdotal Records*. Board of Education, New York City, May 1949.

Kvaraceus, W. C. "The Changing Report Card," *Educational Trend*, Issue No. 952. Washington, D.C., Arthur C. Croft Publications, 1952.

Laas, M. "Parents Write a Manual on Parent-Teacher Conferences," *National Elementary Principal*, **37** (September 1957), 221-25.

Langdon, G., and I. W. Stout. *Teacher-Parent Interviews*. Englewood Cliffs, New Jersey, Prentice-Hall, Inc., 1954.

Langdon, G., and I. W. Stout. *Helping Parents Understand Their Child's School*. Englewood Cliffs, New Jersey, Prentice-Hall, Inc., 1957.

Lewis, R., and McCrea, D. "Three Around the Conference Table," *Elementary School Journal*, **61** (November 1960), 72-75.

Lyon, E. C. "The Best Report Card," *National Parent Teacher*, **47** (May 1953), 15-16.

Martyn, K. A., and H. J. Bienvenu. "The Parent Conference—Progress Report, Not Psychotherapy," *Elementary School Journal*, **57** (October 1956), 42-44.

Maves, H. J. "Contrasting Levels of Performance in Parent-Teacher Conferences," *Elementary School Journal*, **58** (January 1958), 219-24.

McCleary, L. E. "A New Technique in Reporting Pupil Progress," *School Review*, **63** (March 1955), 160-63.

McConnell, S. A. "What Do Parents Want to Know?" *Elementary School Journal*, **58** (November 1957), 83-87.

McCowen, E., and R. C. Bryan. "Reporting to Parents on Pupil Progress," *Elementary School Journal*, **56** (September 1955), 32-34.

Moray, J. "Pupil-Teacher Conferences," *Elementary School Journal*, **58** (March 1958), 335-36.

Morris, L. "Evaluating and Reporting Pupil Progress," *Elementary School Journal*, **53** (November 1952), 144-49.

Morrissy, E., and J. B. Robinson. "Reporting Pupil Progress in Elementary Schools," *Baltimore Bulletin of Education*, **26** (June 1949), 1-10.

Morse, A. D. "Let's Abolish Report Cards!" *Education Digest*, **17** (October 1951), 17-19. *National Elementary Principal*, **37** (September 1957), entire issue.

N.E.A. Research Division. "Reporting to Parents," *NEA Research Bulletin*, **39** (February 1961), 24-25.

Otto, H. J., and others. *Four Methods of Reporting to Parents*. Bureau of Laboratory Schools, Publication No. 7. Austin, Texas, University of Texas, 1957.

Parker, B. F. "The Parent-Teacher Conference," *Elementary School Journal*, **53** (January 1953), 270-74.

Passow, A. H., and M. L. Goldberg. "Overcoming Blocks in Communication," *Childhood Education*, **32** (October 1955), 60-63.

Phillips, B. N. "Characteristics of Elementary Report Cards," *Educational Administration and Supervision*, **42** (November 1956), 385-97.

Plimpton, B. "A Comparative Study of Alternative Methods of Communicating with Parents of First-Grade Pupils." Unpublished doctoral dissertation, University of Chicago, 1957.

Ploghoft, M. "The Parent-Teacher Conference as a Report of Pupil Progress—An Overview," *Educational Administration and Supervision*, **44** (March 1958), 101-05.

"Reporting," *NEA Journal*, **48** (December 1959), 15-28 (issue feature).

Research Bulletin of the National Education Association. "Promotion and Reporting Practices," Chapter V, 148-52, of "Ten Criticisms of Public Education," *Bulletin*, **35** (December 1957), 131-74.

Richardson, S. "How Do Children Feel About Reports to Parents?" *California Journal of Elementary Education*, **24** (November 1955), 98-111.

Roelfs, R. M. "Steps in Changing Pupil Progress Reports," *School Executive*, **73** (October 1953), 51-53.

Rogers, D. "Common-Sense Considerations Concerning Report Cards," *Elementary School Journal*, **52** (May 1952), 518-22.

————. "Report Card Dilemma," *Journal of Education*, **136** (May 1954), 237-38.

Rogers, V. M. "Improved Methods of Reporting Pupil Progress," *School Executive*, **70** (October 1950), 19-22.

Romano, L. "Finding Out What Parents Want to Know," *Elementary School Journal*, **58** (November 1957), 88-90.

Rothney, J. W. M. *Evaluating and Reporting Pupil Progress*. What Research Says to the Teacher, No. 7. Washington, D.C., Department of Classroom Teachers and American Educational Research Association, National Education Association, 1955.

Schiff, H. J. "Improving the Quality of Parent-Teacher Conferences," *Chicago Schools Journal*, **39** (November-December 1957), 87-91.

Stout, I. W., and G. Langdon. *Parent-Teacher Relationships*. What Research Says to the Teacher, No. 16. Washington, D.C., Department of Classroom Teachers and American Educational Research Association, National Education Association, 1958.

Strang, R. *Reporting to Parents* (revised edition). New York, Bureau of Publications, Teachers College, Columbia University, 1952.

————. "Reporting Pupil Progress," *School Executive*, **72** (August 1953), 47-51.

"Teachers Go Home!" *School Management*, **2** (December 1958), 40-41.

"Testing and Evaluation," *Educational Leadership*, **20** (October 1962), 2-37 (issue feature).

Topp, R. "Let's *Tell* Parents Their Children's I.Q.'s," *Phi Delta Kappan*, **40** (June 1959), 342-45.

"Toward Creative Evaluation," NEA Elementary Instructional Service. Washington, D.C., National Education Association (January 1958).

Troyer, M. E. *Accuracy and Validity in Evaluation Are Not Enough.* The J. Richard Street Lecture for 1947. Syracuse, Syracuse University Press, 1947.

Tyler, R. W. "Educational Measurement: A Broad Perspective," *National Elementary Principal,* **41** (September 1961), 8-13.

————. "Helen Is Smarter Than Betsy," *NEA Journal,* **42** (March 1953), 165-66.

U. S. Office of Education, Division of State and Local School Systems. "Reporting Pupil Progress to Parents," Education Briefs, No. 34 (December 1956). Washington, D.C., U. S. Department of Health, Education and Welfare. Mimeographed.

Weckler, N. "Problems in Organizing Parent-Teacher Conferences," *California Journal of Elementary Education,* **24** (November 1955), 117-26.

Westerberg, V., and others, "Reporting to Parents," *Teachers College Record,* **28** (March 1957), 71-73.

"What's All the Fuss About Report Cards?" *Changing Times* (November 1955), 39-42.

Whigham, E. L. "What Should Report Cards Report?" *School Executive,* **77** (May 1958), 21-23.

Wilson, C. H. "Our Report Cards Are Failing," *NEA Journal,* **46** (November 1957), 491-94.

Wilson, J. A. R. "Let's *Not Tell* Parents Their Children's I.Q.'s," *Phi Delta Kappan,* **40** (June 1959), 343-44.

Woodbury, R. W. "Preplan Your Parent-Teacher Conferences," *Instructor,* **67** (September 1957), 6.

Wrinkle, W. L. *Improving Marking and Reporting Practices in Elementary and Secondary Schools.* New York, Rinehart and Company, 1947.

Yauch, W. A. "What Research Says About School Marks and Their Reporting," *NEA Journal,* **50** (May 1961), 50, 58.

Nongraded School Organization

Anderson, R. H. "The Junior High School," *Architectural Record,* **129** (January 1961), 126-31.

————. "Ungraded Primary Classes," *Education Digest,* **21** (November 1955), 47-50.

————. "Ungraded Primary Classes: An Administrative Contribution to Mental Health," *Understanding the Child,* **24** (June 1955), 66-72.

————. "The Ungraded Primary School as a Contribution to Improved School Practices," *Frontiers of Elementary Education II,* 28-39, Vincent J. Glennon, ed., Syracuse University Press, 1955.

————, and J. I. Goodlad, "Self-Appraisal in Nongraded Schools: A Survey of Findings and Perceptions," *Elementary School Journal,* **62** (February 1962), 261-69.

Association for Childhood Education International. *Continuous Learning.* Bulletin No. 87. Washington, D.C., The Association, 1951.

———. *The Primary School: Stop! Look! Evaluate!* Bulletin No. 61, Washington, D.C., The Association, 1952.

———. A Symposium, "Experiments in Reorganizing the Primary School," *Childhood Education,* **15** (February 1939), 262-71.

Association for Supervision and Curriculum Development. *A Look at Continuity in the School Program,* 199-214. 1958 Yearbook. Washington, D.C., The Association, 1958.

Austin, K. C. "The Ungraded Primary School," *Childhood Education,* **33** (February 1957), 260-63.

———. "The Ungraded Primary Unit in Public Elementary Schools of the United States." Unpublished doctoral dissertation, University of Colorado, 1957.

Bahner, J. M., "An Analysis of an Elementary School Faculty at Work." Unpublished doctoral dissertation, Department of Education, University of Chicago, 1960.

Bardwell, R. "Lock-Step Has No Place in Education," *Wisconsin Journal of Education,* **92** (May 1960), 12-15.

Bennett, H. K. "Making the Transition Requires Administrative Planning, Courage and Patience," *Nation's Schools,* **49** (January 1952), 60-65.

Billings Elementary Schools, School District No. 2, Yellowstone County. *Continuous Growth Plan in Reading.* Billings, Montana, 1956.

———. *The Primary Department Continuous Growth Plan.* Billings, Montana, 1953.

Blackstock, C. R. "A Field Study to Initiate an Ungraded Primary School in Brazosport." Unpublished doctoral dissertation, College of Education, University of Houston, August 1961.

Brearly, H. C. "Are Grades Becoming Extinct?" *Peabody Journal of Education,* **31** (March 1954), 258-59.

Brooks, F. E. "A Faculty Meets the Needs of Pupils," *Educational Leadership,* **11** (December 1953), 174-78.

Brown, B. F. "Ungraded Secondary School," *National Association of Secondary Schools Bulletin* (April 1961), 349-52.

Buffie, E. G. "A Comparison of Mental Health and Academic Achievement: The Nongraded School vs. the Graded School." Unpublished doctoral dissertation, School of Education, Indiana University, 1962.

Buford, F. "We Looked at Our Schools," *National Elementary Principal,* **34** (December 1954), 20-22.

Carbone, R. F. "Achievement, Mental Health, and Instruction in Graded and Ungraded Elementary Schools." Unpublished doctoral dissertation, Department of Education, University of Chicago, 1961.

———. "A Comparison of Graded and Non-graded Elementary Schools," *Elementary School Journal,* **62** (November 1961), 82-88.

Carlson, W. H. "Interage Grouping," *Educational Leadership,* **15** (March 1958), 363-68.

Clark, C. W. *Ungraded Primary School.* Eugene, School of Education, University of Oregon, 1960.

Cocklin, W. H. "A Study of an Ungraded Primary School." Unpublished doctoral dissertation, University of Pennsylvania, 1950.

Collins, E. "Individual Differences in a Third Grade and Their Implications for Grading and Nongrading." Unpublished master's thesis, Emory University, 1956.

Cory, L. M. "Primary Department," 16-17. *Annual Report of Superintendent to Board of Education.* Hamilton, Ohio, Hamilton City School District, 1948-49. Mimeographed.

Davidson, H. A., M. L. Schriver, and H. J. Peters. "Should Johnny Compete or Co-operate?" *NEA Journal,* **49** (October 1960), 30-32.

Dean, C. D. "The Continuous Growth Plan," *Montana Education,* **27** (November 1950), 8, 23-24.

————. "The Continuous Growth Plan Replaces the Graded School in Billings," *Montana Education,* **23** (February 1947), 12-14.

Dean, S. *Elementary School Administration and Organization.* U.S. Office of Education bulletin, November 11, 1960.

Dean, S. E. "Organization for Instruction in the Elementary Schools," *School Life,* **42** (May 1960), 8-9.

DiPasquale, V. "Schools Without Grades," *Better Homes and Gardens,* **33** (September 1955), 28, 33-34.

Eldred, D. M., and M. Hillson. "The Nongraded School and Mental Health," *Elementary School Journal* **63** (January 1963), 218-22.

"Experiments in Reorganizing the Primary School," *Childhood Education,* **15** (February 1939), 262-72.

Faith, E. F. "Continuous Progress at the Primary Level," *Phi Delta Kappan,* **30** (May 1949), 356-59.

Ferguson, D. A., and N. Neff. "The Nongraded School Administers to the Dull-Normal Child," *School and Community,* **47** (October 1960), 16-17.

Five Milwaukee Teachers. "We Plan for Living and Learning," *Childhood Education,* **26** (September 1949), 19-23.

Fries, H. C. "A Continuous Progress School," *American School Board Journal,* **119** (July 1949), 52.

Gilbert, J. H. "The Multigraded Developmental Plan Focuses on Pupil Achievement," *Chicago Schools Journal,* **43** (February 1962), 209-14.

Ginther, J. "Sloganism in Education," *Elementary School Journal,* **62** (February 1962), 240-42.

Glencoe Public Schools. *Flexible Grouping and Individual Differences in the Glencoe Public Schools.* Glencoe, Illinois (September 1950). Mimeographed.

Goodlad, J. I. "Developmental Reading in the Ungraded Plan," *Reading in the School of Tomorrow,* 12-17. Kent State University Bulletin (November 1957).

Goodlad, J. I. "Illustrative Programs and Procedures in Elementary Schools," *The Integration of Educational Experiences,* 173-93. Fifty-seventh Yearbook of the National Society for the Study of Education, Part III. Chicago, University of Chicago Press, 1958.

————. "More About the Ungraded Unit Plan," *NEA Journal*, **44** (May 1955), 295-96.

————. *Planning and Organizing for Teaching*, publication of the Project on the Instructional Program of the Public Schools, National Education Association (scheduled for publication in 1963).

————. "In Pursuit of Visions," *Elementary School Journal*, **59** (October 1958), 1-17.

————. "Toward Improved School Organization," pp. 60-127, "Elementary School Organization," *National Elementary Principal*, **41** (December 1961).

————. "Ungrading the Elementary Grades," *NEA Journal*, **44** (March 1955), 170-71.

————. "What About Nongrading Our Schools," *Instructor*, **70** (May 1961), 6.

————, and R. H. Anderson. "Educational Practices in Nongraded Schools: A Survey of Perceptions," *Elementary School Journal*, **63** (October 1962), 33-40.

————, and R. H. Anderson. "1958 Progress Report: The Nongraded Elementary School," *NEA Journal*, **47** (December 1958), 642-43.

————, F. E. Brooks, I. M. Larson, and N. Neff. "Reading Levels Replace Grades in the Non-graded Plan," *Elementary School Journal*, **57** (February 1957), 253-56.

————, and K. J. Rehage, "Unscrambling the Vocabulary of School Organization," *NEA Journal*, **51** (November 1962), 34-36.

————, and O. Sand. *Patterns of School Organization*, 55-minute tape recording. Washington, D.C., Department of Elementary School Principals, National Education Association, 1962.

Gore, L. "The Nongraded Primary Unit," *School Life*, **44** (March 1962), 9-12.

Green, D. R., and S. V. Simmons. "Chronological Age and School Entrance," *Elementary School Journal*, **63** (October 1962), 41-47.

Hearn, N., and G. Reid. "The Webster Story," *Michigan Education Journal*, **32** (December 1954), 179-85.

Heathers, G. "The Dual Progress Plan," *Educational Leadership*, **18** (November 1960), 89-91.

————, and M. Pincus. "Dual Progress Plan in the Elementary School," *Arithmetic Teacher*, **6** (December 1959), 302-05.

Herrick, V. E., and others. "Administrative Structure and Process in Curriculum Development," *Review of Educational Research*, **30** (June 1960), 258-74.

Hillson, M., and F. M. Van Devender. "A Reading Levels Accomplishment Program for Shamokin, Pennsylvania." Shamokin, copyright by the authors, 1961.

Hoflich, J. E. "Ungraded Primary," *National Catholic Education Association Bulletin*, **57** (November 1960), 8-25.

Imhoff, M. M. "The Primary Unit," *Selected References*, No. 1 (revised, May 1957). Washington, D.C., U. S. Office of Education.

Ingram, V. "Flint Evaluates Its Primary Cycle," *Elementary School Journal*, **61** (November 1960), 76-80.

Johnson, L. V., and M. A. Bardenstein. "The Ungraded Elementary School," *The Delta Kappa Gamma Bulletin,* **26** (spring 1960).

Kant, L. E. "The Ungraded Primary School in Wisconsin." Unpublished master's thesis, University of Wisconsin, 1955.

Kelly, F. C. "Doing Away with Grade Levels," *NEA Journal,* **37** (April 1948), 222-23.

————. "The Primary School in Milwaukee," *Childhood Education,* **24** (January 1948), 236-38.

————. "Ungraded Primary School," *Educational Leadership,* **18** (November 1960), 79-81.

————. "Ungraded Primary Schools Make the Grade in Milwaukee," *NEA Journal,* **40** (December 1951), 645-46.

Kennedy, D. F. "Does the Nongraded School Better Meet the Aims of Elementary Education?" Unpublished master's seminar paper, University of Maryland, 1957.

King, R. A. "Ungraded Primary Extended to Full Six-Year School," *School Management,* **3** (February 1959), 58.

Kopp, O. W. "Grouping Pupils in the Elementary School," *New York State Education,* **54** (May 1957), 540-42.

Lane, H. A. "Moratorium on Grade Grouping," *Educational Leadership,* **4** (March 1947), 385-95.

Lane, R. H. "Experiments in Reorganizing the Primary School," *Childhood Education,* **15** (February 1939), 262-71.

Lindvall, C. M., and others. *Meeting the Needs of the Able Student Through Provision for Flexible Progression.* Pittsburgh, Coordinated Education Center, University of Pittsburgh, 1962.

Mercille, M. G. "The Primary School Unit," *Bulletin of the School of Education, Indiana University,* **25** (January 1949), 13-18.

Milwaukee Public Schools. *The Primary School.* April 1956. Mimeographed.

————. *A Study of Primary School Organization and Regular Class Organization at Primary 6 and 3A in Eight Schools.* Milwaukee, Wisconsin, Mimeographed test results in Milwaukee Public Schools, July 7, 1952.

Morse, A. D. *Schools of Tomorrow—Today,* Chapter 2. Garden City, New York, Doubleday & Company, Inc., 1960.

Nelson, T. L. *Pupil Progress in the Ungraded Primary Program.* Berkeley Public Schools, Berkeley, California, September 1952. Mimeographed.

Offt, G. J. *The Ungraded Primary School as a Means of Providing for Individual Differences.* A seminar report presented to the Faculty of the Department of Education, Westminster College. (Unpublished; available from Dr. Lewis H. Wagenhorst, Chairman of Department.) New Wilmington, Pennsylvania, June, 1956.

"Organizing for Effective Learning," *Educational Leadership,* **17** (April 1960), 402-38 (issue feature).

Palmer, D. S. "Advancing Each at His Own Speed: The Ungraded Program at Maple Park," *Washington Education,* **71** (December 1959), 14-16.

Park Forest Public Schools. *The Ungraded Primary School in Park Forest, Illinois.* School District 163, Park Forest, Illinois. Mimeographed brochure issued annually.

Perkins, H. V. "Nongraded Programs: What Progress?" *Educational Leadership,* 19 (December 1961), 166-69, 194.

The Principals Look at the Schools, a working paper prepared for the Project on the Instructional Program of the Public Schools. Washington, D.C., National Education Association, 1962.

Robinson, A. "Should Teachers Be Promoted, Too?" *NEA Journal,* 42 (October 1953), 26-27.

Ryan, W. C. "The Ungraded Primary Class," *Understanding the Child,* 24 (June 1955), 65.

Sanders, D. C. "Patterns of Organization," 68-85, *Elementary Education and the Academically Talented Pupil.* Washington, D.C., National Education Association, 1961.

Sister Mary Alice. "Administration of the Non-graded School," *Elementary School Journal,* 61 (December 1960), 148-52.

————, and A. D'Heurle, "New Ventures in School Organization: The Ungraded School and Use of Teacher Aides," *Elementary School Journal,* 57 (February 1957), 268-71.

Skapski, M. K. "Ungraded Primary Reading Program: An Objective Evaluation," *Elementary School Journal,* 60 (October 1960), 41-45.

Slater, E. M. *The Primary Unit.* Curriculum Bulletin No. 3. Storrs, Connecticut, University of Connecticut, 1955.

Smith, L. "Continuous Progress Plan," *Childhood Education,* 37 (March 1961), 320-23.

Smitter, F. "What Is a Primary School?" *California Journal of Elementary Education,* 17 (February 1949), 139-45.

Stimpson, E. B. "An Evaluation of the Provo Primary Unit." Unpublished master's thesis, Brigham Young University, 1951.

Stoddard, G. D. *The Dual Progress Plan,* New York, Harper and Brothers, 1961.

————. "Dual Progress Plan in Elementary Education," *Educational Forum,* 25 (March 1961), 271-76.

Symonds, P. M. "What Education Has to Learn from Psychology," *Teachers College Record,* 56 (February 1955), 277-85.

"The Gradeless School," *Newsweek,* 52 (September 15, 1958), 76.

Thimblin, L. M. "The Ungraded Primary School: An Experiment in Flexible Grouping." Unpublished course paper, Northwestern University, 1954.

Thompson, E. "The Ungraded Plan Helps Provide for Continuity of Learning," *NEA Journal,* 47 (January 1958), 16-18.

Tucker, M. B. "The Shoe Didn't Fit," *NEA Journal,* 45 (March 1956), 159-61.

Ultican, T. "Ungraded Primary Plan," *School and Community,* 48 (October 1961), 22.

Wagner, G. "What Schools Are Doing in Developing the Continuous Growth Program," *Education,* 79 (May 1959), 595-96.

Waller, E. A. "Ungraded Primaries," *Wisconsin Journal of Education,* **81** (January 1949), 8-9.

Weaver, J. F. "Non-grade-level Sequence in Elementary Mathematics," *Arithmetic Teacher,* **7** (December 1960), 431.

White, E. *The Russell School Ungraded Program.* Alameda County Schools, Court House, Oakland 7, California.

Wilson, A. T. "The Ungraded Primary School," *American Teacher Magazine,* **43** (February 1959), 5-6, 20.

Wood, H. B. *Foundations of Curriculum Planning and Development.* Seattle, Cascade-Pacific Books, 1960.

Woodbury, R. M. (ed.). *Organization of the Elementary School in Terms of Pupil Progress.* Cambridge, Massachusetts, New England School Development Council, 20 Oxford Street, April, 1952.

Worcester, W. "School Organization for Primary Education." Unpublished doctoral dissertation, Yale University, 1942.

Wrightstone, J. W. *Class Organization for Instruction.* What Research Says to the Teacher, No. 13. Washington, D.C., Department of Classroom Teachers and American Educational Research Association, National Education Association, May 1957.

Yeomans, E. "A New Plan for Progression in the Lower School," *Shady Hill News* (Cambridge, Massachusetts, November 1960), 2-4.

INDEX

Entries in italics are communities or schools reporting nongraded elementary programs.

Ability, pupil
  and graded structure, 4
  grouping by, 15, 17-20, 90-91, 99
  and nongraded structure, 90-91, 99
Achievement, pupil
  and graded structure, 4-15, 27-28
  grouping by, 18, 73, 90, 91-93, 99
  in homogeneous classes, 17-20, 91-92
  and intelligence, 24
  and nongraded structure, 91-93
  and nonpromotion, 34-35
  and readiness to learn, 8, 9, 27-28
  recording of, 134
  and success vs. failure, 159-61
  variation in, by grade, 8, 9, 13, 27-28
  variation in, by pupil, 8-9, 15, 17, 27-28, 88, 91-92
  See also Reading achievement
Adjustment, pupil
  and promotion policies, 37-39, 162-63
  recording of, 135
  reporting of, 124
Administration, school
  functions of, 61
  and graded structure, 61-63
  and nongraded structure, 176-77, 188-90
  purpose of, 41
  and reporting, 103
Admission policies, 63-64
Anxiety, 24, 157, 165
Appleton, Wis., 57-58, 71, 191, 194
Average learners, 149-51, 154

Batavia Plan, 50
Bay City, Mich., 129, 130
Behavioral objectives, 80-82, 83-84
Boards of education, 181-83, 183-85

Cabool, Mo., 92, 191, 194
Chicago, University of, Laboratory Schools, 50
Child development
  and achievement vs. potential, 138-39
  and curriculum content, 86, 88
  and educational theory, 51, 157-59
  and graded structure, 3-15, 20-24, 27-28, 156
  and nonpromotion, 162-63
  norms of, 105-06
  See also Mental health
Chronological age
  grouping by, 18, 65
  vs. other measures, 3-4
Classification, pupil. *See* Grouping
Classroom, nongraded, 89-98, 99
Coffee County, Ga., 191, 194
Combination grades, 71-77
Community, 181-85
Continuous promotion. *See* Social promotion
Corona, Calif., 130
Cumulative record folder, 74, 113, 132-35
Curriculum
  components of, 79
  differentiation in, 91-92
  and graded structure, 80, 83, 84, 87-89

and nongraded structure, 77-78, 83-89, 207-08, 212-13, 223-26

objectives of, 80, 103-04, 107, 109, 140

organization of, 52, 79-89

See also Educational theory

Cycling, teacher, 66-68

Dalton Plan, 50-51

Dalton Schools, 81

Davidson County, Tenn., 130

Delinquency, 36

Dewey, John, 50, 51

Edmonds, Wash., 191, 194

Educational theory
and child development, 51, 157-59
learning theory, 52, 152-54, 157-61
and school organization, 51-52, 61-63, 175-76, 205-06

Elementary education, philosophy of, 20-21, 24-25, 28, 39-40, 98-100, 161, 166-67

Englewood, Fla., 71-78, 81-82, 95-96, 208

Englewood, N.J., 97-98

Evaluation
of grouping procedures, 90, 99
of pupil progress, 94-96, 99, 103-14, 186-87, 208

See also Reporting

Failure, 35-36, 157-61. *See also* Non-promotion

Flint, Mich., 97, 130

Fort Wayne, Ind., Francis M. Price School, 98

Franklin School, Lexington, Mass., 98, 130

German educational system, 46, 48

Gifted learners, 145-49, 154-55

Grade norms, 104-07, 149-51, 155-56

Graded school structure
and achievement, 4-15, 27-28
as administrative device, 61-62
admission policies in, 63-64
and child development, 3-15, 20-24, 27-28, 156
and curriculum, 80, 83, 84, 87-89
description of, 1, 2-3
history and early criticism of, 44-52, 203-05
measurement in, 103-07
and mental health, 142-51, 163-68

modifications in, 15-20, 73-77, 178, 204-05

vs. nongraded structure, 58-59, 213-23

and parents, 28, 31-32

and promotion policies, 39-41, 162-63

and pupil motivation, 151-56, 161

reporting in, 102-03, 137-38

and teachers, 62-63, 87-89, 164-68

Green Bay, Wis., 92

Grosse Pointe, Mich., Monteith School, 195

Grouping
by ability, 15, 17-20, 90-91, 99
by achievement, 18, 73-74, 90, 91-93, 99
by chronological age, 18, 65
evaluation of, 90, 99
interclass, 15-20
multi-age, 68-70, 75
and nongraded structure, 64-70, 89-100
parental acceptance of, 73, 76
by pupil interest, 90, 93-95, 99
by random selection, 65
by reading achievement, 17, 64-65, 66, 92-93
by social relationships, 65-66
by study-work skills, 90, 95-96, 99
and team teaching, 97-98, 99

See also Heterogeneity, Homogeneity

Heterogeneity
demands of, on teachers, 95-96
in homogeneous classes, 17-20, 91-92
by subject area, 92, 99

High schools, 24-27

Home. *See* Parents

Home visits, 122-23, 125

Homogeneity
in graded classes, 15-20, 91-92
in nongraded classes, 64-70, 89-98
by subject area, 92-93, 99

In-service teacher-training, 125-28, 177-80, 181

Intelligence quotient (I.Q.)
and achievement, 24
grouping by, 18, 90
vs. other measures, 3-4
recording of, 134

Interest grouping, 90, 93-95, 99

Kindergarten, 63, 113, 186-87

Laboratory Schools, University of Chicago, 50
Learning process
and standards, 206
timing and pacing of, 84-85, 87-89, 99
Learning theory, 52, 152-54, 157-61. *See also* Educational theory
Lexington, Mass., Franklin School, 98, 130
Longitudinal curriculum development, 80-99 *passim*, 105-06, 107

Mann, Horace, 46, 48
Marking systems, 104, 118-20, 205
Measurement, 103-07. *See also* Evaluation, Reporting
Mental age
and achievement, 8, 9, 27-28
vs. other measures, 3-4
readiness to learn equated with, 4
variation in, within grade, 6, 9, 13, 27-28
Mental health
of pupils, 142-64, 186-87
of teachers, 164-68, 187
See also Child development
Milwaukee, Wis., 53, 54, 57, 71, 177
Monitorial system, 45-46, 48
Monteith School, Grosse Pointe, Mich., 195
Motivation, pupil, 151-56, 157-59
Multi-age grouping, 68-70, 76
Multigrading, 71-77, 211

Nongraded school structure
admission policies in, 63-64
adoption of, 170-202
advantages of, 209, 219-23
analysis of, 210-13
classrooms in, 89-98, 99
and community, 181, 183-85
and curriculum, 83-89, 91-92, 207-08, 212-13, 223-26
evaluation of, 56-59, 209
vs. graded structure, 58-59, 213-23
grouping in, 64-70, 89-98
history of, 49-52, 53-56
introducing parents to, 73, 76, 171-74, 181-83, 184-85
introducing pupils to, 185-88
introducing teachers to, 177-80, 188-90

and kindergartens, 63, 186-87
and "levels" plan, 212
measurement in, 103-07
and mental health, 142-51, 162-63, 186-87
obstacles to, 209
organization of, 77-78
practices in, 206-10
and pupil motivation, 156, 160
reasons for, 2, 52-53
recording in, 133, 134, 135
reporting in, 77, 102-03, 123, 140
and rural schools, 54
and standards, 27, 205-06
states using, 55
teachers, use of, 66-68, 96-98, 99
Nonprofessional assistance, 129-30
Nonpromotion
and achievement, 34-35
and delinquency, 36
and personality, 162-63
and pupil adjustment, 37-39
pupil attitudes toward, 35-36
reasons against, 33-34, 157-59
reasons for, 32-33
Normal schools, 46-47, 48
Norwalk, Conn., 130

Objective, curricular, 80, 103-04, 107, 109, 140. *See also* Curriculum
Organization, school
appropriateness of, 56
and educational theory, 51-52, 61-63, 175-76, 205-06, 210-11
and mental health, 142-51, 165-67
purpose of, 41

Pacing of learning process, 84-85, 87-89, 99
Parents
communication of, with teachers, 103, 106-13, 114-28
conferences of, with teachers, 123-25, 126-28, 131-32, 136-37
and graded structure, 28, 31-32
and grouping, 73, 77
and nongraded structure, 171-74, 181-83, 184-85
on teacher cycling, 67
Park Forest, Ill., 71, 126, 131, 135, 177
Price (Francis M.) School, Fort Wayne, Ind., 98
Primary School Plan, Milwaukee, Wis., 71

Promotion policies
 and achievement, 27
 and educational philosophy, 39-40,
  182
 and graded structure, 39-41, 205
 and pupil adjustment, 37-39, 182
 variation in, 30-31, 32-34
 See also Nonpromotion, Social promotion
Public school education, development
 of, 46, 48
Pueblo Plan, 50
Pupil. *See* Ability, Achievement, Adjustment, Child development,
 Grouping, Mental health, Motivation, Variability
Pupil-teacher conferences, 136-37

Quincy Grammar School, Quincy,
 Mass., 44, 45, 48-49, 203-04

Racine, Wis., 122-23, 127
Readiness to learn. *See* Mental age
Reading achievement, 17, 64-65, 66,
 92-93
Recording, 128-35
Reporting
 administrative nature of, 103, 116
 in graded schools, 102-03, 137-38,
  204-05
 importance of, to teachers, 116-17
 mechanics of, 128-35
 in nongraded programs, 73, 76, 102-
  03, 123, 140
 process of, 113-28
 purpose of, 103, 138
 types of, 117-25, 136-37
 types of data used in, 110-13
 See also Evaluation, Measurement,
  Recording
River Forest, Ill., 126-28
Rural schools, 54, 68

San Francisco Normal School, Calif.,
 50
*Sarasota County, Fla., Englewood
 Elementary School,* 71-78
Schools. *See* Administration, Elementary education, Graded school
 structure, Nongraded school

structure, Organization, Second-
 ary schools
Secondary schools, 24-27
Shorewood, Wis., 131-32
Slow learners, 143-45, 154
Social promotion, 40, 53, 162-63, 166
Study-work skills, 90, 95-96, 99
Success, 159-61

Teacher aides, 129-30
Teachers
 communication of, to parents, 103,
  106-13, 114-28
 conferences of, with parents, 123-
  35, 126-28, 131-32, 136-37
 conferences of, with pupils, 136-37
 cycling of, 66-68
 and graded structure, 62-63, 87-89
 mental health of, 164-68, 187
 and nongraded structure, 59, 87-99,
  170-74, 177-80, 208
 and promotion policies, 32-34, 39-
  41
 and reporting, 116-17
 and team teaching, 67, 68, 97-98,
  99, 211, 223
Teacher-training
 and graded structure, 46-47, 48
 history of, 46-47, 48
 in-service, 125-28, 177-80, 181
Team teaching, 67, 68, 97-98, 99, 129-
 30, 211, 223
Textbooks, 47, 48, 49
Timing of learning process, 84-85, 87-
 89, 99
Torrance, Calif., 69
Transfer students, 64

*University City, Mo., Nathaniel Haw-
 thorne School,* 92

Van Dyke, Mich., 127
Variability, pupil, 20, 21-23, 73-74,
 211. *See also* Ability, Achievement
Vestal, N.Y., 117-18, 199

Western Springs, Ill., 53
Winnetka Plan, 50-51